# DAY TRADING STRATEGIES FOR BEGINNERS

2 Books
Day Forex and Swing Trading Strategies
for a Living. The Ultimate Guide
to Safely and Quickly Start
to Create your
Long Term Passive Income

MARK P. ANDERSON

# FOREX TRADING FOR BEGINNERS

## Table Of Contents

# SWING TRADING FOR BEGINNERS

## Table Of Contents

# FOREX TRADING FOR BEGINNERS

A Complete Guide
to Forex Trading for Beginners,
how to Become a Successful Trader
and Create Passive Income
for a Living. Learn how
to Build the Right Mindset

MARK P. ANDERSON

# Introduction

For international trade to take place effectively, countries need to have access to a market that enables them to convert local currencies to other currencies. This means that forex trading is an important factor in facilitating trade between different countries. For example, if a company in the United States was to import goods from Germany or any other European country, it can easily pay for the transaction in Euros rather than dollars by converting U.S dollars into euros.

**History of Forex Trading**

Currency exchange has always been an important part of trade throughout history. It enabled people from different regions to trade in items such as food, cloth, tools, and many other essentials. For instance, if Egyptian merchants were trading with Turkish merchants, and the Turkish merchant's currency was worth more than the Egyptian currency in terms of value, the Turkish trader would be able to purchase more goods with fewer coins because the value of his coins would make them superior in terms of purchasing power.

Throughout history, the value of currencies has been set against commonly recognized measures such as gold or silver. Gold was typically used to fix the value of a currency by providing a measure that could equate a certain quantity of gold to a certain amount of money. Silver was also used as a measure of value for different currencies.

As early as the fifteenth century, banks had been opened to facilitate trade between different countries. The year 1880 is considered the beginning of the foreign exchange, and it saw the establishment of the gold standard. The gold standard meant that the standard economic unit of account was established based on a fixed quantity of gold. This standard was widely used in the 19th century and as well as in the early part of the 20th century.

The increase in the volume called for a better trading system, and this is what prompted Reuters to introduce computer monitors into the forex trading market from 1973. Hitherto the introduction of computers, telephones, and telexes were the main platforms that were used for trading quotes.

By the end of the first quarter of 2010, at least 36% of the trading volume in the forex trading market was attributed to the U.K., making it the largest foreign exchange trading center at the time. The United States, over the same period, accounted for at least 17% of the global foreign exchange trade while Japan was third in terms of volume with a contribution of 6% of the total traded volume.

Recent years have seen a remarkable increase in the total turnover of forex trade. By April 2010, the turnover of the options and futures market had reached the $ 166 billion mark. As it stands, over 2% of OTC turnover in foreign exchange is accounted for by forex currency derivatives.

While there are numerous different currency pairs from all around the world, there are just 18 that is considered by most to be of the greatest importance. While this doesn't mean that you should try and trade all of the pairs at once, it does mean that you will need to be aware of them and what they are doing so you have a better forecast of the market as a whole. Even better, the 18 pairs are all from just eight countries. While this doesn't make successful Forex trading any easier, it will make it easier when it comes to knowing where to put your focus.

## CHAPTER 1:

# What Is Forex Trading?

Forex is short for foreign exchange and is an exchange of currencies. For example, when you are traveling from one country to another, you will need to exchange your home currency for the other country's currency. If you live in the United States and are traveling to Europe, you will need to exchange the American dollar for euros.

Forex is one of the largest trading markets. One reason is that each country has a currency. The other reason is that most people understand currency and how it works. Also, everyone participates in forex in some way, be it on an individual or business level. The market is open 24 hours a day from Monday morning to Friday evening.

What do we trade in the Forex Market?

The answer is simple – MONEY. Yes, the forex market is all about money in different currencies. For beginners' trading in forex can be confusing because one is not buying anything physical, which is why many tend to be skeptical about forex trading. Well, this book will clarify such ideology. You can consider buying forex as when you buy a share in a country. It is similar to buying a company's stock in the market. The rate of a particular currency represents a direct reflection of the thinking of the market about its present and future health of the currencies economy.

Remember the Japanese yen example I made at the beginning? Let us assume you decide to buy the yen, what it means is that you are investing in the Japanese economy by buying a share of the country.

In order words, you are "banking" on the Japanese economy that it will do well. You are buying this yen intending to sell it in the market to gain profit.

Generally, the exchange rate of a particular currency against other currencies represents the economic conditions of the economy.

## Principles of Forex Trading

***Learn the Market's Trends***

One needs to be able to predict the changing nature of the foreign exchange market to be successful in Forex Trading.

Accordingly, a person should understand the general direction of the marketplace. Trends can be uptrend, downtrend, or sideways trend. Identifying a pattern can profit a person in that he or she will be able to trade with the trend. Uptrends are trends that move upwards, indicating an appreciation in currency value. Downtrends move downwards as an indication of depreciation in currency value. Sideways trends show that the currencies are neither appreciating nor depreciating.

***Stay Focused and Control Your Emotions***

Forex trading is a challenging marketplace that can cause a person to lose confidence and to give up in the toughest of times. That is understandable given that traders put in their hard-earned money. As a result, when a person experiences loss, he or she can lose focus when negative emotions become overwhelming. It is, therefore, essential for one to become aware of the negative emotions that result from Forex trading so that he or she may minimize the emotional effects of loss and remain focused.

***Learn Risk Mitigation Tactics***

To achieve the profits that a person anticipates, the person needs to minimize the likelihood of financial loss. Since the forex market keeps on changing, the risks, therefore, keep on changing. The most crucial risk management rule is that a person should not risk more than he or she can afford to lose. Traders who are willing to invest more than they make become very susceptible to Forex Trading risks.

Consequently, a person can mitigate potential losses by placing stop-loss orders, exchanging more than one currency pair, using software programs for help, and limiting the use of financial leverage.

### *Establish Personal Forex Trading Limits*

A person should know when to stop Forex trading. One can stop Forex trading when he or she has an unproductive trading plan, or when he or she is continually experiencing losses.

An ineffective Forex trading plan may not bring trade to an end, but it will not function as well as a trader may expect. In that case, the trader can consider stopping the trade, constantly changing markets, and the decreasing volatility within a particular foreign trading tool may also cause a trader to take a break from Forex trading.

Besides, when a person is not in a good physical or emotional state, he or she may want to think about taking a break to deal with personal issues.

### *Use Technology to Your Benefit*

Being up-to-date with existing technological developments can be gratifying in Forex trading.

Given that forex markets utilize the online forum, high-speed internet connections can increase Forex trading performance significantly. To make the most of Forex trading, a person must take it as a full-time occupation, and he or she must embrace new technologies. Similarly, receiving forex market current information with smartphones makes it possible for forex traders to track trades anywhere.

Forex trading is an aggressive enterprise that needs a trader to have an equally competitive edge. Therefore, a forex trader needs to maximize his or her business's potential by taking full advantage of the available technology.

### *Make Use of a Forex Trading Plan*

A Forex trading plan comprises of rules and guidelines that stipulate a forex trader's entry, exit, and money management principles.

A trading plan provides the opportunity for a forex trader to try out a Forex trading idea before the trader risks real money. In so doing, a trader can access historical information that helps to know whether a Forex trading plan is feasible and what outcomes he or she can expect.

When a forex trader comes up with a Forex trading plan that shows potentially favorable outcomes, he or she can use the trading plan in real Forex trading situations. The idea is for the forex trader to adhere to the trading plan.

Buying or selling currencies outside of the Forex trading plans, even if a trader makes a profit, is poor trading, which can end any expectation the plan may have had.

CHAPTER 2:

# How Forex Works

There are a lot of terms used that are new to a trader who is just starting and are vocabularies to them. It would do well to an aspiring trader to acquaint themselves with the new terms and understand the meaning behind them and how to use them appropriately when trading. This will prove essential to avoid miscomprehension of certain concepts when trading. To new traders, the terms may be a little bit difficult and also have a completely different meaning than the expected one from its word-formation.

## A Pip

A pip is the lowest measure of the value of the movement of currency under observation. The term pip is, however, an abbreviation of the term-percentage in point. A pip, as the lowest measurable value of the movement that the currency makes, always measures ad 1% of the currency that a trader wants to exchange.

When in the forex market, a currency increases or decreases by a single pip, the inference has the meaning that the currency either increased or decreased by 1%. A great example is when the market analysis tools show that the U.S. dollar has increased by a pip. This is to means that the U.S. dollar has increased in its value by $0.0001.

That is how a pip is inferred, and it's meaning. Trade is always made in terms of pips, and a trader can make trades with many pips as possible. This is because the pips are the lowest value that is measured by the currency.

## The Base Currency

The base currency is the type of currency that a trader has and is currently holding. The base currency is likely the currency of the country that you're from. If a trader is from the U.S., his or her base currency will be the U.S. dollar. If the trader is from the U.K., the base currency of the trader will be the pound. The base currencies of traders, therefore different across many traders around the globe due to different geographical differences.

## The Asking Price

The asking price is a term that is used to refer to the amount of money that your broker firm will demand from or will ask from you when you are making a trade. A broker always demands this price or this amount of money when they are accepting the pair of currencies to be traded from you—the price id for buying the quote that you've made of the pair of currencies. A note to be made is that the asking price, made by the brokerage firms, is always higher than the bid price.

## Bid Price

The bid price is mostly used about the brokerage firms, where it is the amount of money that the brokers will be willing to buy or to bid the base currency that you are currently holding. The broker firm sets the bid price according to their ability to bid on the base currency.

## Quote Currency

The quote currency, unlike the base currency, is the currency that a trader wants and is willing to purchase in exchange for his or her base currency. If a trader wants to exchange U.S. dollars for getting South African Rand, the currency of South Africa, the Rand is the quote currency. It is always stroked against the base currency when trading and when the currencies are made into pairs.

## The Spread

This is the commission that the broker firm receives from being a platform where forex trading can take place. When referred to, the spread means the difference in value between the bid price made by the broker and the asking price, also quoted by the broker.

These are but a few but the major terms that are used in the forex trading world. Knowing this alone will not be enough. You have to be familiar with more words and phrases that can be found in books concerning forex trading.

## Finding the Right Broker Firm

To trade forex, you will have to have a brokerage firm that will be an online platform from which you'll open and close the trade. Finding the right broker firm is an important process, for other brokers can be a sham out to cheat people of their money. It is, therefore, paramount that a trader carries out research on the available broker firms and picks out the best and one that is highly recommended for its services. When deciding on which broker firm to go with, look at the ask and the bid price that the broker quotes, and other important aspects, including the margin and the leverage level that they offer, the customer service should also be top-notch for the broker, which will be great for a trader who is just starting. Most of the broker companies also offer studies on how to carry out forex trading, and those come in handy to the new traders.

## Making an Analysis of the Worldwide Economy

To make gains and profits and gains in trades that you are going to make, analyzing the economic trends of the worldwide economy is of great importance to be fully aware of the factors that may trigger the currencies to increase or decrease in value. This is important in making a correct prediction on the pair of currencies you're exchanging, whether they will make a profit or a loss. Factors that are important to look into when evaluating the global economy are like the political climate of countries whose currencies have strong value, natural factors that may influence the economy of countries, the Gross Domestic Product of the country whose currency you want to exchange with your base currency, and other minor factors such as the investment rate of the said country. Evaluating which countries are looking up to growth and development opportunities is also important in determining the quote currency to use, impairing up currencies to make a trade. Also, on the analysis of the worldwide economy, when the currency of the country you seek to purchase in exchange for your base currency is doing well and is set to increase in its value, convert your base currency into the quote currency.

On the other hand, convert the quote currency into the base currency in case its value increases. Various online sites have analysis tools on the economic performance of different countries that you may seek for them to be your quote currency. Others rank counties in terms of their GDP that makes it easier for you to choose the countries that are projected for growth and development. Being in touch with the trending news globally is a plus in getting information relevant to trading forex. A new forex trader may subscribe to a few forex trading channels and outlets to be constantly on toes of events and happenings that may trigger the value of currencies to either increase o decrease, which may result in the reversal of the outlook of the trade made. Having relevant information at all times is key in making gains and preventing the loss of your money, and probably your account is cleared.

## Opening the First Trade

Pairing currencies and making the first trade; opening and closing a trade happens when the quote currency to be paired by the base currency has been paired, and there is a suitable trading window. Opening a trade is making an order to purchase a certain currency and in exchange for your base current through your broker firm. You'll have the analysis tools that are commonly offered by the brokers in software programs. The execution of making an order in some platforms might be instant, while in some other platforms, it might be a tad bit slower. Nonetheless, most brokerage firms offer live prices and values of the currencies that are to be traded, and their exchange rates and the instant changes to their values are displayed. The first trade for a new trader might just be one, or others might open up new trades over a short period. Just several enough trades should be opened, in which the new trader is comfortable and at ease in trading.

CHAPTER 3:

# How to Develop the Right Mindset to Operate in Forex

It is an inevitable reality that your success or failure in forex trading will largely depend on your state of mind. In other words, if your psychology of Forex trading is not correct, you will not earn money! Unfortunately, most dealers ignore this important fact or do not know how important it is to have an appropriate mindset for the success of Forex trading if you do not have the right trading mentality, whatever the quality of your trading strategy, because no strategy will ever make cash if it is used by a professional with bad psychology.

Note: Leave me your comments and comments below after reading today's lesson!

Many people seem to be unaware that they are negotiating with a state of mind that stops them from making money in the markets. Instead, they think that if they find the right system or indicator, they will magically start printing money on their computers. Success in business is the result of developing good business habits, and habits are the result of good business psychology.

## Step 1: You Must Have Realistic Expectations

The first thing you must do to develop the right Forex trading mentality is to have realistic expectations of trading. I mean this; do not think that you will leave your job and start earning $ 1 million a year after two months of live trading with your $ 5,000 account. It doesn't work this way, and the sooner you base your expectations, the sooner you start making money consistently. You must accept that you cannot negotiate and leverage the path to business success. If you do both, you can make money fast, but you will soon lose everything and more. Accept the reality of the money you have on your trading account and the amount you are willing to lose by trading. Here are some other things to consider:

**Trade Only With Disposable Risk Capital.** The capital disposable is money you do not need for your living expenses, including retirement and other long-term things. If you do not have capital available or risky, keep doing demos until you have, or stop trading together, but whatever you do, do not trade with money because you will be delighted of the loss. Always assume that you can lose the money you have on your account or in a trade, and if you agree with that, then you should go, just make sure not to lie to you. OK, exchanging "scared" money (money you cannot afford to lose) will cause intense emotional pressure and loss.

The fact is that your last company has absolutely nothing to do with your next business. You must avoid becoming euphoric or overconfident after a winning or vengeful negotiation after a lost negotiation. The fact is that every time you trade, this should only be considered as a new execution of your trading margin; If you only had three consecutive winners, avoid risking more than usual in your next exchange simply because you feel very confident, and avoid returning to the market immediately after a lost exchange just to try to get back what you lost.

**Do Not Get Too Focused on Your Trades.** Do not take trades in person; it's not because you lose in a few trades in a row that you're bad at trading, even if you win in three trades in a row, it does not mean you're a negotiator "God" safe from losing. If you do not risk a lot by negotiating and do not trade with the money you require for other things in your life, you are probably not very attached to your business.

## Step 2: Understand the Power of Patience

**Learn How to Trade on Daily Charts First.** By learning to trade first on daily chart periods, you will naturally take a broader approach to markets and avoid the temptation to over-trade. Beginning traders must especially slow down and learn to trade the daily charts first. Daily charts give the most practical and relevant view of the market. You do not have to trade every day to get a solid return every month.

**Use Your Bullets Wisely.** To truly harness the power of patience in developing the right business mindset, you need to understand that patience will instill you with positive business habits. Patience strengthens positive trading patterns, while emotional negotiation reinforces negative ones. Once you have begun to negotiate patiently, you will see the judicious use of your "bullets." You just need a few good transactions a month to get a respectable return on the markets; once you have it patiently, you will learn to appreciate NOT being in the markets because then you are "looking for prey." This contrasts with the frustrated trader who stays up all night watching the graphics as a zombie who simply does not accept that he has to trade less often.

## Step 3: Be Organized in your Approach to the Markets

You MUST have a business plan, a business journal, and you must plan the bulk of your stock market before you can enter. The more you plan before you register, the more likely you are to make money in the long run. You will ALWAYS interpret the market more precisely when you are not in business, so planning everything increases your chances of making money because you work more on logic than on emotion.

**Keep a Professional Trading Log.** You need a history, you have to record your transactions, and you must do it in a forex trading journal.

This is an essential element to forge the right Forex trading mentality as it provides a tangible document that you can view and instantly get rough feedback on the performance of your trading.

**Think Before Shooting, Not After.** All the planning and pre-emption I just mentioned is akin to thinking before shooting. A weapon is a very powerful weapon. We all know we have to think before we shoot, even if we just hunt or shoot at close range. Similarly, markets can be very powerful "weapons" to win or lose money. So, you want to think as much as possible before starting a job, because once you enter, you will naturally become more emotional and will not want to be able to conclude pitiful transactions constantly. If you plan your actions before joining, you should not regret your operations, even when you lose trades. I never regret the exchanges I receive because I only negotiate if my advantage is present, and I am always comfortable with the amount of money I have risked in any transaction.

## Step 4: Do Not Have Doubts About Your Business Advantage

Finally, do not start trading for real money if you do not know how to trade your advantage. You will not develop the appropriate trading mindset if you enter the trading of an active account without being 100% sure of what you are looking for. Whatever your benefit, make sure you can redeem it on a demo account for at least three months or more before uploading it. Not just "dive" without feeling completely comfortable with your approach, that's what most traders do, and most of them also lose money.

**Have 100% Confidence in Your Advantage.** I have 100% confidence in my price action trading strategies, but that does not mean I'm fool enough to believe that ALL trades will win. Still, I am completely confident that every time I negotiate, my advantage is present. I do not compromise my business advantage by making settings that seem "almost" good enough ... I just do not work in this case. I take only the price action patterns that I feel in my instincts as valid high-probability representations of my benefit. Therefore, I am never afraid or worried about the negotiations I enter, even if I lose.

**Price Action Trading Helps to Develop an Appropriate Trading Mindset.** My benefit is price action, and I am convinced that the simplicity of price share trading has helped me develop and maintain a mindset of proper Forex trading. We do not need tons of confusing indicators on our charts, and we do not need Forex trading robots or other expensive software. All we need is the raw action of market prices and our magnificent human spirit to interpret it; it is up to us to exploit this power.

CHAPTER 4:

# Start Trading in Forex

Like any other endeavor where there are risks and benefits, education is key to achieve success in currency trading. Education is what distinguishes the trader or investor with a successful playing hand of strategies from the amateur, essentially gambling with his own money. Sure, the foreign exchange can be thought of as a type of gamble just like the stock market: you are risking your money, and you may make more money based on this risk, or you may lose it all. The key to making money rather than losing it is approaching currency trading with an understanding of the basics of how it works as well as the right strategies that you will consistently use to come out in the blue or, at the very least, cut your losses when the market turns against you. Again, developing and honing trading strategies takes time. Still, the goal of this e-book is to pinpoint some of these strategies for you so that you are ahead of the game compared to someone else who, unfortunately, is likely to be learning by trial and error. Someone in this latter case may never develop an understanding of how important it is to stick to a strategy. Not to beat a dead horse, but our goal is to provide you with the Jedi mind tricks to allow you to become a lightsaber-wielding trader on Forex. To be honest, half of wielding that lightsaber is merely understanding what a lightsaber is and when not to use it.

Alright, just to give you an idea of how important it is to approach currency trading with a strategy, think about this one: buying low and selling high. That's a strategy, and it makes sense, right? You purchase a currency when the price is relatively low (compared to the U.S. dollar), and then you sell high, or when the price comes up. Of course, there are a few variables here that may make this simple strategy less straightforward than it may seem at first glance. For one thing, variation in exchange rates may be so low that this buying low and selling high may represent a change of only a few cents when dealing with thousands of dollars' worth of currency. To be honest, it may be less than one cent even. Secondly, knowing when to sell is not always easy. When did your currency start to experience a downturn, when is the right moment to sell? Let's say you purchased Euros because the exchange rate was favorable compared to the U.S. dollar, the Euro gained in value, so you made money, but now the value of the Euro is dropping. What do you do? Do you sell now? Do you wait to see if the Euro will swing back up again? How long do you wait? Not so simple, is it? You may find that, before you know it, the Euro is worth less than what you paid for it, and instead of buying low and selling high, you bought high and ended up selling low.

But that's jumping the gun a little bit. We have not learned enough about the foreign exchange to have a set of strategies to use yet.

## Foreign Exchange Brokers

Although we put forex brokers last in our list of the things you need to get started in trading, we will discuss this list item first as it is a key to understanding and making the best use of the others. What is a forex broker? Well, as you, the trader, is little more than a tiny ant in the foreign exchange game, you will be involved in trading through an intermediary that has more access to information than you do. You are not a Jedi yet; you are not even an apprentice, Jedi. You are an ant or a centipede scurrying across the floor that the professional traders in their fancy Wall Street offices will try to step on in their thousand-dollar Ermenegildo Zegna shoes. These guys are talking about Fibonacci retracement and sentiment analysis, and you don't even remember what you had for breakfast. You will not be interacting with these guys. Your intermediary, the broker, has access to the interbank information upon which the currency trading bids and asks are based. Sure, the $25,000 you have to start with is a lot of money, and you worked hard for it, but you have to understand that the banks are dealing in the millions and billions and the sorts of figures that you will most likely be handling are infinitesimally small to them. So, the broker (also called the broker-dealer) is the person or platform that you will be dealing with rather than dealing directly with the banks that hold the currency. You will register with a broker or brokerage platform, and you will use their electronic platform to engage in your trades.

Like any other market that deals with money, there are many options when it comes to choosing a forex broker. Though it is not the purpose of this e-book to choose the forex broker for you, we can help you by explaining the different types of brokers and how their platforms operate. If you have experience trading on the foreign exchange, this information may be something that you already know, but for many of you, it will be completely new. Although there are several types and variations among broker-dealers, the two main divisions are between the "Dealing Desk" brokers and the "Non-Dealing Desk" brokers. We will delve into the differences between the two in a second. Within the category of Non-Dealing Desk or No Dealing Desk, brokers are two subdivisions called Straight-through Processing (SCP) and Electronic Communication Network + Straight-through Processing (ECN + SCP).

Understanding how dealing desks work will require you to understand some of the concepts involved in currency trading. Dealing desks operate using a spread, also called a spread trade, which is essentially a buy and a sale tied together. Spreads are not confined to currency trading as they are an important aspect of all futures and commodity trading schemes. The easiest way to think of a spread is that you are selling one currency and buying another at a value that links the buy and sale together. In a Dealing Desk operation, you would place an order for the trade that you would like, for example, USD-JPY, and the dealing desk would fulfill your order. Dealing Desk brokers are also called Market Makers because they are operating as a market themselves, not merely linking different parties together. This is the reason why some traders choose not to work through a Dealing Desk. Technically, the Dealing Desk broker may end up on the other side of a trade from you, meaning that your profits and their profits are inversely linked. In reality, there is little to no benefit to a Dealing Desk broker to work against a trader as you are still their client, and they are dealing with such a high volume of trades that they would essentially be indifferent to you.

In contrast to Dealing Desk, brokers are the No Dealing Desk brokers that primarily link various parties together. In other words, rather than selling you a currency, they are linking you to someone else who has that currency and matching your bid with their ask. That means if you are interested in paying a certain amount for currency, they try to match you with a party whose ask is close to your bid. Close, but not too close, as will become clear in a second. The most common form that this link takes is the Straight Through Processing (STP) type of No Dealing Desk broker. Taking the example of a Euro-US dollar trade, if you are attempting this trade using an STP platform, you will be able to place your ask (the price you are willing to sell the Euros for). The STP broker has liquidity providers that are willing to buy currency at a certain bid. The STP will have multiple liquidity providers and will match your ask with a liquidity provider's bid.

Obviously, you will not see all of the information that the STP broker has because the exchange is structured so that they would get a small cut of the transaction. So if you are asking 1.3999 for your Euros, the broker will match you with a provider that is willing to pay 1.4001, and the broker would keep the 2 pip difference. Notice that we used the term pip here. No, not a pimp. Pip. This term is used in foreign exchange to indicate the difference between one currency value and another. In this case, we talked about your ask and the provider's bid being different by 2 pips, but pips could also be used to indicate the falling value of a currency. For example, if you are holding Japanese yen and the value of the yen falls relative to U.S. dollars, you would say that you lost 4 pips today or 8 pips or whatever it is.

Another type of No Dealing Desk broker is the Electronic Communication Network (ECN), representing the early electronic forex platforms of the '90s. In this type of platform, the broker is not acting as an intermediary between the parties buying and selling currency as they are in the STP scenario. This is sort of like an auction where participants can post their best bids and asks and make trades. As the information is public compared to in the STP set, the broker does not take its cut from the difference between the bid and the ask, but by charging a small commission. As a trader, you are not participating directly with the ECN, though you have access to the information. To participate directly in the buys and sales (i.e., without a broker), you need to be an ECN subscriber, and only traders working on behalf of financial institutions and broker-dealers can become ECN subscribers. Many No Dealing Desk brokers operate through a combination of STP and ECN.

## CHAPTER 5:

# Choose Your Trading Style

One of the most important things the trader needs to do is they need to develop a trading plan. Typically, most traders don't develop a trading plan. I am sure that most readers are going to agree that the type of person that would scoff at using a demo platform for a couple of weeks to learn the basics of trading is also going to be the same person that fails to develop a trading plan. Well, let's consider the following. Concerning determining your success or failure as a Forex trader, having a trading plan is going to be one of the most important factors. Simply put, having a trading plan is one of the most important things that you are going to need to get you a handle on when becoming a new Forex trader.

So what are some of the things that are going to go into the Forex trading plan? The first item that you should, including your plan, is the balance you intend to keep in your Forex trading account. Keep in mind that when I say balance, I mean the total of cash plus positions held. So, no matter what it is, let's say, $5000 or $10,000, pick a number to stick with for the next three months at least. Of course, if you find out that you are a successful Forex trader, you are going to want to increase the amount in your balance.

So, having a balance enforces a bit of discipline with your account. Firstly, if you end up taking some losses, you should stick to your plan, and as soon as it's available, deposit more money in the balance to bring it up to the level that you have determined. So if you set out and determine that you want to balance of $5000, and you take a loss, and your balance drops to $4000, stick to your plan and add another $1000 to the balance. However, in your first year of trading, I don't believe that you should add money to your account on a whim. You can reevaluate the situation every three months and adjust as necessary. But for the three months, maintain the balance at the level that you have determined. The key point here is to avoid letting emotion drive you into pouring money into Forex trading out of excitement. Sometimes new traders get overwhelmed by excitement; maybe they've made a trade that is earning money. Amid their excitement, they might drain their bank account to fund more trades. And what happens more often than not is they end up getting into losing trades because they are overexcited, and then they find themselves in a position where they have lost money.

So, besides the amount of money that you're going to invest, let's take a look at some of the other things that we need to consider, including a trading plan. The first thing that I would mention is you should have a goal for profits. At first, we aren't necessarily talking about actually meeting the goal. But you need to have a good idea of where you are going so that you can take steps to correct your course if you are not moving in the right direction. Second, your initial goals of profit should be modest. I know that many traders are anxious to get going, and they would love to drop their day job, but to have a realistic chance of doing that, unless you happen to be a whiz at trading, it's probably best to start with small goals that you have a chance of meeting, and then each time you meet the goal, you can elevate to a new level.

So maybe you start small, like shooting for a profit of $500 over a month. Once you meet the goal, you could raise the level. So using this example, maybe after you have reached $500, then you change it to $1000. Over time, you'll find that soon enough, you will be able to get in the situation where you can trade for a full-time living.

The next thing that we need to put in our trading plan is our fixed loss and profit levels. This is going to be highly important for enforcing discipline. It's only going to be up to you, so I can tell you what to do to be successful, but I can't be there with you when you make your trades. Some readers are going to read this and nod, but not follow the advice. If that's you, more than likely, you are not going to end up as a successful trader.

So, you should take a level of profit that you are willing to accept and be happy about. This can be done in absolute terms, or it could be done in percentage terms. If we are talking about absolute terms, then you could set up a level of pips that you're willing to accept as a profitable move. Or as a percentage, you simply set the percentage gain or return on investment you're willing to accept with each trade. This is not something you are going to write down and then file away. Rather, you need to make this a rule that you follow with every single trade that you enter. Many platforms allow you to set up take profit levels with the trade, so you can use that feature and put a take profit order, which is a limit order, and then have it automatically executed. You should figure out a maximum loss that you are willing to except on each trade. This can be done on a percentage basis. Then with every trade that you enter, you can enter a stop-loss order, so that it is automatically executed.

The next thing that should be included in your trading plan is a list of currency pairs you're going to focus on. Besides, your trading plan should include the main strategy that you're going to use for most of your trades.

Keep in mind that your trading plan does not have to be written in stone. But I would advise sticking to it for at least three months. So each quarter, you can revise the trading plan as you see fit. But then stick to it for three months, so that you can give it enough time to find out if it's working or not.

CHAPTER 6:

# Basic Strategies

Market fluctuations are an inevitable part of forex trading. These unexpected changes can pose risks for both novice traders and experienced traders and require a trading plan to execute successful trades. It is easy to fall into the school of thought that equates success in trading to using complex strategies. More often than not, more straight forward strategies are easier to adopt, follow, and more effective. Whichever strategy you opt to use in your trading, there are basic elements that every beginner should consider before they start trading. These are:

**Trading Capital Management.** You need to decide on the amount of initial investment you want to begin trading with. This will also involve setting a guideline on the amount that you can use per trade.

**Time Management**. Forex trading requires commitment in terms of time that you will spend analyzing and predicting market trends so that you can use the information to guide your trades. Successful trading cannot be accomplished without proper planning or preparation, both of which demand that you put some fair amount of time into your trading.

**Do Not Over Trade**. While you're getting the hang of things in the forex market, it is wise to limit the number of trades that you execute. Entering into multiple trades per day is bound to deplete your capital without any gains. Starting small helps you manage your capital and get better at trading without unnecessary risks.

**Learning.** Staying informed and being able to identify market indicators will improve your chances of success. Familiarizing yourself with various analysis platforms will empower you to trade more profitably.

**Consistency.** Sticking to your trading plan will help you keep emotions at bay. The main strategy should be to stay within your strategy, work within your budget, and not let overconfidence or anxiety distract you from the plan.

**Patience.** Market changes are inevitable parts of the forex trade. Ensure that you exercise patience and avoid making rash decisions.

As a beginner in forex trading, It is also important for you to consider three essential components that will enable you to profit even when market movements are marginal. These components are:

1. **Liquidity.** The liquidity of a particular trade will make entering and exiting trades easy and will not be costly for you.
2. **Volatility.** Volatility typically impacts on the potential profit or loss you stand to make on a trade.
3. **Volume.** High trading volume usually indicates that there is a significant interest in the trade can be an indicator of a price movement either upwards or downwards.

The most successful traders enhance their trading skills through consistent practice and self-discipline. Self-analysis is a useful tool that you can use to determine what drives your trades. Some of the basic strategies to consider for any investor starting in the foreign exchange market are:

***Follow the Trend***

When you are just getting started in forex trading, being able to follow the general market movements will help you in making profitable trades. When you establish the direction of the trend, then the trades you enter should be in the general direction of the trend. Market direction can be extended or limited to a short duration, so the expected length of the trend should guide you on whether to adopt a long term or short term trading plan. Based on the time frame selected, you can then determine the type of charts to use.

***Moving Averages***

Moving averages provide buy and sell signals to the trader. They will help you understand the current market trends. You can obtain buy and sell indicators using moving averages by plotting different means on the same chart and observing the points at which they cross.

***Oscillators***

Oscillators help us to identify the markets that have either been overbought or oversold. Oscillators will guide you on the best entry point into a market.

The Relative Strength Index (RSI) and the stochastic oscillators are popular among forex traders. They vary on a scale ranging from 0 to 100. A Relative Strength Index that is more than 70 will indicate that the market has been overbought, while when the index is below 30, it is indicative that there is no overbooking.

A change in the market trend will be signaled by a divergence where the signal from the oscillators different from the price direction.

***The ADX Index***

The Average Directional Movement Index can be used to establish whether or not a market trend is strong when the ADX index exceeds 25, the implication that the trend is strong. The ADX index does not indicate in which direction the trend is moving.

***Retracements and Corrections***

When a trade corrects either up or down, it propagates the past market trend. Using a trend percentage, you can determine the level of the correction in a particular market. In the forex markets, investors tend to follow Fibonacci retracements, which are 38% and 62 %.

### *Buy Low and Sell High*

Profit is primarily obtained when you can dispose of an asset at a greater price than what you paid for it. Buying low and selling high can be a very effective strategy in forex trading because it allows you to spend less while making more.

The problem with this strategy is knowing when you are at a low and when you are at a high. The price can fall significantly and look like a good opportunity to buy, but as soon as you enter a trade, the price falls further, and you make a loss. This can be very frustrating. This can put you in a cycle where you keep on buying as the price continues to fall, meaning that you will then make multiple substantial losses.

To effectively apply the strategy of buy low and sell high, you need to avoid buying something that is still falling. Three main strategies can reduce the risks that come with a buy high and sell a low model of trade. These indicators include pivot lines that establish resistance levels and support levels and the Relative Strength Index, which signal market direction. The assumption that "the price can't go any lower" can cause you to lose money on bad trades by giving you a false sense of the market. Using the following indicators will prove useful in gauging the best exit and entry points on a trade.

### *Pivot Lines*

When it comes to predicting possible support and resistance levels to mitigate risks and increase potential returns, pivot lines are an efficient indicator. You can find an entry point into a trade by identifying a high low or an exit point by identifying a low high by using pivot lines.

When limits do not guide your trading, your risk exposure increases, and you are more likely to lose on your trades. Support and resistance levels provide you with a safeguard by giving you an indicator of the range you need to operate within. A trade moving in the right direction and making you money can go bad if you do not exit the market at the right point.

### *RSI*

The Relative Strength Index is an indicator of the strength of the market direction. Traders can identify strong entries that favor the RSI bias. Adding a trending line to the RSI is a simple but effective way to establish the directional bias on the Relative Strength Index.

### *Trendlines*

Depending on the market movement, a trader can determine the best buying opportunities that will net him the best possible returns. The best buying opportunities are usually present when the market is in a rising trajectory, while the best time to buy is when there is a downward trajectory in the market movement.

Trendlines are a useful indicator when trying to pinpoint a better probability entry or exit point.

### *Stop-Loss*

Market fluctuations and volatility in the foreign exchange market are a constant risk factor for investors in the currency exchange market. Mechanisms such as stop-loss can be used by traders to prevent trades from incurring high losses that can be occasioned by fluctuations in the market and market volatility.

Rapid market movements characteristic of the forex trading market lead to rapid changes in especially in situations when trends change directions. In these cases, a stop-loss mechanism can be used to close a trade at the indicated final level at which you can accept a loss. By setting a final level at which you can accept the loss, you, in effect, minimize the risk exposure occasioned by volatile market changes.

When choosing an effective and appropriate stop-loss limit, you should keep the following factors in mind:

- The length of the trade, longer trades are generally riskier
- The target price
- The size of your account and current balance

- The number of open positions you have
- The size of your order and whether it matches your account balance and time frame
- The general market sentiment at the time of entering the trade (for instance, is it volatile, awaiting news or other external factors?)
- The time frame available before the market closes. (for instance, is it almost weekend?)

When placing stop-loss limits, you can apply the following strategies:

***Static Stops***

This type of limit involves using fixed prices as a stop level. The static stop remains in place for the duration of the trade until the target price or reached, or the stop limit is reached. A static stop mechanism is straightforward and enables forex traders to stick to a minimum one-to-one risk-to-reward ratio.

***Trailing Stops***

In these types of stops, changes can be made to the limit price specified depending on the direction in which the trade is moving. Trading stops are not fixed to a particular price and provide a flexible mechanism that can be adjusted to suit the market direction if it presents an opportunity for the trader to make better returns on his trade.

***Fixed Trailing Stops***

In these kinds of stops, the limits set will be changed incrementally as the trade moves in a direction that is profitable to the trader. You can, for instance, put a trailing stop that changes after every 15 pips gained in the trade. This process continues until either the stop level is hit or the trader manually closes the trade.

## CHAPTER 7:

# Beware of the Brokers and the Platforms You Use

Picking the right broker for you can be a daunting task, especially if you are not clear about what you should be looking for. On the whole, finding a good broker isn't too hard when you know what you are looking for.

However, the question begs: why do you need a broker in the first place?

This is a reasonable question. The reason why you need a broker to enter the FOREX market is that you, as an individual, are not officially permitted to trade in the FOREX market unless you have the backing of a licensed institution. In this case, the brokerage firms that offer access to their platforms are the institutions that will back your trading activity.

It's like you're playing your home games in someone else's stadium. It's still your home turf even though you don't own the stadium. In this regard, the access you are granted to the platform enables you to place trades for yourself. All you pay to the brokerage firm is the right to use their platform.

That's all.

So, you aren't hiring a broker to manage your portfolio. What you are doing is simply "paying to play." A good way of looking at it is by comparing it to poker. When you play professional poker, you need to buy your way into the game. This is in addition to the blind you have to pay for each hand.

Similarly, FOREX platforms will charge you for access to enter the platform. Once you are in, then you can place your trades with the trading capital you have at your disposal. This will then enable you to make a profit. The best part of this type of setup is that the profits you make are yours. You don't have to pay a commission to some broker for their "expertise." By reading this book, among other publications out there, you will gain the same type of knowledge that brokers have. Therefore, you won't have to waste your money by paying commissions. That goes straight into your pocket.

As such, there are some important points to consider when looking for a brokerage firm that can grant you access to the FOREX market.

1. **Membership Fees.** All FOREX trading platforms will charge you some kind of membership fee. This fee is generally used to keep the platform running. Thus, the price you pay is what keeps the lights on. Regular brokerage firms will charge you a flat fee for the use of the platform. This can either be an annual fee or a recurring monthly payment. In other cases, discount brokers may charge you a one-time signup fee. However, they'll get you on the back end with their fees per trade. When you opt for a full-service broker, you'll pay a higher upfront fee, but you'll get a great analytics package that offsets the cost of the platform itself. Also, depending on the type of platform, you get algorithmic trading, expert advice, and even the opportunity to do copy-cat trading. Most discount brokers simply offer you access to the platform, and that's it.

2. **Fees per Trade.** When you conduct individual trades, you generally end up paying a fee per trade. In some cases, you may end up paying a couple of bucks on each trade regardless of the size of the position. In other cases, you pay pennies per trade. The best way to maximize your value when it comes to fees per trade is to purchase bundles. Most platforms offer

bundle packs like 10 trades for $1.99. These offer the most value as they allow you to control your expenses. If you go on a trade-by-trade basis, you'll find it hard to keep tabs on the amount of money you are paying per trade. So, it's best to see if you can lock in the price you pay for each trade you place.

3. **Reputation.** This is one of the most important aspects to consider. Sure, you might be tempted by the neat look offered by Joe's Trading Platform. But if you don't have any idea of who they are, you might be walking into a scam. The best trading platforms have a good reputation for backing them. You can even call up the Better Business Bureau in your area and get information on the parent company. Legit companies are always in the business of transparency as they know how valuable a good reputation can be.

4. **Free Demo Account.** This is a deal-breaker. If a platform does not offer you a free demo account, then it's better if you pass on them, at least in the early going. When you don't have access to the free demo version, then you will be playing for real right from the start. This can be dangerous, particularly when you don't have a lot of experience. So, a demo account will always be your best bet. Most platforms will require a credit card number or some other type of payment option though they won't bill you until after the trial period has ended. Take full advantage of this time as you are playing with house money. Therefore, you can afford to make a few mistakes. That way, you know what to look out for when you live with the real thing.

Please keep these points in mind as they will save you a lot of headaches along the way. In particular, ensuring that you are dealing with a reputable company is the most important thing you can do to protect yourself from unnecessary risk.

## Signs of a Legitimate Broker

When you are selecting the brokerage firm you plan to do business with, there are several signs you can look out for. So, let's take a look at these signs:

1. **You Can Get Full Information on the Parent Company Running the Platform**. This is a biggie. If you cannot find out who's behind the platform, then you are better off staying away from them. When you know who is running the show in the background, then you can rest assured you are dealing with pros. The main issue to keep in mind is that not being sure of who you are dealing with can lead you to give your money to unlicensed firms. This will not only result in you losing your money, but you may also end up sharing sensitive personal information.

2. **They Are Licensed.** This is another important thing to consider. If the firm you are dealing with cannot produce any official licensing information, then you had better run away as fast as you can. Please keep in mind that platforms pop up every so often. Now, they might be licensed for a while. But after they scam enough people, they lose their licensing. Yet, they advertise themselves as if they were duly licensed. So, a cursory check at their licensing information should provide you with the assurance you need. In particular, a walk through the Securities and Exchange Commission's (SEC) website should provide you with the assurance you seek.

3. **The Price Makes Sense.** When you are dealing with officially licensed firms, the price will reflect this. While we're not saying that it will be expensive, we are saying that the price will be on par with the market. This is why you need to beware of prices that are too good to be true.

Of course, there is always the chance that you are dealing with promos. However, the price should be a major tip-off.

4. **Users Will Be Happy to Leave Both Good and Bad Comments If Given a Chance.** As such, finding a good amount of comments about them will help you determine if they are right for you. In contrast, if you can't find any information on them, then you might very well be dealing with a fraudulent company. This is why user feedback is so important.

5. **They Have an Active Presence on Social Media.** If they are legit, you'll find them all over social media. This is a great way of knowing who you're dealing with. Even if they are new in the market, you'll them making an effort to gain traction on social media. In some cases, legitimate brokers will go out of their way to ensure engagement. Such efforts are always a positive sign.

## Signs of an Illegitimate Broker

When you're shopping for a brokerage firm to grant you access to the market, it might be tempting to go with the cheapest option you can find. At first, this may seem like a good idea, but one the whole, please bear in mind that you get what you pay for. So, here are the most important signs to watch out for when looking to spot illegitimate brokers.

1. **They Don't Offer a Demo Account.** This is a key issue when it comes to determining if you are dealing with a legit broker. Any time you sign on for a new account, you should get a chance to try out the platform for free during a short trial period. This period is generally 15 days though it could be longer depending on the type of promotion the company may be running. In some cases, you may get a full access 7-day pass.

As long as you get the free trial period, you can rest assured that you'll have the chance to test the entire system out first and then make up your mind. If the broker asks for money upfront, then you may be getting yourself in trouble.

2. **They Don't Disclose Their Licensing Information.** This is an automatic deal-breaker. If you can't get any information on their licensing, then it's best to just get away from their platform. Clever scammers may appear to sell you access to a platform, but you might find out that it's just a test platform or some other type of demo software that doesn't trade the real thing. So, you might get scammed into believing you are really trading when you're really not. Also, you may be dealing with a once reputable broker that either has an expired license or a revoked one. So, make sure you do your homework on this one.

3. **They Don't Provide Any Information About Their Leadership or Board Members.** When you're dealing with legitimate companies, they are generally publicly traded firms. As such, this type of information is available on their website. You can easily find out who's on their board and what type of credentials they have. Additionally, you can find links to social media pages like LinkedIn. While this isn't exactly a guarantee either, illegitimate brokers are usually scant with the amount of information they provide.

## CHAPTER 8:

# Manage the Loss

Always make sure that you have your stop losses in place when you begin to trade. These will ensure that you keep your losses to a minimum and help you to keep any of your profits as well. These stop points tell the market when you want to exit, even if you are asleep and can't watch your computer all the time. The stop losses can do a great job of keeping you in the game, limiting your losses, and preventing more risk than is necessary.

First, you must step a stop loss for losing money. This needs to be placed at the point where you are comfortable losing that much money. When the market goes down and reaches that point, your trade will be closed, and you will just have to settle that loss.

Even if the market continues to go down, your stop loss took you out and ensured you didn't lose more money.

If you had gotten into the market without the stop loss, you might have wanted to stay in the market and hoped that things got better. Or the downturn may have happened while you were asleep, and you wouldn't be able to fix the issue. Either way, this stop loss can help save you a bunch of money.

You should also put in a stop loss for your profits as well. This will be at the place where you are most comfortable with the profits that you make.

Doing this ensures that if the stock reaches that certain point, you will be able to walk away with a profit.

This way, if you are away from the computer for some reason, and the currency hits your profit point, but then takes a sharp turn down, you get to take the profit because the system took you out before the downturn occurred. This helps you to maintain your profits and can do wonders for keeping your emotions out of the game.

CHAPTER 9:

# How Much Can You Make in Forex?

The primary objective for every Forex trader is to make money. However, one should understand that Forex trading is not a cheap means of getting rich, or we can say that it is not a short cut to success.

Let us support these with a few points below:

***It Is a Skill Learned Over a Period***

Only skilled traders make money here. In addition, however much you are skilled, you cannot achieve success overnight. It is not a piece of cornflake as you may wish to believe, because if it were the case, every trader in this business could be a rich man.

Even experts encounter losses periodically because there is no trick to the business. It needs a lot of experience and practice to major in it. First of all, you need to gain knowledge and put it into practice via a demo account and master it well.

***Every Expert Loses Money On Some Trades***

Approximately 90% of Forex traders have lost money at a certain interval in the business. This could have been a result of poor or lack of proper planning, lack of proper training, lack of proper discipline, lack of a trading edge, or simply because of poor or lack of proper money management skills.

***Forex Trading Is Not For the Poor***

It is as simple and clear as it is. The mini account should have to a tune of $10,000 as trading capital before you join the business. Does it sound imaginary? Yes, that is the reality. You cannot begin with few coins in your account and dream of being the next millionaire.

Forex market is known for its speculation capacities because of its robustness, liquidity as well as the nature of currencies movement in powerful trends. Another aspect is the number of traders who make a killing has been limited to a few individuals.

Those individuals who make gigantic earnings are the ones who invest without paying attention to the risk factors in the business.

It is well now that we are aware of the gimmicks of the business, it is good to go ahead and identify some of the most used terminologies in Forex trading that we shall be referring to hare and there.

***Major & Minor Currencies***

Major currencies refer to those currencies that are ever frequently being traded in and that are very liquid and volatile on the market. There are at least eight currencies in this category, namely: EUR, USD, GBP, JPY, CAD, NZD, CHF, and AUD.

As opposed to this, any other currency on the market is what is called the minor currency.

***Base-Currency***

In any pair of trading currencies, the first currency is what we refer to as the base currency. For example, EUR/USD, in this case, the base currency is the EUR. This implies the base currency is quoted against the other currency. For instance: if the USD/EUR rate is 1.12300, this means that 1 USD is worth EUR 1.12300.

Note: In the foreign exchange market, it is the U.S. dollar, which is always quoted as the base currency. This indicates that quotations are ever expressed in terms of one U.S. dollar against the other currency stated in the pair.

***Quote-Currency***

This is the second in any pair of the quoted currency. It is also called the Pip currency, which signifies the loss or unachieved profit that is always presented here.

### *Pip*

This is the least entity of price for any given currency as you have seen; almost all quoted-pair have got 5-figures with a decimal point following the first digit. For example, EUR/USD is 1.1234. This indicates that a single pip is equal to the slightest change in the 4th decimal place, which is .0001.

### *Bid Price*

The bid price actually is the price where the currency pair on the market is expected to be bought. It is at this price that the base currency I sold off by the traders. The currency is indicated on the left side of the quote.

### *Ask Price*

The opposite of bid price: This is where the Forex market is set to give out any currency pair. You can buy the base currency at this very price. This is always shown on the left side of the quoted currency.

### *Bid/Ask Spread*

When you hear of a spread, what comes into your mind should be the difference, and in this case, it is that difference of the Ask and Bid prices.

### *Cross Currency*

This is a currency quote where neither of the quoted currencies is in U.S. dollars. This comes with very unique yet high price characteristics, which means that the trader has already run both traders in USD. In most cases, the cross-currency quotes usually incur the high costs of the transaction.

For example, EUR/GBP is called a long-buy, which is the same as to buy a EUR/USD pair and sell it GBP/USD currency pair.

### *Transaction Cost*

A bid/ask spread an example of a round turn transaction cost. Round turn here, we mean a buy or sell trade with the offsetting sell or buy-trades of the equivalent sizes and in the same pair of currencies.

***Margin***

Every time you come with a new trading account/margin account with brokers, you need to deposit some considerable amount in it. This amount may vary depending on the broker you are investing with. This could go from a small amount as one hundred dollars to one hundred thousand dollars.

Whenever you initiate a trade, there is always a percentage of the balance in your account of that margin account that is put aside and will be used as the initial margin necessity in the upcoming new trade.

***Leverage***

It is a ratio of capital investment to the needed security deposit. It is also the ability of the trader to take care of huge dollar amounts of financial assets using significantly low capital.

It comes in ratios depending on the brokers you are involved with and also the country in which you are trading. Usually, it is in ratios of 500:1 to 2:1 in that order.

All that said and done, we need to embark on how to make money, or money-making process in Forex trading. By now, you must be well versed with the technical terminologies as used in the whole of Forex trading, and that you are now free to advance your knowledge in other areas comfortably.

Forex trading is much similar to any kind of trade in financial markets, for example, stocks markets, and therefore, if you had any prior knowledge of the same, then you stand a greater chance of learning the trade so easily.

The main agenda of the trade is to trade one currency against the other through exchange with a primary expectation that there will be price changes. What we mean here is that you will have high hopes that the currency you bought will have its price go higher than the one which you sold for you to make some profit.

Example: let's say that you are interested in trading with the U.S. dollar against Euros. Assuming you bought 10,000 US dollars at a rate of 1.1700 and after like one week, you realize that the rates of exchange have gone high, like say 1.2600 and that you would wish to dispose of the money, then you will earn 900 US dollars.

This can be arithmetically represented as follows:
EUR 10,000*1.17 = US $11,700 and EUR 10,000*1.126 = US $12,600.

## What Time Do I Need to Buy or Sell Currencies?

One of the key factors to consider before selecting the currency to trade-in is the country of origin of the currency in question. As we know, a currency belongs to a specific country. It originates somewhere there's an economy.

The economy of the country affects the strength or the weight of its currency. So it is good to an economic mapping of the country at which you would wish to have their currency traded in before you make any necessary move.

You can do this by conducting what we call Forex fundamental analysis that is usually done by the financial brokers and have the information relayed to the prospective clients for decision making.

The country's economy may be affected by factors like international trade, lack of employment, general productivity, interest rates as well as manufacturing, just to mention but a few.

## Know the Game

We will be showing you an example of how the real trade is made some factors that you need to consider as you initiate the trade.

Suppose you are done with your feasibility study and established that the economy of the U.S. is going to weaken, you could decide to initiate a buy EUR/USD. This means that you will have to purchase the Euros with an anticipation that the U.S. dollar will drop in value as compared to the Euro.

You can do the vice versa if you believe that the Euro may weaken in value as compared to the U.S. dollar.

## Margin Trading

As we had briefly defined margin before, we now wish to go deeper into the business with margin.

You will understand and appreciate the use of margin in Forex trade.

When you need to buy eggs, say in a grocery, you will discover that it is hard to get it as one unit. Instead, they are bundled together, similarly in foreign exchange trade, and you will ever find the currencies bundled in the format 1000 or 10,000 to 100,000-units based on your account type and perhaps the type o brokers you are dealing with.

In margin trading, you do not necessarily need to have this entire amount before you trade. You can have capital on a borrowed basis called the margin. You can go in for greater accounts having very limited capital.

It is very easy to conduct big transactions, efficiently and smoothly even with low initial capital. Assuming the market signals is indicating the rise in the pound against the U.S. dollar, you go-ahead to open an account placing a lot of say GBP/USD 100,000 units that you have bought by the British pound at a margin of say 2%, you will hence wait as the rates go up.

In this case, if bought GBP/US- one lot equivalent to 10,000 units at 1.40000 as the price, it means that you have purchased the 100,000 British Pounds at $140,000 US dollars. Suppose the requirement of the margin was 2 percent; this means that U.S. $2,800 will be spared for opening the trade (2% of $140,000).

This implies that you can control a lot of 100,000 pounds by use of U.S. $2,800. When the market is favorable to you, and you happen to sell of your currencies, you may end up with a closing position of say 1.40500, and you will have earned $500. Whatever it is, whether it is a profit or loss, is all deposited in your account.

CHAPTER 10:

# Strategies to Create a Passive Income With Forex Trading

According to experts in the field of Forex Trading, it is possible to create a passive income through this form of financial trading. However, before jumping headlong into this type of financial trading, prospective traders need to ask themselves whether it is suitable for them, in addition to learning as much as possible about this line of business.

A passive income is the income stream traders or investors get at regular intervals and require little or no effort on their part to maintain it. Some of the common types of passive income include dividends from stock owned in a listed corporation, rental income, and interest income from bonds.

Other less common forms of passive income include royalties from a music record or publishing a book, or dividends from a non-listed company run by a family member or friend. Passive income may also arise from a new business model or income from a multi-level marketing network, where the income originates from other people's activities. Some internet marketers, such as affiliate marketers, also receive passive income from internet traffic that continues to stream in from blogs they posted a long time ago. Nowadays, traders can make a passive income through the forex market.

In fact, one does not have to participate directly in the trading process or have tons of experience in this field of business. Forex traders can earn a passive income from this form of financial trading in several ways, with some requiring more work or input from the trader. Some of these include:

## Forex Signals

These are short messages new traders can use to determine the best currency to trade and the right time to trade. Traders can receive important trading information through email, text messages, or any other type of communication, including social media platforms such as TX forums, Twitter, and other leading financial trading platforms.

These signals or messages are usually brief snippets of information, which instruct users to take specific actions, such as purchasing EUR/USD at a certain price. Sometimes, these signals feature various types of orders, such as a market order, pending order, or limit order. There are tons of sites that teach traders how to read and understand forex signals.

These signals can also be premium or free, with the former leading to better trades. Many providers of forex signals freely send important trading information to investors to boost their reputation in the financial trading industry. Forex signals are also great for people who want to earn a passive income trading options but do not have the time or opportunity to learn much about Forex Trading.

However, it is important to perform adequate research into providers of forex signals to avoid losing money. Forex traders, however, should approach these signals with utmost caution to make a good passive income.

## Forex Robots

One of the best ways to make a passive income from the forex market is using a tool known as a forex robot, which performs automated trades on a trader's behalf. Once traders set up these forex robots, they do not have to do much else; however, they should keep an eye on the trades the forex robots are making for them.

To get started, traders need to perform adequate research into the software available for forex robots. They need to choose software that will meet their needs, in addition to being reliable when it comes to executing the right forex trades. After setting up this software, it will make forex trades based on preset signals.

In addition, it will use its acquired knowledge to purchase or sell at specific times, earning users a passive income in the process. However, it is important to understand that not all forex robots make passive income for investors as claimed. In the same way that a human can make a losing trade, a forex robot can also make the same mistake.

It is also important to understand that many so-called forex robots are frauds, which is why respected news platforms such as the Wall Street Journal and Forbes refuse to promote or advertise them. Unfortunately, this is particularly true when it comes to free forex robots.

These sites try to give an honest opinion of different investment platforms and outline all the benefits and limitations of each platform. They also offer a detailed analysis of how these platforms work and how traders can get started on them, which is especially helpful to new traders.

## Social Trading

The social trading network works in the same way as a social networking platform. Instead of sharing selfies or pictures of pets playing the piano, however, social traders share important information about forex or financial trades. This allows others to copy them and make passive income as well.

New forex traders simply need experienced traders they trust and copy their trading strategies to make money. In addition to making a passive income, they will also learn when, why, and how successful traders make their trading moves, which will give them more insight and understanding into the forex industry.

However, finding traders who can trust and emulate is not as easy as it may sound. New traders need to set aside adequate time to perform thorough research into different social trading platforms, in addition to learning more about forex traders they want to work with and copy.

In certain situations, they might need to spend some money on the trader whose trading strategies they copy. However, this commission is negligible and not a big concern for new traders who want to make a passive income. Forex trading is something that most people are looking for ways to make some extra cash look into.

However, most of them do not know where to start. This discussion provides three great ideas for Forex trading beginners to consider. Each of the options above requires a different investment in terms of time and effort. The most important thing to remember is that beginners should perform adequate research before picking a trading platform or strategy to use.

Nowadays, Forex trading is one of the best ways for people to make a passive income working online. Millions of traders are earning a passive or active income every day through Forex Trading. This line of business is just like any other online money-making concept, but its profit potential is unrivaled. With modern technological advances and the availability of detailed information, anyone can make a passive income through Forex trading.

## CHAPTER 11:

# Strategies to Forex Trading

Would you like to trade, but you don't really know where to get your hands on to start? Well then, what it takes is calm and cold-blooded and a good trading platform.

If you intend to save money and start getting important results immediately, you can do it only with the best strategies. No market is indomitable for you, and no profit target is unattainable for you, continue reading and choose now to become an ace in trading thanks to the use of this strategy.

Why a strategy?

Maybe you've heard of the fact that many people lose money in trading. Well, we are certainly not here to deny the evidence, and we want to inform you as honestly as possible; the reality is there for all to see and offers disconcerting numbers as regards the winning and losing financial operators in the field of trading.

In recent years, above all, an unexpected catastrophe has occurred: about 90% of those who trade end up losing their capital in a period that can vary from 6 months to a year. Only 10% of financial operators manage to bring home satisfactory results, in other words, to earn well and consistently over time.

But at this point, a question arises: how is it possible that there are such negative statistics on online trading?

What is the reason for this almost catastrophic fact that seems to leave no hope to those who approach financial products for the first time?

From the analyzes carried out by the experts, a trend is clear: in recent years, there has been a boom in adhesions in online trading, a real race towards the riches of the financial markets that seems not to want to stop in front of anything, but are the new arrivals ready to trade online?

It seems not, and the most meaningful explanation lies in the fact that a strategy is not used.

Let's find out together why using a strategy is a guarantee of success, but also the reasons why you can do it too.

## Trading Strategies

Financial markets are made on stairs, some go down, and some go up.

The trivial paraphrase of a famous saying that we have reported above can help understand how things are going in trading. The fact that most retail traders lose does not mean that no one climbs the ladder, which means rosy prospects for their trading account in terms of profits and earnings, which would be unthinkable with any other online business, but let's try to understand why many traders lose and few who earn.

First of all, it should be noted that this boom, known from online trading, has led many people to start a trading business without any preparation. We are talking about people who are simply attracted to the prospects of earnings who probably got to trading thanks to some deceptive advertising and used their capital as if they were at the racecourse to make a bet.

Fortunately, online trading is something else or something that has nothing to do with a bet or any recreational activity.

Trading is a serious income opportunity that must be exploited professionally through the implementation of strategies.

This is a word that summarizes several meanings:

- **Strategy Is Not Tactics:** a strategy is a method studied in detail that has been developed to achieve specific objectives along a long-lasting path. A tactic, on the other hand, is only a technique that is adopted to obtain a short-term result that often is not based on particular criteria, so the tactic is similar to a bet.

- **Investment Plan:** strategy also means having a precise investment plan, all based on the capital available. The plan should include the monthly and annual objectives, the balance of income and expenditure, and the planning of the daily investment activity, including a study on financial assets.

- **Money Management Strategy:** Managing investment capital is a primary aspect when trading. Too many beginners underestimate this aspect, and it is no coincidence that ALL pay the consequences. Investments must therefore be weighted and well thought out, and the money must be rationalized for each open position on the market.

- **Technical Strategies:** In the final analysis, but not for importance, we must mention the fact that by strategies, we also mean the "technical" ones, that is those based on the use of technical indicators that are used for the study of the trend of financial assets on the short and medium-term, which are fundamental for intraday and multiday trading.

## The Advantage of a Strategic Approach

Choosing to strategically approach trading allows you to obtain great advantages and satisfactory results, but we want to close the discussion regarding the importance of strategies by revealing a little secret that 90% of retail traders who lose money every day ignore or choose to ignore. Learning strategies can take some time and a certain amount of patience, but managing to trade strategically offers you a little known advantage which, however, is decisive: a strategy like the ones that allow you to know there is guarantee success on average in 75% of market positions for two reasons:

- These are exactly the same strategies that are used by experts in the sector with the only difference that they are explained to you in an understandable way without leaving room for empty technicalities that are ultimately only counterproductive and prevent clear and long-lasting learning over time.

- The strategies are all based on the most important and proven technical and fundamental analysis tools of the financial markets. Even the use and understanding of these technical tools will be easy for you because our explanations are geared towards newbies in the sector. However, an expert certainly does not need to contact us.

We asked expert traders to write trading guides that are practical and effective.

In the field of trading, there is so much misinformation and bad information that we have decided to make the maximum clarity by offering strategies for all beginners looking for serious earning methodologies. If you are not willing to learn and apply strategies with commitment, then trading is probably not for you, but if you want to be serious here, you will find all the material you need. Read on and find out all about scalping and intraday strategies and much more.

CHAPTER 12:

# Choose the Right Broker

Following are a list of things required for becoming a successful Forex trader:

**Trading Plan:** A forex trader should have a trading plan that should be prepared well in advance. The trading plan should list out his entry and exit conditions as well as his money management rules. This is of utmost importance, and he should religiously follow his trading plan to the tee. In order to become a successful forex trader, he should never deviate from the trading plan.

**Discipline:** This is one of the most important qualities needed to be a successful forex trader. A trader should be disciplined and methodical in the way he goes about with forex trading. He should not only meticulously plan his trading, but should also be disciplined enough to follow it.

**Ability to Do Analysis:** A forex trader should have the ability to analyze the technical charts and other financial data to become a successful forex trader. He should invest in himself and learn how to use the financial tools that would help in becoming a better trader. Trading is a very competitive job, and one needs to be always one step ahead of others to be successful.

**Emotional Stability:** It is very important to keep emotions and trading separate. In order to be successful, the trader should be able to trade like a machine and not let emotions affect his trades. He shouldn't let losses affect him, nor should he get overly excited about the winning trades.

**Hard Work:** Nothing beats hard work for becoming a successful forex trader. The trader should be prepared to put in a lot of hours and research the forex market thoroughly before each trading day. Most successful forex traders have a pre-trading session wherein they analyze the global markets, check charts, read various financial newspapers, note down key economic events of the day, etc. before they start their trades.

**Good Knowledge of Charting and Analysis Tools:** In order to be a successful forex trader, it is very important to have good knowledge on the usage of charting and other analytic software. The usage of this trading software raises the odds of success considerably, so it is important to have a good understanding of them.

**Constant Learning:** Trading field requires constant learning. The trader should be prepared to learn throughout his trading career. Something that might work now might not work after 5 years. So it's very important to constantly adapt and keep learning to be a step ahead of others. A good trader should be on the constant lookout of learning new things that might help him with his trading, be it the usage of trading software or a new way of analysis.

**Mastering Fear:** It is very important to master fear to be a successful forex trader. The trader should be prepared to take losses now and again and should understand that it's part and parcel of the game. The inability to book losses and holding on to a losing position can result in more losses. The trader should also be ready to take a trade when a good opportunity arises and should not allow fear to hold him back.

**Thinking on Your Own:** It is very important to think on your own and make trading decisions and not just blindly follow the crowd. As the saying goes, "buy into the fear and sell into the greed!" Now, this does not always mean doing the opposite of what others do. It just means that the trader should have an open mind and should have the ability to think on his own and make decisions accordingly.

**Awareness of Global Events:** Forex markets are affected by the major international events that occur. The key economic events are happening globally, as the forex markets are traded globally and affected by these economic events. A few examples of the key economic events are the Federal Bank interest rate decision, ECB rate decision, GDP data of key economies, job data of key economies, inflation data of key economies, etc.

**Never Blame the Market:** The market might behave irrationally, but the trader should be responsible for reading the market cues and making trading decisions. Instead of playing the blame game, he should learn from each mistake and learn from it. The trader should understand the risks associated with trading and have a proper money management rule in place.

**Trading Journal:** It is important to maintain a trading journal and make an entry of all the trades he makes. The reasons for taking that particular trade should also be noted down. This would help in analyzing the trades later and help in avoiding the mistakes made. This would also help in identifying the good trades made and look for similar patterns later on.

**Choosing the Right Broker:** It is important to choose the right broker. Some of the factors that should be considered while selecting a broker should be a) low brokerage, b) fast and reliable trading terminal, c) ease of trading and good research, and charting software's that the broker provides.

**Money Management Rules:** This is perhaps the most important among all things that are mentioned now. A money management rule is basically the rules that define the maximum loss a trader can afford to take per trade or at a point of time. Most forex traders never risk more than 2- 5 % per trade.

They also never risk more than 10-20 % at a particular point across all trades. It is very important to follow these rules; else, you run the risk of wiping out your entire trading account in a matter of days, if not hours! It is always better to limit your losses and live to fight another day!

CHAPTER 13:

# Developing Your Trading Plan

You now have the fundamental principles of Forex trading under your belt, and you are aware of what you are trading in and why. So how do you translate that into a practical application?

Every successful trader enters the marketplace with a clear plan in their mind, and the reason they can then describe themselves as successful is that they follow it dutifully and religiously.

Now, while it's true that you can find software out there that will make those decisions for you, I strongly recommend that you avoid the temptation. Much as with those crash diets that never help lose more than a couple of pounds and the wonder medicines that do little else than taste unpleasant, those software programs tend to be snake oil. After all, if they really did work, everyone would be using them, and everyone would be millionaires.

Instead, you're going to have to create your own plan and then rely on your hard work to research the markets, your intuition, and your ability to assess the risk to provide the rest.

Getting started is relatively simple. You will need to provide yourself the answer to two questions:

- What is the maximum loss you are prepared to make in a single position? (In percentage terms.)
- What will be your stop-loss position on your trades?

Every trader needs to know the answer to those questions, although everything else is fluid and personal. Your ability to analyze the market, the time of day you trade, your capital and risk ability – these things are all distinctly personal, which means there is no possible way to develop a plan that works for absolutely everybody.

Not to mention that the same strategy won't necessarily work in every market and on every trade or with every currency pair. You will need to develop a fluid mindset that can adapt your plan accordingly to the realities of the market.

So, with that in mind, how do you develop your personal strategy? Start with the two questions above, as these are designed to make sure that the capital in your trading account remains intact. Answer those questions with a mind to your trading account and to how much you can afford to lose before you no longer have the capital to continue trading. Your answers are the only ones to which you must adhere religiously, come what may. Consider your capital to be your prized possession and worthy of protection at all times.

A quick example to show you how those questions then apply to actual trade. Let's assume that you've decided that your maximum risk on a trade is going to be $45, which equates to 2 percent of your capital (I would recommend never going above 5 percent), and that you've decided your stop-loss position will represent three times the average pip movement of that currency pair.

Now let's assume you're looking at a trade that moves on average five pips within your chosen timeframe. You would therefore have a stop loss position of 15 pips. If you divide the maximum loss you're prepared to make by the number of pips, you get the number 3, which translates to $3 per pip.

So what does that mean? It means that you want a contract that balances out at $3 per pip.

You can, of course, then play with your equation. For example, if you enter into a contract with less risk than you're prepared to take, you can then increase your position later if your predictions bear out, adding more contracts until you reach that $45 maximum.

Don't forget that the answer to these questions represents the maximum risk you're prepared to take, so you don't actually have to meet those numbers exactly as long as you don't exceed them.

## Step by Step Trading Plan Decisions

With those two basic questions asked and answered, you have numbers to play with that will guide you through individual trades.

But what of your overall strategy? To develop that, you'll need to ask yourself some questions that you may have already been thinking about as you worked through this book.

1. How much capital do you want to invest, and how much time do you want to spend trading? The decisions you make about your trading need to fit with your lifestyle and responsibilities, so it's best to work this out first and then develop your plan to fit around these basic needs.

2. How do you want to perform your analysis? You've been introduced to the basics of both fundamental and technical analysis in this book, and I did suggest that a combination of the two is a good idea. Before you decide which to use, experiment with them for a little while. Make theoretical trades based on what you have learned through research and see how they pan out. Traders don't all use one or the other of these systems, and that's for a good reason – our brains all work in their own unique ways, and you may find yourself making better decisions using one over the other.

3. What are your financial goals and targets? It's paramount as a trader that you are consistent in your approach, and making sure you have these goals will ensure that you are. As a quick note, your goals should be based on the number of pips you want to gain, not a solid figure in dollars or pounds. As your capital grows, you'll be investing in bigger contracts, so the pips will represent larger amounts of money. This is how you will grow your capital: by consistently following the same strategy as you go along and seeing how that strategy brings bigger gains over time.

4. Do you want to be a long or short term trader? This is going to affect how you perform your research and what you are looking for and, ultimately, will dictate what it is that makes you decide to enter into a trade.

5. What currency pairs do you want to trade-in? Keep in mind the risk associated with each pair and also your personal circumstances – there's no point trading on a currency that's barely moving during the time you're able to trade, for example.

With all these questions answered, you must now take on board that all of your tradings are going to come down to the idea of risk. It is based around how much risk you are prepared to take in general – the answers to those first two questions – and how much risk a particular position represents. If you keep this in mind during every trade decision, you can't go too far wrong.

Make those high-risk choices if you want to, but make sure that you're aware they are high risk before you do and that you're not taking any greater risk than your plan dictates.

CHAPTER 14:

# Beginners' Mistakes to Avoid

The investor who faces the world of financial markets should be considered as a person who wants to learn how to play tennis. You are obliged to know the rules of the game, have the necessary materials, and attend teacher/student lessons, telling them what they should and shouldn't do.

This paragraph and the following paragraph are instead dedicated to the things that should not be done, that is, the mistakes that traders and investors tend to repeat with a specific frequency.

1. **Not Accepting Losses.** One of the biggest problems facing the trader is not to close at a loss trades that prove to be incorrect. It is a difficulty related to both the economic and psychological aspects (many people find it extremely difficult to admit that they have made a mistake). Many traders build operating strategies with stop-loss only "theoretically": that is, they identify a level of support and, mentally, think of closing the position if prices fall below that threshold. Then, when prices actually break the support, and you have to suffer the loss, they prefer to wait for something to change. Some people think the market is wrong. Others seek some technical motivation to assume that it is just a false signal. Others increase positions to mediate the load price. Nothing more wrong. The truth is that, frequently, the strategy that was built turned out to be wrong, and we need to get out of that position immediately before the situation worsens further.

2. **Not Following Pre-Established Rules.** The lack of an operational plan built at the table, in which you define where it is determined how much to invest in the single operation; what is the maximum risk you are willing to take; what are the operational levels that you intend to use in your operation (entry-level, initial stop-loss, take-profit), lead the trader to make mistakes dictated by the emotionality and stress of having to then manage the position in real-time. Doubts arise, doubts, uncertainties that have nothing to do with the analysis that was carried out in firm bowls and which had led to the judgment as interesting a specific technical situation.

3. **Not Learning From Mistakes.** Often operators make the same kind of error (they enter the market earlier than they should, they get into a late position, close the area soon, they do not comply with stop-loss, and so on), and from their mistakes, they fail to draw due lessons. To be able to analyze in detail your operations, it is advisable to keep the accounting of the various transactions, marking the entry-level, the stop-loss, the possible take-profit, and the reason for which the transaction was made. Only the correct registration of all trade can allow you to objectively evaluate the results obtained, identifying the situations on which you are profitable and those on which you make mistakes and suffer losses.

4. **Not Being Patient.** One of the difficulties that the trader often encounters is to know how to wait for urgent situations to be created. Staying on standby for a while can be mentally unnerving. This leads the trader to trade even when there are no conditions, just because he has to do something. In some cases, you also risk going into overtrading (i.e., operating frantically, without a basic logic), for the desire to recover prior losses or to want to continue a possible positive streak of operations.

5. **Not Letting Their Profits Run Fast Enough.** One of the basic rules of trading claims to "cut losses and let profits run." When the market goes in the intended direction, it is appropriate (I would say necessary) to exploit the situation, but following pre-established rules (taking partial profit, for example, after prices have made a favorable movement, proportionate to the initial risk to which you are exposed). One of the techniques that can be used is to simulate your table operation (what in technical jargon is called paper trading) to be able to evaluate whether the targets/take-profits that are used in their operations are too close or too far from the movement made by the market. In some cases, it will be found that you have closed your positions too early, while in others, you have set too ambitious targets.

6. **Not Following Strict Money Management Rules.** Only careful money management can allow financial markets to survive for a long time. The trader who takes too high risks, who does not correctly relate the size of the individual positions to the total capital at their disposal, which does not respect the set stop-loss, is inevitably destined to suffer losses. To achieve positive returns consistently, you need to be extremely disciplined and rigid in your operations. If these rules are not followed, inevitably, our equity-line (the cumulative line of profits and losses, which records the outcome of the various transactions) will be very volatile: there will be periods when good results are obtained (however high risk), but also periods in which you suffer substantial losses.

7. **Following Rumors/News Instead of Your Analyses.** Many traders are often distracted by the river of news that is constantly coming into the market and tend to be influenced by the opinions expressed by other analysts. It should never be forgotten that trading means working on prices: the latter must,

therefore, be closely followed, analyzed, and studied. You have to understand how they formed and what their future behavior might be. Everything else is just "noise" background noise, which can certainly generate volatility (on the occasion, for example, the dissemination of important macro data or as a result of some particularly relevant corporate choices), but it is rarely able to change the technical structure of the market. If the latter is set to rise, it will find a way to rise even in the presence of a negative environment (indeed, a market that does not fall when negative news comes is a symptom of strength and indicates the will to rise, with buyers who have exploited this news to accumulate upward positions); if instead the market is set to fall, it will find a way to fall even in the presence of a positive environment (indeed, a market that does not rise when positive news comes is symptomatic of extreme weakness and indicates the willingness to go down, with sellers who have used this news to liquidate any long positions or open new short positions).

8. **Using Complex Analyses.** Novice traders, often in search of the Holy Grail, fill their screens with technical indicators/oscillators, numerous trendlines) that intersect with prices, complex graphical methods that are difficult to decipher. Nothing more wrong. The chart should be as clean as possible, with prices needing to have the highest visibility possible, with some trend lines that help identify the main trend and identify the main levels of support or resistance, and few, very few indicators that can provide useful operational information. The goal is to achieve a chart/layout that is as clear and as simple as possible, where the key levels that have been formed and on which you intend to operate must be evident.

9. **Not Being Clear.** When you decide to open a new position (and therefore put your money at risk), you need to have a clear and accurate picture of the situation. If you have doubts, uncertainties, indecisions, it is better to give up. If the technical picture is mixed, it means that the market itself is undecided about what to do. Under these conditions, it is preferable to stay at the window, waiting for the scenario to clear up or unlock. The basic rule is that we enter the market only when the probability of success is in our favor, that is, when the analyses conducted (graphical analysis, quantitative analysis, and volumetric analysis) are all agreed in highlighting that prices are destined to rise (for long operation) or to fall (for a short operation). In general, it is preferable to miss an opportunity rather than take a risk by betting that prices will take the desired direction. Trading only achieves positive results if you take advantage of favorable situations and reduce your level of risk as much as possible.

10. **Changing From One Strategy to Another.** The trader must build a solid analysis methodology and a sound operational strategy. The latter requires you to operate only when there are technical situations that the operator has learned both to recognize (for example, a breakup) or a reversal bar), and to exploit. This means that, in the face of similar situations, you will have to operate similarly, always using the same tools (graphs/quantitative/volumes), taking on the same level of risk, and managing the position in the same way. It is, therefore, not necessary to change the way it operates just because the latest results have been negative. Losses need to be managed and analyzed, but they must not make us abandon a methodology that, over time, has proven to work.

CHAPTER 15:

# The Trading Strategy

You need a trading strategy to place your trades. You can have all the trading requirements to make you a successful trader, but without the right trading strategy, you won't get any profits at all.

Never start your trades when you do not have a strategy in place.

## Developing the Right Trading Strategy

Day trading strategies are important for beginners and advanced traders. The good news is that the process is easy. The bad news is that coming up with the right profitable strategy is harder than you might think.

### *1. Choosing the Right Market*

There are various viable day trading markets that you can explore. These include stocks, Forex, and futures. One of the top questions that new traders ask is, "which is the best market?" Under this heading, we shall look at the different markets and the pros and cons of each.

However, the best market depends on how much money you have, interests, and time. We also look at the potential of each market.

### *2. Pick a Market You Have a Lot of Interest In*

Day trading is tough. No one should lie to you that it is something you can do without all the prerequisites.

When you come across something challenging, the best thing is to have an interest in it. If you aren't passionate about day trading, it is prudent that you put your time into something else.

When starting out, pick a single market and focus on it. Once you have mastered the first market, you can then branch out to other markets, but remember to focus on one market at a time. Trying to learn too many markets distracts you, and you lose out. Start with the market you have more interest in, stick to it, and build the skills. If you like the market and it is working for you, and then you don't have any reason to trade anything else. Trading multiple markets won't give you more income.

### *3. Understand the Income Potential*

All the different types of markets are giving you the chance to make money out of your trades. Forex, stocks, and futures all give you the same day trading income potential. Therefore, do not think that you will have more money trading futures or stocks with a poor strategy.

Thus, income potential shouldn't be your driving force when it comes to choosing a market; instead, you need to check on how much capital you require to enter a particular market.

Stocks are more capital intensive than other types of trades. Next is futures followed by Forex.

To trade stocks, you need at least $25,000 in US markets. However, other markets are less stringent, and you can start with even $10,000. However, the US market presents the best for day trading, so it is wise to run trades on it. Many low-level brokers will allow you to open an account with just $1,000 and give you the option to trade at $500. But this isn't advisable because you can't cushion yourself against losses.

Start with enough capital so that you give yourself a fighting chance.

To trade Forex as a day trader, you need to start with preferably $1000 or more so that you can start building an income. Here, many brokers can open accounts for as little as $100. Remember that all markets have the same profit potential. So, the lesser you invest in any market, the lower the possibility of making money. Just because you can start with a minimum amount doesn't mean you must go with that amount.

## When Can You Day Trade?

Futures and Forex markets give you 24-hour periods to trade for 5 days a week. You can actively trade stocks between 9.30 and 4 pm ET.

After you consider which market to trade and how much capital to put in, you also need to look at the time you need to invest in the market. Some times of the day are best suited for trading. Some markets are flexible, with Forex being the most flexible of all of them.

Day trading, especially in currency pairs, offers you the most options when it comes to day trading. Time also matters. For instance, lunchtime isn't a good time to trade.

For day trading stocks, the market usually opens at 9.30 am EST. Sometimes opportunities occur in the hour before this time, but most of the time, the action occurs between 9.30 am and 11.30 am EST.

If you plan to run trades, then focus on them and sit down to actually trade for several hours with total focus. Do not trade from a computer while focusing on another job since you will be distracted.

### *Look at Market Correlation*

If you are using multiple markets to trade, you need to consider the correlation of the markets that you have selected to trade. Products that move together increase the level of risk that you face.

### *Liquidity and the Risk*

The way the market moves is important as well. You need to know the normal trading range per day, the value of per tick, and the volume that is traded each day. You also need to understand the level of liquidity of the order book.

These factors make up the execution risk, which is a factor that determines how easy it is to get in and out of the market at a certain price without too much slippage. Trade risk refers to what you need to risk to know whether a trade will work out or not.

### *Selecting a Timeframe*

When you decide to go into day trading, you need to choose a timeframe of fewer than 24 hours. Some of the popular timeframes run from 1-minute to 60-minute timeframes. A smaller timeframe gives you smaller profits but low risk as well. Additionally, you have access to more trading opportunities compared to choosing longer timeframes.

When you start day trading, you might want to go for a smaller timeframe to make sure you do not overwork your account. The best timeframe is 15 minutes, which is small enough to capture the best moves and long enough to get rid of any clamor in the market.

However, the 15-minute trend might not work for you the way you want it to do. Make sure you experiment with a lot of time frames so that you choose the best one for your needs. The time frame should also be in line with your trading strategy. For instance, you might find that a plan that won't work on a short timeframe may work on a longer one.

So, start working on your strategy while targeting the shorter time frames, say 15-minute trades, and then change it first before you can change any rules.

### *Choosing the Right Trading Approach*

After you select the right market, you need to choose the perfect trading approach that you would like to use. After this, the fun begins. This is the perfect time for analyzing the various stocks to see which ones are the best investments. You want to determine what each of the companies is all about and what makes its stocks move.

You have to choose between fundamental or technical analysis. Both of these instruments have advantages and disadvantages.

CHAPTER 16:

# Risk and Money Management

## Budgeting for Profit

Budgeting for profit means that you have to understand how the Forex market works.

If you want to make profits when Forex trading, there are a few tips you can use. For instance, ensure that you start small. This advice applies mainly to those who are new to Forex trading; you can only be successful at trading millions when you have learned how to handle a few dollars as you can be successful in trading dollars when you have learned how to trade pennies. If you are lucky enough to buy many small stocks, there is a probability that they could tremendously increase in value, earning your profits. Luckily, there are traders today who allow you to open an account with just a few dollars. If you constantly use the account, over time, your profits will begin to grow, and you will begin to experience success.

Additionally, if you want to succeed, you should be a regular investor. This does not mean you have to put in huge chunks of money for trading each time. It simply means that you could add manageable amounts to your investment every week — for instance, $10 or $20 per week. Being a regular investor not only refines your craft but also grows your account when the profits are compounded over time. When you invest small amounts, you will not feel the pinch, but the rewards will be great regardless.

Another tip when budgeting for profit is to be patient. As has been highlighted above, starting small is a good move. However, many people get frustrated because of the slow process. To enhance your tolerance, trade small, but do not view these small amounts as dollars. Instead, view them as percentages. If you get a profit of, let us say $1 when you have a $10 account, then you have made a 10% profit.

On the other hand, if you lose a dollar, then you have lost 10%. You will then have learned a valuable lesson about Forex trading at a low cost of just a dollar. Also, when you trade in smaller amounts, you learn to deal with the hurdles associated with learning how to trade Forex.

## Risk Management

Risk management involves reducing the size of potential losses while getting the most benefit out of a single trade. Risk management is highly debated as a topic in Forex trading and, yet, it remains important as an aspect of trading because of the volatile nature of the Forex market. To understand risk management in detail, read on.

One of the fundamental rules of managing risk when trading Forex is to ensure that you only risk what you can afford to lose. Interestingly, many traders make the mistake of investing more than they can afford to lose, especially when they are learning the trade. As a Forex trader, however, you can avoid some of the fundamental mistakes made by traders and become an outstanding trader yourself. You should know when to cut your losses. Cutting losses can be made in two ways. The first is when you impose a mental stop and decide that the right thing to do would be to limit the drawdown, then you can take on a trade. Another way to control losses is by using a trading platform that allows you to lock in stops when your losses reach a particular level.

To control risks, you can also use the correct lot sizes. When accounts are advertised by brokers, they make it seem like a good idea to open an account with, let us say, $300 and use leverage to enhance mini-lot trades. They make it look like this technique will help double your money in just a single trade. This kind of thinking can sometimes deviate from reality. As a new trader, it is important to start small so that you have many options for managing the trade.

You should also be able to track your overall exposure. Reducing lot size is a good step to take. However, other steps, such as opening many lots with currency pairs, could have serious implications. For instance, when you go long on USD/CHF and short on EUR/USD, you are exposed twice to the realities of the dollar movement. Should the dollar tumble, you will suffer double losses, which can be painful. If, however, you keep your exposure limited, you have a better chance at reducing risk and increasing your chances for success in the future.

Trading with a plan is also essential. This is because when you have a plan, you can easily avoid emotional responses, which are a natural part of trading Forex. Having a trading plan will help you know what steps to take from the beginning to the end of your trading session before you open a position. An additional benefit of trading with a plan is that it will keep you from speculations and possible overtrading as a result of there being an open position. Understand that in Forex, you have to have strong will power. Your trading plan is not going to work magically. You must have a plan and follow it to the letter for this risk management strategy to be effective.

Another risk management strategy that you can employ is understanding the nature of the currency pairs you have decided to trade. Understand the events scheduled to take place in the day and even week ahead and how the data looks. Look at your trade plan's time horizon and consider liquidity conditions. Have a clear view of what the market has priced in and out because anticipating market events can alert you of possible disruptive circumstances even if it is not a complete indicator of how you can win a trade. By understanding that risk varies across currency pairs, based on different factors such as liquidity, data sensitivity, and volatility, you will be better placed to understand the analytical tools and strategies that are best for you.

Also, you can trade with an edge. This means that you do not have to be in the market all the time despite the fact that the currency market operates round the clock. Block the noise, and do not let it pull you in. You can do this, for instance, by picking a spot and timing yourself. Also, look for setups in which there is a clear risk/reward scenario to avoid an unnecessary headache. Being an opportunist in the real world can be a problem, but that does not mean this strategy cannot work in the digital world of Forex trading. You can take your time looking at the coming trade opportunities and use these chances instead of getting caught up in the market moves of a single moment.

I look forward to future opportunities because there will be more opportunities, and it pays to be ready.

Sometimes in life, it is good to take a step back from situations because it provides an individual with moments of clarity. Therefore, it is advisable to occasionally take a step back from Forex trading. Yes, this means that you need to take time off from the markets completely for a while, and no, you will not miss out on important trades. On the contrary, when you take this break, you may find that it was much needed, you are more objective when you trade, and you have a clearer perspective that keeps you from emotionally investing in a market position. Also, you can use this downtime to develop other skills, such as your understanding of fundamental analysis and to prepare yourself for fresh trading opportunities.

It is important that as a trader, you take your profits regularly. When you take your profits, you are, in essence, reducing your exposure to risks in the market. You may find that your trade plan has an aggressive profit target but imagine what would happen if events do not play in your favor. It is, therefore, a better idea to protect what you have already worked for. After all, nobody has ever gone broke while making a profit.

This is a tactic that can be referred to as taking money off the table. If you keep your profits in your margin account, you are likely to be subject to future trading decisions and are susceptible to unknown risks. Taking money out of your account keeps you in a position where you can trade in comfortable sizes. As you trade, remember that trading is not purely a game of profits. You can use the profits you make to do other things. For example, you can invest the profits into another venture once you withdraw them.

Additionally, you should ensure accuracy by double-checking. By now, you must have understood that currency trading takes place in a fairly fast-paced environment. It is even faster, thanks to electronic trading. There is, therefore, the risk of human error when inputting orders and trades, and this may have serious implications for you as a trader. For instance, what would be the benefit of putting in place a stop-loss order if it not entered for the right amount of currency? Make it a part of your routine to double-check your order and trade entries to avoid unnecessary mistakes that may prove costly to your Forex trading venture. Ideally, it would be good to double-check figures when you enter them and just before submission. Mistakes happen, but this does not mean you need to let minor errors become the source of your downfall.

## Leverage

By now, you must have an idea of what leverage is and what it can do for you in Forex trading.

In Forex, leverage can be described as the ratio of the trader's funds that you are allowed to use to the size of the broker's available funds. In essence, leverage is whatever capital you borrow to increase your returns. In reality, the leverage size usually exceeds invested capital to a large extent. Leverage is not fixed in all companies and may largely depend on the trading conditions provided by the Forex brokers. You are using leverage can sometimes be a risky affair because, just like a double-edged sword, it may work to your favor or not. Below, we highlight how leverage works and how it can affect your bottom-line.

CHAPTER 17:

# Beginners' First Investment

In the midst of the recent investment boom, the number of people who want to effectively increase their own assets by investing in financial products such as stocks and Forex (Foreign Exchange Margin Trading) is increasing very much.

However, it may be difficult for beginners to invest in high-risk assets all of a sudden. So, you should start by improving your skills with index funds.

It is also true that many people think that asset management is very difficult. There are so many terms to learn, and it's a very difficult choice to learn from and what kind of financial products to buy. Especially for those who are not so bright in finance or the economy, it may be difficult at first.

This anxiety should be even higher because it could severely damage valuable assets. In such a case, let's consider the purchase of the mutual fund managed by a professional fund manager by all means.

A professional fund manager will choose the best combination of financial products from around the world on your behalf. Among investment trusts, index funds are highly recommended as products that investment beginners should purchase for the first time.

This is a product that invests in indicators that we frequently hear, such as the Nikkei Average, TOPIX, and the Dow In New York.

As you invest, you always need to understand these indexes. That's why it's very useful for beginners to learn about economics and investments. The characteristic of index funds is that commodity prices are determined in conjunction with various indicators in the economy.

Index funds make their investment decisions easier to understand than individual stocks, and price movements are much more stable. Therefore, anyone can easily invest. When purchasing and managing such index funds, it is not so much the profit trend of individual companies as the movement of the global economy as a whole.

Learning in a field called macroeconomics becomes very important. Stock prices will change significantly due to economic indicators and policy announcements from major countries, including Japan. It is very important to properly assess the linkage between daily news and stock prices and to conduct training to properly understand what kind of stock price movement will be made when it comes out.

This knowledge of the economy as a whole is essential for investing. Investment beginners first organize their knowledge in this field in a body-shaped manner and then learn about investment and stock price linkage by purchasing an index fund linked to macro indicators.

Index funds have ETFs (listed mutual funds) on similar products, but the risk is very low because the price movement is milder than that. For stable and wonderful asset management, it is very important to start with such an index fund.

Financial instruments are more or less subject to fees. Financial products pursue returns, but of course, there are risks. It doesn't make sense to risk and offset the revenue you earn with commission costs. You can enjoy making your own investment by reducing the financial burden as much as possible.

Investment trusts may incur a fee of several percent at times. Recently, there are many products called no-road funds that do not charge a fee, so it is important to make effective use of this.

I think many people start their own investments from mutual funds, but surprisingly, it is the fees and costs of mutual funds. Since it is very expensive for a general mutual fund, it is necessary to check the product guidance called the prospectus about financial products at the time of purchase and to confirm the cost of the fee, etc. properly.

We should think about this point properly and make investments that are a little less wasteful. The main principle in long-term investment is that not wasting a small amount of profit leads to significant profits. If you are like this, let's consider using no-road funds as a priority.

With no-road funds, you can not waste money on your investment strategy. The main feature of no-road funds is that there is no commission at the time of purchase, and such products are increasing rapidly in the market.

In general investment trusts, there are purchase fees that occur at the time of purchase and commissions, such as trust fees deducted monthly. The purchase fee can be as high as a few percent at times. Investors must make more money than this fee when they ultimately make a sale. It is a natural idea to purchase products with a low commission.

In addition, trust fees are the costs deducted monthly. If you think about long-term holding, this is nothing better than cheap. In the midst of intensifying competition, various products are appearing on the market more and more. It is a gateway to investors who are wise to choose products with low commissions on the premise of long-term holdings.

Let's think about how to do our best to make as much money as possible. By choosing a mutual fund that is paid a no-road and monthly distribution, you can manage assets stably.

It is very important not only to be blinded by the profits of your asset management but also to have a proper awareness of risks and costs.

Considering the relationship between cost and return, it is important to give proper consideration to fees.

Mutual funds vary from product to product, but it is also one of the great pleasures because it contains an amount close to the dividend called a distribution. The timing of dividends varies depending on the product, such as once every month, every other month, or once every six months. If you are investing in distributions, let's carefully consider the span of such payments.

It is a very important method of asset management to make your investment more and more efficient in mutual funds. Distributions are a very important source of revenue. Let's use it as a reference when you enjoy thinking about your investment.

It also compensates for losses incurred due to lower prices, so you should make good use of them. Some profits rise in price as a major advantage of mutual funds, but there are also dividends and distributions.

You can get both income gain and capital gains mentioned earlier, and the market can compensate for unrealized losses with distributions. Let's enjoy both sides and increase investment efficiency more and more.

Distributions are paid at different times, depending on the product. The timing and number of distributions paid depend on the product. There are a lot of products that the distribution enters every month in the inside, too. Have fun incorporating distributions into your investments. The fund which the distribution enters every month feels very advantageous.

If you hold such a fund for a long time, you can manage your own assets at a very reasonable time. To make investments aimed at distributions, it is important to invest from a long-term perspective.

Again, the important idea is the dollar cost averaging method. It is very important to think about appropriately diversified investment in your asset management from a long perspective. It is very important to protect your assets over a long period. Let's enjoy and do wonderful asset management.

As for the payment status of the distribution, you can easily find it by examining the product. Let's make fun of investment, including distribution, by taking advantage of the advantages of mutual funds that can easily invest in various products around the world.

Stock investment is very risky. If you think about such dangers enough, by incorporating mutual funds well into your usual investments, you can make reliable investments while successfully enjoying the benefits of distributions and other benefits.

If investment trusts are incorporated into asset formation regularly, you can make more reliable investments on your own while making effective use of distributions and other materials.

CHAPTER 18:

# Needs to Know About Forex Trading

Forex trading is an avenue that is making people earn a more significant income. There are many platforms where you can put that little penny in the trading and amerce that profits. However, it needs you to be that wise speculator who knows who reads the indicator promptly and knows the point to make that trading. Remember that forex trading is all about the trading of currencies. Therefore, you have to be knowledgeable about how the different currencies perform. The following are the basics where a beginner should know.

You should first be interested in knowing how the currencies behave in the market. That is where one ought to recognize the values of different currencies. The major currencies traded across the globe shows significant value in the market. Some of these currencies include the Us dollar, pound sterling, Swiss franc, Japanese yen, and the euro. That is not to say that other currencies are not traded, but this one has the commanding value in the forex exchange. Therefore, it requires the broker and the trader to be updated on the value of the stated monies. This is because, in some instances, the currencies may deteriorate and increase their worth significantly. Another thing to contemplate is how the paired currencies behave with each other. For example, in the forex chart, you may see the Us dollar combined with the euro or any other pair.

Another thing you ought to know is the type of indicators available and how one can make trading. These indicators follow specific movement criteria. First and foremost, before knowing that indicator thinks of the scales used in the chart. The chart represents a graphical diagram with both the independent and the depend scales. The independent scales are normally plotted on the horizontal axis and the dependent scale on the vertical axis. Therefore, you have to know the different variables in trading. Some of these variables are the price movement, the volume, and many others. Check on these charts ad test the movement of these variables appropriately.

Concerning the indicators, you should be aware of how these indicators behave. They are of different types and are influenced by the variables you use. For a beginner, it is essential to have that knowledge of how they behave is crucial. You have to know the different types of these indicators so that you can follow their trend. Think of the indicators like the Moving Average Convergence and Divergence. This indicator measures the two exponential moving averages. There is the Bollinger band indicator that measures the standard deviation of those currencies of the currencies. In some terms like the volatility market, you also need to know them. Remember that the volatility of the currency is its behavior to have either a sharp increase or decrease in the market. That is where you can either gain a sizable profit or loss.

That is not to forget the relative strength index, which is beneficial for ascertaining the overbought and the oversold. These indicators are very many in particular, but when you have their information is nothing that should stop you from earning—even the types of charts like the candlesticks. Line charts and bar charts should be at your fingertips. There are different charts for every level of your trading. For example, in your case, as a beginner, you can use the thence stick or the basic charts.

Another thing is the trend analysis. You should analyze the direction in which the indicator flows whenever you make a trade. That should help you in analyzing the peak times and recession periods of a paired currency. You also can anticipate the next performance of the paired currency if you are experienced in reading the behaviors of the indicators. You still use this information to know the right point of the market entry and the exits of the point—those brokers who analyze the trend accordingly and are in a position of obtaining a sizeable return.

## Which Qualities Make You a Successful Beginner in Trading?

After knowing the basics, you do not just start trading when you have the minimal qualities required in this business. You will realize how you will get frustrated when you stake a lot of cash, then the trading fails. At other junctures, you need to apply essential speculation tactics. That is the knowledge of probability and analyzing the statistics for you to stand a chance in trading. Some of these qualities are:

**Be That Guy Who Is Good in Decision Making.** Remember that the facility needs intelligence and critical thinking. You may find yourself succeeding a lot in a particular segment of trading. However, not to realize that it may be a trap where even after making sublime returns, you will eventually gain a hefty loss. Some other times you need not consider only short-term profit but fight for long-term returns. You may identify a promising venture but where whose returns are realized on a long-term basis. However, if you are that person who needs quick money, you will not be patient on that venture but look for short term profits. Moreover, those who take time in making a decision realizes a pattern trend and make the right move.

**Be That Risk-Taker Who Does Not Fear to Make a Loss**. If all people were risk-averse, then there would be no forex trading. Hey, remember that this business is like a gamble. I am sure that many people do not like hearing this term, but whenever you are dealing with uncertainties, you are gambling. No matter what you do, you have to sacrifice that penny expecting two possibilities, which are either a win or a loss.

Even other renowned investors cite that 'you have to stake big to win big.' Therefore, be a risk-taker who stakes big and hopes for massive earnings of returns. Even if you fail seldom, do not give up, but eventually, you will win.

**Be Persistent.** When you are persistent, you normally are tolerant. You never give up hope even after failing many times. While your needs are learning from your mistakes, do not repeat the same strategy you did, which failed you. Be that person who sees the failure as a lesson to improve their ways of staking. Adopt a trial and error strategy, which will eventually give you a winning edge. You do not expect to keep winning all the time. You will undoubtedly lose in some instances. You will realize you will keep developing tactics of trading with this trial and error strategy. You will, too, familiarize yourself with the trend analysis, and, therefore, with what is stopping you from knowing how to make that currency trade.

**Timing Is Also Operational in the Business.** You have to flexible enough to identify a profitable opportunity. The way the currencies behave is like a pendulum that goes in every direction; you can use a stopwatch and identify the specific time the trading signals a return and risks or an entry point and an exit point, because those seconds or minutes you waste may be the advent of your failure. Make a demo trade in which you do not have to input some cash, look at the behavior of the currency, and how they react in any substantial change. You may identify the correct timing when you need to stake, and, therefore, you will have that confidence to risk your money in the trading.

**Intelligent Speculation Is Required for This Job.** This trading requires you to be wise in reading the trends and having a knowledge of statistics and probability. Those brokers are reputable in making the wise traders are the one who clearly predicts the next behavior of the trading because their experience in reading the scales and indicators further enhances effective trading. Intelligence speculation is a skill that is learned by various strategies, and one of those strategies is the trial and error method, where you will consequently have that experience of trend analysis. Knowledge of the different currencies, charts, and indicators gives you that winning margin. Lastly, you can consult specialists to train you about the analysis of currency trading.

**Adequate Preparation Is Needed in This Exercise**. How best can you be in a particular exercise if you are not that fully prepared? You must be that person who is willing to set your record straight. Efficient preparation starts with the person who keeps the trading records and can analyze the performance of the currencies using them. Always appreciate the usage of the demo account in which you practices trading. In this, you are not fearful of losing your cash. Once you are used to frequent rehearsals, you are comfortable with making the trading.

## What Are the First Steps for a Beginner in Trading?

First, you have to have good preparations. Trading does not fall on the moon; however, you need to have the gadgets for trading. You need to have that electronic device. It can be either your phone, laptop, eye pad, or any other gadget. Make sure you have the best source of the internet because you need to make many references to the currencies from the network. Make sure you are comfortably sat and good to go.

Choose the best agency company in forex trading. Remember, there are many companies online that broke those currencies. To get such firms, one must conduct an extensive study of them. You also need to consider if they are registered and licensed. Moreover, consider their brokerage fee and their essential features. It should have the necessary charts, variables, and indicators which must satisfy the trader. Consult other traders to recommend you the best brokerage firm. When you are satisfied with this, create an account with them. Assess they provide a demo account that is necessary for the trading rehearsal.

The demo account is very vital for you to practice trading. Remember, you cannot put your money in a venture that you do not know; therefore, you must understand it first. If you are satisfied with it, then start the trading program. The good thing with the demo account is that you are not afraid of any risks since you have not staked any cash. Check at the trading platform and its chart.

Open the chart or the diagram and try to choose the currency pair. Most of the time, the currencies are found in the top of the graph, its sides, or below the chart. Look at the available currencies and think about them. You have to be keen in choosing the pair. You can even research how the values of different currencies and how they behave with each other. Do not forget to check their volatility and how they fair when traded. Choose those pairs and fix them at the graph.

CHAPTER 19:

# How Can Beginners Manage the Risk?

Forex trading is quite similar to stock investing. The higher the amount of money you invest, the greater your potential profit or loss will be. In currency trading, you need to invest in making a profit. Drawdowns—a decline in a fund or an investment—also happen in currency trading. If you have limited funds, losing a lot will make it hard for you to get back on track.

It is common for beginners to think that Forex trading is easy and fast. But, in truth, becoming good at trading currencies and making profitable trades requires patience, knowledge, time, and commitment.

You also need to consider your broker's trading conditions.

Risk management is integral in Forex trading because the market is unpredictable. Risks can make you lose your capital.

Speculators are the most vulnerable to trading risks. This is because they tend to invest more than what they can afford.

The use of risk management in currency trading separates successful traders from the people who deplete their trading account. When you can manage existing trading risks properly, you can control the amount of capital you can lose on a Forex transaction. Even if you experience the worst-case scenario in a trade, you won't go bankrupt.

### *1. Only Invest Your Excess Money*

This is the very first unwritten rule in Forex trading: Only risk the money that you can afford to lose.

Many beginner traders believe that their first few trades will bring in extra cash.

However, like seasoned traders, beginners will experience losses if they trade carelessly. If you trade using your monthly budget, stop right there! Forex trading is inherently risky. Don't take risks by using the money for your basic necessities.

### 2. *Your Risk/Reward Ratio Should Be Set at 1:3*

RRR is an essential tool in currency trading because, as a Forex trader, you have to mitigate and eradicate downside risks.

The RRR helps you set your take-profit and stop-loss orders based on your preferred risk tolerance. Although the ratio depends on every trader, the RRR of 1:3 is the most widely used. With this, you can earn three times as much as your capital.

For example, if the difference between your entry-level and stop-loss order is 20 pips and the distance between your Forex entry point and take-profit is 60 pips, then your risk\reward ratio is 1:3. This implies that you're willing to risk 20 pips to get 60 pips.

### 3. *Maintain the Risks*

If you can't completely eradicate a risk, then it's advised to just maintain it. The majority of beginners will increase their investments after making a profit in earlier trade.

If luck is on your side, you can win big by risking everything. However, this is the best way of wiping your trading account clean.

Three winning streaks don't mean that your next trade will be successful. As a beginner, you have to study the trends, the price movement, and the reasons behind your success.

If you become an expert in predicting future prices, and you have an eight-five percent win-rate, only then should you try investing all of the funds in your trading account.

Beginners like yourself should always trade like you're making your first-ever Forex trade. Don't include your gains in your investment.

### *4. Control and Understand Leverage*

Foreign exchanges are leveraged markets. Because of margin trading and leveraging, you can borrow money more than your capital investment.

As collateral, the broker or financier will only ask you to set aside a small percentage of your entire trading account.

When leveraging, you'll make huge profits. If you only make $30 per trade with your $500 trading account, you can earn $90 by borrowing $1000. This strategy is best combined with the 1:3 RRR.

### *5. Two Percent Investment*

As a beginner, the best tactic you can do to manage the risks is to invest only a small percentage of your account on each transaction. By doing so, you can avoid losing streaks and prevent a huge drawdown in your trading account. This can kill your account and make it difficult to reach breakeven. It's recommended to only trade two percent of your account.

CHAPTER 20:

# Secrets to Be Profitable in Long Run

## Finding Success in Forex

Since you understand the basics of Forex Trading, you are ready to learn the strategies that traders use to attain success on the market—understanding what you are attempting to accomplish with your trades as well as appreciating that less is more when it comes to trading. Before we jump into the strategies that will aid you in turning a buck in currency trading, let's just spend a moment reiterating some of the important concepts that have led us to this point. There are many key points that you need to understand before you even start talking about strategies.

## Successful Trading Strategies

When all is said and done, you are the one responsible for turning your venture into foreign exchange into a successful endeavor. That is actually one of the great things about forex. You do not have a boss screaming down your neck, telling you to do something that you do not agree with. You can come up with your own trading plan based on your research and your knowledge. That being said, success can come more quickly for some than for others, and a lot of the time, this has to do with approaching this endeavor with the right strategy.

***Strategy 1. Buy Low and Sell High***

If you began currency trading today with $25,000 in your pocket and access to a trading platform, all ready and raring to go, how would you know what is low and what is high? It's your first day. Naturally, for you to understand what would represent a good low investment and conversely what is high, you need to have some knowledge of the exchange rate history of that currency. Maybe the exchange rate for Japanese yen seems low, but actually, compared to last year or a few months ago, it's a little high. Now it would not be the right time to buy. Maybe the pound seems low right now, but yesterday the British government announced that the first round of the Brexit negotiations with the EU failed, and therefore, the pound may have room to go lower than it is when you logged onto your trading platform. Maybe you should wait and see what the pound is later today or tomorrow and buy then. The point here is that buying low and selling high requires understanding the patterns associated with that currency and what might cause it to go up or down, and that's merely the buying side of things. Once you have bought low, you need to figure out when you are going to sell. This is where a good trading plan will come into play. A good plan will prevent you from selling too soon, or even not selling soon enough.

### *Strategy 2. Focus on Not Losing Money Rather Than On Making Money*

This may not be an easy strategy to understand initially, in part because not losing money and making money seem like two sides of the same coin. They are, but they are not identical. One of the personality types that is associated with difficulty in finding success in trading is the impulsive type. This type of person wants to make money, and they want to make it quick. They have a vague strategy about how they plan on doing that, but the most important thing to them is that they have a high account balance to make as many trades as they need to turn a profit. This is the wrong approach because currencies are not the same as stocks. The value of a currency may change very little even over a week, so a strategy that involves a lot of trades to make money is usually not the best strategy. You want to have a crystal clear idea of when you are going to but, yes, because you want to make money, but mostly because you don't want to lose. Every market that involves exchanges, like the stock market, has some implicit risk, and currency trading is risky, too, because you may be tempted to give up the advantage you have to try and make money quickly.

***Strategy 3. Develop a Sense of Sentiment Analysis***

Alright, the third strategy was going to be about Fibonacci retracement, which is a type of technical analysis of the market, but as this is the basics of currency trading, we are going to go into a different strategy that is not any easier than a Fibonacci retracement, just different. Sentiment analysis is a term that is used in many different specialties, not just finance, and it is not easy to describe. It is essentially a type of analysis that is not based on a chart showing exchange rates over time (technical analysis) or on an understanding of a factor that might today be affecting the value of a currency (fundamental analysis). Sentiment analysis attempts to gauge the tone of the market, the direction the market is heading in by parsing all of the available information. A key to understanding sentiment analysis is likening it to public opinion. The economy may be booming, people have more money in their pocket, so the currency of this hypothetical country should increase in value, but maybe it doesn't. Maybe there is something that is causing the market to be bearish and which, therefore, might cause the currency to drop. As you perhaps can tell, as this analysis is not based on any concrete information, it can be thought of as intuitive, and no one has intuition on day 1. Let's just be honest about that. Intuition comes from experience. But the purpose of this strategy is to introduce to you the idea that not the foreign exchange market, like any market, is not going to behave like a machine because it's not a machine. Markets are places where human beings come together, and humans are unpredictable, often in a frustrating way. Perhaps one day, currency trading may be handled by machines (that wouldn't be fun), but that day is far off, and so you will have to develop your own sense of where the market seems to be going and use this as a strategy to achieve success in this endeavor.

CHAPTER 21:

# Tips and Tricks to Trade Like a Pro

Throughout this book, you have been able to learn some of the basic skills that will enable you to make it in the Forex market. However, that alone is not enough. To be an exceptional Forex trader, you have to be equipped with some tips and tricks that will enable you to maneuver around. You have to learn that the best traders are disciplined and practice a lot. They don't just do trade analysis but also perform self-analysis to clearly understand what motivates and drives their trade. By doing a self-analysis, you will also help you to keep both greed and fear out of the trade equation. Here are some of the essential skills, tips, and trips that will make you trade like a pro:

## Begin By Defining Your Goals

Before starting your journey as a Forex trader, it is important to have a clear idea about what you would like to achieve and how you intend to get to this destination. Ensure that you have clearly drawn your goals and mastered them in mind. After defining your goals, try to assess through the different trading methods available. Select the best method that fits you and ensures that this trading method will enable you to achieve your set goals. This is because each trading method has its own risk profile, which will require you as a trader to develop some attitude as well as an approach to be a successful Forex trader. For instance, if you are this type of person whose instincts do not allow you to go to sleep when there is an open market position, clearly, you are the best fit for day trading. However, if you are this type of person who is ready to take time and wait for some periods for trade to appreciate, then you are the best fit to be a position trader.

It is appropriate that you be sure of your personality. Your personality must fit your trading style. Forex trading at times is stressful; thus, be sure that your personality matches the method of trade you have chosen.

## Choosing a Broker and a Trading Platform

It is appropriate that you chose a reputable broker. I advise that as a beginner, start by taking a considerable amount of time to do deep research on the differences between the available brokers. Try to understand the different policies that each broker has, as well as how each of these brokers goes about making a market. You have to understand that doing trade in the over-the-counter market differs from exchange driven market. Again, I advise that you be sure of the trading platform your broker is using to know the suitable analysis that will fit you. For instance, if you trade by analyzing Fibonacci numbers, just ensure that the platform your broker is using also supports the drawing of Fibonacci lines. Try to understand good brokers with poor trading platforms, poor brokers with good trading platforms, and good brokers with good trading platforms. Ensure that you choose a good broker with a good trading platform.

## Before Moving to Multiple Currency Pair, Focus More on One Currency Pair

By now, I believe that you have noted that the Forex trade world is complicated. This is probably attributed to the mixed-up nature of the currency market, the different goals different participants have, and the wide and diverse characters. Unless you are a genius, it will be very difficult to understand all the financial and economic activities going around the world. Therefore, to be a successful Forex trader, you must try to stick your Forex trade activities with the currency pairs you are familiar with and have a good understanding of. It is an even greater advantage if you start with your nation's currency. However, if this is not what you want, I prefer that you chose the widely and most liquid traded currency pairs.

## Clearly Determine Your Entry and Exit Points

Often many beginners are usually confused by the information presented in the charts in the different timeframes. This is due to the scenario that most of the time, the information presented in these charts are so conflicting.

There are times when what is shown on the weekly chart as the buying opportunity can be shown up on the intraday chart as a sell signal. It is advised that as a Forex beginner, if you have chosen to shift your trading to a daily chart, say from a weekly chart, ensure that you synchronize these two charts. What I mean is that, suppose your weekly chart gives a buy signal, be patient for the release of a daily chart to confirm a similar signal. Just be sure to keep your timing in sync.

## Study the Forex Market and Its Fundamentals

Having a deep understanding of the fundamentals of the Forex market and the technical factors affecting the price action is of great importance. Without a reasonable understanding of the Forex market, you are likely to be affected negatively. However, don't be afraid of the consequences of erroneous application or the consequences of failing to understand the technical or fundamental studies. Learning is a gradual step, and as we make errors, we get to learn more.

You must have proper money management skills as well as emotional skills as these play an important role in the analysis. It is also appropriate that once you make profits, learn how to protect them. I suggest that if you have no skills in money management, learn. Money management will teach you how to minimize your losses and maximize your profits.

I prefer that you develop a bible of money management and put it as a trading library's centerpiece. This will guide you on ways of ensuring that you don't gamble with the profits you have earned hardly as well as cut your losses short.

## Be Sure To Calculate Your Expectancy

Basically, expectancy will help you to determine your system's reliability. It is advised that as a trader, you should try to roll back and check your trade history. From here, get a measurement of your winning trades and losing trades. Try to compare the profitability of your winning trades versus the loss of the losing trades. For instance, you can have a look at the last ten trades you have made. Suppose you have not yet made any actual trades, I advise that you go back on your chart. Try to check whether the trading activities would have resulted in losses or profits. Now proceed to total the winning trades found and then divide this total wins. The below formula will guide you:

Expectancy (E) = $[1+ (L/W)]\times P-1$

Where we have W and L as the average of the winning trade and losing trade respectively and P being the winning ratio percentage

Case Example

Having made ten trades, out of these ten, you have won 7 and lost 3. The percentage win ratio is [(10-3)/10], which is equivalent to 7/10 (70%). Suppose that these seven trades earned you $4,200, your average win will be ($4,200/7) = $600. Again suppose your losses summed to $1,500, the average loss in the ten trades made will be [$1,500/ (10-7)] = $500. Now apply the use the formula we used to get the expectancy.

$E = [1+ (600/500)] \times 0.7 - 1$

$E = [1+1.2] \times 0.7 - 1$

$E = [2.2] \times 0.7 -1$

$E = 1.54 - 1$

$E = 54\%$

This means that your system is likely to give you a positive 54% expectancy, and your expected return will be about 50 cents per dollar you invest.

## Always Begin With Small Sums

The best tip for any Forex trader wishing to be a professional trader is by beginning with a small account and then increase the size of your account through profits. Don't start by investing heavily. Don't be confused by the idea that larger accounts will lead you to greater profits. It is perfect when you are able to increase your account size through trading choices. Otherwise, I don't see the need of you pumping money to an account that will only lead you to strain your finances and emotions.

## Focus On Minimizing Losses

Once you have decided to invest in Forex trade and you have funded your account, in your mind, your money is at risk. Therefore, avoid making this trading money to be money used for your regular living expenses but rather look at it as vacation money. Develop an attitude in you that directs you towards trading. With this attitude, you will be psychologically prepared to accept small losses. This is a basic step in risk management. A trader who gives their focus on trade and accepts small losses are more successful than those who focus on constantly counting their equity. To be a professional trader, you must recognize the available markets. However, to recognize the markets, begin by first recognizing yourself. Assess yourself and be aware of your capital allocation for Forex, as well as your tolerance to risks. Just ensure that they are not lacking or excessive. You have to master your financial goals and understand why you are engaging in Forex trading.

## Be Motivated By Positive Feedback Loops

By having trade plans that are well executed, you definitely will create a positive feedback loop pattern. As always, success breeds success. You will feel confident when the trade is profitable.

Furthermore, take losses but ensure that they are small according to your trade plan. This will help you build a positive feedback loop.

## Be Consistent With Doing Weekend Analysis

The Forex markets are usually closed on the weekends. When closed, take your time to have a deep study on the weekly charts to identify the patterns or news that can have effects on your trade. For instance, you may notice that a particular trade pattern is indicating a double top, but the new and pundits, on the other hand, are making suggestions that there will be a reversal in the market. In the real sense, this kind of reflexivity could only be there to promote some pattern prompting the pundits to reinforce it. Therefore, be patient and, according to your best plan, set up your things and follow your objectives.

## Always Keep A Printed Record

When I began doing Forex trading, I always printed all the trade charts. Printed records provided me with a great learning tool. I would, therefore, advise you as a beginner to always print out the charts and then list all the reasons as to why you are making the trade. List the fundamental reasons you feel swayed your decisions. In your printed chart, mark your entry and exit points. Also, ensure that on the chart, you include emotional reasons for taking the actions you took. For instance, if you were anxious, panicked, or you were just greedy, put them all there. By objectifying your trades, you will be able to develop strong mental controls as well as a discipline that will guide you in executing a trade in accordance with your system and not your emotions of personal habits.

CHAPTER 22:

# 10 Achieving Goals In Forex Trading

With all said and done, there are rules to abide by for one to reach their potential and, most importantly, realize their potential. Below are 10 rules that help in achieving goals in Forex Trading.

## 1. Trust the Process

Forex trading is a business, and it takes time to grow and be stable, which means that there is more than just waiting for profits. Profit oriented businesses end badly mainly when a forex trader does not meet the threshold they had set, and it is a bad approach for any business. Any business is not only buying and selling as it involves huddles and logistics to make the whole institution work and doable. Money oriented forex traders tend to give up easily when they do not meet their target at the close of business or even at a certain set period. However, one can set a timeline and work towards meeting the set target without having to achieve a specific point, which might turn to be the opposite. To achieve your goals, some points are process-oriented and help in reaching the high note in forex trading and are outlined.

***Outline Daily Activities***

Day to day activities can only be achieved when put down on paper for a specific task in forex trading. Having in mind the right thing to do on a specific day is good as it helps in avoiding distractions and other things that may come in between a business day. This means that the more you know what you are doing on a busy day, you will not waste time doing other things that do not help achieve your goal and the needs you want to build your forex trading skills.

*Analyze the Market*

As pointed out earlier, trading with emotions is bad for business as it does not go by the plans and strategy, but with the reaction of business gone wrong or even a big win. Being greedy is so bad in forex trading, and it is advisable to analyze the market first before trying out forex trading and giving a shot on the most promising patterns. When you play by the rules, you train the mind to follow the right procedures and even helps in becoming more discipline in forex trading. Training the mind helps in a vulnerable situation, which will make you hold on when there is a crisis.

## 2. Be Defensive

This is another important rule to follow in forex trading, for it is the core purpose of joining the business and what will keep you survive storms that will come your way in one way or the other. This simply means that you should not trade everything, including your capital, defend your initial capital, and aim at making profits. When you make a target and do not meet it, then at least you tried, but trading profusely just to meet the target with limited time is not good at all, as it is an offensive approach. You should always protect your capital as it is the only thing keeping you in the business, and one mistake can send you to factory reset, i.e., going back to the drawing board wondering when the rain started beating you.

## 3. Have a Trading Plan

Just like any other venture, Forex trading needs a business plan that has been tested to be working and giving impressive results. The plan involves things that you need to do from A-Z. This may include the rules of engagement, trading pattern, market analysis, and other key aspects that make the business run well. After making the trading plan, you can test it virtually to see if it will go well with the market and if it is good, then give it the green light and start the forex trading. But make sure that you outline the plan as it is the backbone of the whole venture.

## 4. Know That Trading Is a Business

Forex trading is like a business and should be treated as such for one to get the best out of it by giving the attention it deserves. Other researches have talked about not comparing trading with job opportunities or hobby to be done in leisure time. This means that one must not expect a salary and work on getting profits and paying attention and not only focusing on it when you are free. With this, a forex trader will learn to prioritize forex trading just like any other business.

## 5. Outline Risk

Make sure that you point out the risk you intend to get yourself into and do not give it too much until you are out of business. Do not risk an amount that you cannot afford. Risking is only for the amount you are capable of and not anywhere near initial capital. Remember, as said earlier, if you lose capital, that means that you are out of business, and you will not want that to happen to you. Only risk an amount that you know if they go, then you will not struggle with bringing back the business into living.

## 6. Use Technology

The modern era of inventions and innovations can be a plus in forex trading as it helps improve the outcome of a venture. Technology has played a big role in forex trading, thanks to innovators who come with new things every day to enhance the world in bringing people closer. With technology, one can trade anywhere in the world monitor charts using a computer or even mobile phones. This means that one can travel all over the world as well as working at the same time. This has been evident for bloggers and travel entrepreneurs who blog for a living and promote products online while they travel. This can be the same for forex traders, and it helps in even having a good time and relaxing the mind while working.

## 7. Have a Stop-Loss

This is somehow similar to outlining risk but specifies the amount that one should be willing to lose in particular trading. In Forex trading, you should only lose what you afford, and it is very important to outline the amount or percentage that one should only lose in trading. This also acts as a disciplined mode as it helps in controlling the mind and emotions not to surpass the limited amount of possible risk.

## 8. Focus on the Bigger Picture

What is the purpose of starting forex trading? Can you do the business to be aligned in that direction? Are you getting some profits and losing sometimes? Then you are on the right track heading to greatness in forex trading. Business is not about just making profits but making impacts on a personal level and getting more skills. So what is your bigger picture? To have gained at least 10 percent in the financial year 2019-2020? Having this in mind, then you can be sure of aiming in the right way as compared to only focusing on maximizing profits.

## 9. Keep Learning Markets

Forex trading is an ongoing process even after mastering markets and getting out of an amateur venture. One does not stop learning at anything, and things keep changing in the forex world. This is important to keep an open mind in everything to do with business. Some of the skilled forex traders can fall prey to crowd psychology, and some markets are unpredictable, making forex trading a learning experience every time one is trading.

## 10. Be a Progressive Trader

Every forex trader wants to earn profit as it is the main reason for venturing in forex trading in the first point, but are you only profit-oriented the first day in the market, or are you moving forward? Learning also can be huge progress as it helps one avoid making similar mistakes and open ways for more profit in the future. A progressive trade is the one that celebrates every win, either small or big, so long as it is a victory. Just like a child, they learn to sit, then the next thing is they start crawling, and with no time, they start walking with few steps and eventually even running. This is the case to forex trading, you move from one stage to the other, and you cannot jump to only making profits. After making a trading plan and testing it, one can join the trading business and encounter ups and downs as it shapes the ultimate goal of forex trading. With this progress, one can be sure of securing a future in forex trading full of experiences and lots of encounters that can prepare you for any hard hurdles that one might come across at the course of trading.

So, are you setting up your mind on winning and achieving your goals? Then you better follow the procedures outlined above by winning small until you master the art of forex trading and eventually smile to the bank after meeting your ultimate goals. Remember that forex trading is not a walk in the park, so you should make the right choices.

CHAPTER 23:

# Common Mistakes and Tips for Beginners in Forex Trading

The forex market, due to its low restriction, makes it one of the most available markets in the world. With an internet connection, phone or computer, and some few dollars, you can begin trading in the market. However, because of its free accessibility does not mean it is easy to make huge returns. When I started trading, I made some of these mistakes, and you have the chance to learn from my mistake. For a fact, I will be saving you thousands of dollars you may have squandered.

## Common Forex Mistakes

Mistakes in forex are unavoidable, but there are always remedies to deal with such a situation. Before you consider plunging into trading, it is important to consider the following mistakes and do everything possible to avoid them in the future. Most people are persuaded to venture into forex trading with fantasies of getting rich overnight.

Undeniably, the opportunities in the forex market are innumerable for you to make money and live the lifestyle you want. Notwithstanding, the forex road is not an easy road to travel because it is full of bumps. If there is anything I can assure you as a beginner is that you will struggle for various reasons, including having a poor forex foundation, poor trading structure, and impatience.

These common mistakes cripple the confidence of most beginners. I could boast that you have a solid foundation if you went through the beginning of this book to the end. However, how you apply the principles in this book depends on you only.

These mistakes are the reasons most traders consider the market a scam. I am sure your testimony will be different because you are learning from the best book on forex trading.

## Tips for Trading Forex

Just as I promised you at the beginning of this book, to help you avoid the mistake I made as a beginner, I have decided to compile most mistake beginners as you make. I will expound on the top trading tips you should inculcate into your trading and improve your performance.

Learning to trade successfully in the forex market is quite problematic for new traders. Most traders have the mindset of getting rich overnight, which is not something realistic. Forex trading can be prodigious, particularly if you are a beginner and do not know the rules guiding the market. These tips will help you in your trading journey as a beginner. It is always advisable not to forget the basics because, without them, you will struggle in the market.

### *Pick Your Broker Cleverly*

If you can choose the right broker, then you are halfway done in the forex market before choosing any broker. Ensure to seek recommendations from professional traders and do your own research because some traders will recommend a particular broker because of their affiliate programs. Take your time as we have various fake brokers looking for traders like you to ripe off. Do not be moved by mouthwatering deals. Rather look for an authorized broker with years of accomplishment.

### *Develop Your Strategy*

A list of tips on forex trading is not complete without mentioning strategy. As a beginner, you need to create your own trading strategy that works for you. Every trader should know what to expect and get from the market. You should set a definite goal because it will help discipline yourself when trading.

### *Learn Slowly*

Forex is not something you learn and stop over time. Every new skill requires consistent learning to grasp the basics. Additionally, you do not have to rush your learning process. Take your time slowly and begin by investing a little amount of money. Remember that slow and steady will win the race as a beginner.

### *Control Your Emotions*

If you allow your emotions to guide you when trading, you will regret it later. I am not telling you that it is easy, but you can control it. You need to stay rational in order to make wise choices during trading. If you let your emotions rule over you, you are bound to expose yourself to pointless risks. Forex trading is risky, but you can control the level of risk that can happen.

### *Do Not Trade If You Are Under Stress*

Hardly can you see someone who concentrates optimally when under stress. Traders who decide to do that will surely make an irrational decision, which will cost them money. Therefore, before thinking of trading, ensure to identify anything that will cause stress and eliminate them before it eliminates your forex account (do not mind me; I am just joking, but there is a sense to it). If you had a stressful day and still had to trade, consider taking a deep breath while allowing your mind to focus on what you are about to do. You can overcome stress in various ways such as exercising, sleeping, and listening to music, hanging out with friends. Whatever the situation is, find a solution to your stress and manage it effectively.

### *Never Stop Practicing*

Do not neglect this tip because it is crucial to your success or failure as a forex trader. Hardly can you succeed on your first encounter in the forex market. Therefore, when you make your first mistake, do not relent because, with consistent practicing, you will be among the top traders. However, you have the adventure of using a demo account to perfect your skill.

### *Risk Is Part of the Game*

If you are not ready to risk, you are not ready for the forex market. Most brokers will advise you that trading is risky, and you should accept that fact. If you think that in forex you are going to have a sweet ride, then you need a reality check. Additionally, I have seen mouthwatering advertisements promising you the "unpromising." Well, you should be realistic about your goals and strategies.

### *Patience Is Priceless*

Do you remember the old adage? "True success is never instantaneous." That holds true in the forex market. It is the product of consistent planning and work, which many beginners tend to overlook. There is no easy path to making a profit in the market. Let patience have her way in you.

### *Upgrade Your Knowledge Continuously*

The more you trade, the newer things you learn. Improve your knowledge by looking at trends, analyzing news, and financial processes. Furthermore, do not neglect the fundamental basis you have learned. Significantly, you should study, practice, and continue this routine. A knife gets dull when it is left idle. Sharpen your trading skill with continuous learning and practicing.

### *Take Breaks*

All work and no play makes Jack a dull student. You can take routine breaks, especially when you are under stress. For those glued to multiple computer winds to analyze data from various sources, it is important to take a break as you may feel pressured.

### *Trends Are Essential*

Trends are important for any trader, and you should not neglect them. The capability to identify these trends makes it a valuable investment for you. I understand there are various trends; it is important to ignore those that will lead to disaster. Trends give you a picture of what may come in the future. With this, you can prepare for the future.

### *Planning Is a Necessary Ingredient*

Forex trading is not sports betting where you gamble the team to win or score. Forex trading is a strategic game that requires painstaking planning and attention to evaluate your next move before taking action. Before starting any trade, formulate a plan that includes challenging questions like:

- What is my primary plan?
- What is plan B?
- What strategy should I employ?
- What are my loss and profit margins?

### *Understand the Charts*

You will trade in various markets, and these require different information to analyze each trade. We have numerous tools you can use to make your trading easier. However, charts are time efficient and serve as the best option for beginners. You should not know them only. You should learn how to read and use them to your advantage.

### *Incorporate Stop-Losses in Your Trades*

Setting stop-loss for trade is an efficient strategy to use when trading. With stop-loss, you minimize your risk and escape any trade that goes haywire. Additionally, avoid greediness by setting the maximum profit and loss range. Once you hit your target, you should avoid the trap of placing another trade.

CHAPTER 24:

# Basic Forex Trading Skills You Need to Learn

There are many ways to become a successful forex trader. For example, if you want to be a forex trader under a financial firm, they usually hire people who have a strong background in the hard sciences, engineering, or math.

In starting your career as a forex trader, there are basic skills you need to learn. This includes the following:

1. Analytical skills
2. Research skills
3. Focus and control
4. Money management
5. Psychology

## Basic Trading Skills

Analytical thinking is a basic skill that every forex trader should have. You must be able to analyze the available data within a limited time frame.

Forex trading is a numbers game, and the platform is filled with patterns, indicators, and charts that you need to analyze quickly. You also need to develop your analytical skills so you can easily identify trends in the forex market.

## Reading Currency Quote

When you are quoting a currency, you are doing it in relation to the currency of another country in a way that the value is defined by the other currency's value.

Hence, if you want to know the forex rate between the Swiss Francs (CHF) and Chinese Yuan (CNY), the forex quotation will look like this:

CHF/CNY = 6.95

This is known as the currency pair. In this pair, CHF is the base currency, while CNY is the counter currency. The former always has a value of one unit, and the latter is what that one base unit is equivalent in its denomination. This fx pair means that CHF1 = 6.95 Chinese Yuan. So if you have one Swiss Franc, you can buy 6.95 Chinese Yuan. Take note that the fx quote includes the currency symbol for the currency pairs.

You can quote a currency pair either indirectly or directly. An indirect quote is basically when the local currency is the base currency, while a direct quote is basically a forex pair wherein the domestic currency is the quote currency.

Therefore, if you are looking for the United States dollar as the domestic currency and the Japanese yen as the foreign currency, an indirect code will be JPY/USD, while a direct quote will be USD/JPY.

In a direct quotation, the quoted currency could vary, while the base currency has a default value of one unit. Meanwhile, in the indirect quote, the domestic currency has a default value of one unit, while the foreign currency has a variable value.

For instance, if the Japanese yen is the domestic unit, a direct quote will be 109.37 USD/JPY, which means that 1 unit of USD can buy JPY 109.37. The indirect for this will be inverse (1/109.37), 0.0091 JPY/USD, which means with 1 JPY, you can buy USD 0.0091.

In the fx spot market, most currencies are traded against the USD, and this is often referred to as a currency base. These are all direct quotes and true to the above CHF/CNY that indicates 1 CHF is equal to 6.95 CNY.

You must remember that not all currencies have the USD as the base. The currencies used by the British Commonwealth, such as the New Zealand dollar, the Australian dollar, and the British pound are all identified as the base currency against the USD. This is how we also quote the euro. For these situations, the USD is positioned as the counter currency, and the fx rate is known as an indirect quote. Hence, EUR to USD is quoted as 1.19, because one unit of euro can buy 1.19 USD.

The exchange currency rates are quoted up to four digits after the decimal place. One exception to this is the Japanese yen because this currency is quoted only up to two decimal places.

If a currency quote is given without the USD as a component, this is known as cross-currency. The most popular cross currency pairs are the EUR/CHF, EUR/JPY, and the EUR/GBP. In general, currency pairs expand the trading horizons in the fx market. But you should bear in mind that they are not that much popular compared to the currency pair that uses USD as the base currency.

## Buying and Selling Price

Like in stock markets, if you are trading currency pairs, you have to refer to the buying rate (bid) and the selling price (ask). Take note that these are still in relation to the base currency. If your strategy is too long (buying a currency pair), the asking price refers to the rate of quoted currency, which should be paid so you can purchase one unit of the base currency, or how much the market is willing to sell a unit of the base currency in reference to the currency quote.

On the other hand, when you go short (selling) a currency pair, the bid rate signifies how much of the quoted currency you can get when you sell a unit of the base currency or how much the market is willing to shell out for the currency (quoted) in reference to the currency base.

Remember, the figure on the left of the slash is the bid rate, while the next two digits to the right of the slash are the asking price.

Take note that it is customary to quote only the last two digits of the full price. The bid is also smaller compared to the asking price. Below is an example:

USD/CHF = 1.3000/05

Ask = 1.3005

Bid = 1.3000

Buying this fx pair signifies that you like to purchase the base currency, and so you have to refer to the asking price to know how much in Swiss francs the market will charge for US dollars. Based on our asking price, you can purchase $ 1.00 with 1.3005 Swiss francs, which is the currency that you are quoting.

But if you want to sell this fx pair or, in other words, you want to sell the currency base using the quoted currency. You have to refer to the bid. This signifies that the market will purchase a $1 base currency for a price that is equivalent to 1.3000 Swiss francs, which is the currency that you are quoting.

The base currency (whichever you are quoting first) always refers to the one in which we are conducting the transaction. This means you can either buy or sell the currency base. You can refer to the specific currency pair rate to find the price depending on what currency you like to use for selling or buying the base with.

## Research Skills

In trading in the forex market, you should not trade on an impulse. You must be confident with your strategy, and you can do this through research. In the past, you can do a background check on the hottest currency pairs by reading books, newspapers, and other traditional forms of information sources.

But with the advent of the World Wide Web, there are now countless sources of information that you can use for your research. However, not all of these sources are reliable and can guide you to become successful forex traders. In choosing a source to consult, make certain that this covers the currency pairs to buy or if it is time to sell your currencies based on different factors such as technical and fundamental analysis.

There are also reliable newspapers and publications that you can read, which includes interpretation of global news and how the current events could affect the forex market. Forex trading involves revisiting past basic economics because politics can also affect the behavior of forex players. Hence, it is crucial that you are updated with significant non-financial news from around the world.

In order to develop a solid foundation in forex trading, you must be updated with important technical and fundamental developments in the industry. Successful forex traders usually have a thirst for information as well as the drive to look for all relevant data, which could affect the trade.

Many traders even maintain a monitoring platform to keep up with major news breakthroughs that can have a considerable impact not only in the forex market but also in the global financial scene.

## Focus and Control

Focus is another important skill for forex traders, which can increase the more that you practice it. With the emergence of numerous online resources promising to guide you on forex trading, you should be able to develop how to identify and focus your lens on the actionable trends that could affect your trade.

There are forex traders that are only focusing on specific types of currency pairs so they can put all of their efforts in projecting the movement of the trade. By focusing on these currencies, traders can develop a competitive advantage compared to traders who don't focus on their trades.

Meanwhile, a successful trader should also learn how to control their emotions and follow a specific strategy or trading plan. This is crucial in handling risks in forex trades by taking profits at specific points or using stop losses. There are strategies in place that allow traders to lose a bit on bad trades but gain more revenue from ideal trades. Bad traders are usually affected by their emotions, which influence the strategic implementation of their trading plan.

## Risk Management

Risk Management is a skill that you should master to safeguard your trading capital from losses. This must be integrated into your trading strategy as early as you can in your forex trading career. Risk management covers strategies such as risk to reward, scaling trades, and stop losses. Mastering this skill will allow you to obtain higher profits and prevent losing money.

For instance, many successful traders don't risk more than 2 percent of their funds in a single trade. This will safeguard your account from any significant downturn and will allow you to safely trade using leverage.

## Psychology

Successful traders are not only adept in the mathematics behind the forex trading platform. They are also masters of understanding the psychology of people behind the trade. Aside from observing the possible behavior of market players, a forex trader should also overcome psychological aspects such as greed and fear.

In forex trading, you should learn how to follow the rules of the game without allowing your emotions to distract your game plan. It is not easy to become a successful forex trader, but if you work through your plan and master yourself, you can win the game through skills and discipline.

CHAPTER 25:

# Time Management and Money Management

## Time Management

Time management, a key feature in Forex trading, is one of the determinants of the gains and losses a trader is to make from the opening and the close of a trading period. It is therefore paramount that a trader has a solid plan in his or her time management in trading to reap off gains.

A trader has to know when to enter and exit the market when to get the necessary information on trading patterns.

### *Match Your Personality and Your Trading Pattern With the Time You Have*

It is suicidal for a trader to operate based on a trading pattern that does not suit their personality and goes against them at all odds. The personality type being referred to in this case is major whether the trader is patient or not. An impatient trader will want to have instant results and gains for trades made and will, therefore, not tarry around for long-term trading systems.

Such traders do not find the trade analysis tools that are long-term to be useful to their course. Impatient traders are mostly associated with swing traders who get antsy and do not stay put to trade for the long-term. Analysis tools that evaluate long-term trade may not be suitable for such traders.

Short term analysis tools are mostly preferred for such traders and will work perfectly to their trading plan. The plan also has to mindful of the time available for the swing traders, which is very limited in most cases, and they, therefore, have to come up with a strategy that works in the available time that they have to trade.

Analysis tools and trading patterns that work for the long-term apply to those whose personality is being patient. Long-term strategies work for these kinds of people. They should, however, take caution not to be blind to current events that may drastically and completely change the trading pattern in existence and therefore results in losses for them.

Their strategy also has to be within a time frame that they are comfortable trading in. On the other hand, swing traders are on the disadvantage because they tend to overdo and overexert themselves in the analysis of the trading patterns, all the while trading for just but a short period.

An advantage to the long-term traders is that they can concentrate on other works while at the same time still trading. It is, therefore, of great importance to match one's personality with their trading pattern, choosing the one that will work for them.

***Consider the Important Trading Analysis***

Irrespective of the type of trader that you are, critical and important analysis on trading patterns and factors affecting trading of Forexes is not to be ignored. Just a small bit of information may change the trading scales to either make profits or losses. Even when a trader is pressed for time, never make a trade on a pair of currencies without thoroughly evaluating them to avoid regretting later.

For the long-term traders, an important analysis is to trigger you to make a change in the currency pairs for a profitable trade. Make use of the little time, if you are a swing trader, and do a proper analysis of the currencies before putting your money at stake for a loss.

Many traders have failed to do so where their efforts to pairing profitable currencies came to naught. Only make a trade when you are confident enough that your currencies are ago after wisely employing your time.

### *Unplug From Distractions When Analyzing Trading Patterns*

Distractions such as social media, the TV, background noise, and many others are to be avoided when making an analysis. They tend to eat up a lot of time when it could have been spent wisely in analyzing and not miss out on an opportunity to make a trade that could have resulted in profits. Unplug from social media for a while trading and shout out all the noise in your surrounding and fully concentrate on evaluating the currencies and making wise decisions on pairing them. This saves a lot of time that otherwise could have been used in multitasking trading and other activities, all the while not fully concentrating on each activity.

### *Come Up With an Information-Sorting Strategy*

There could be information overload on Forex trade and a lot of unnecessary news regarding the same that waste time for a trader goes through all that in a bid to make a successful pairing of currencies. There are also a lot of sites online that offer updates on Forex trading, and if a trader could subscribe to all of them, then all they could be doing is analyzing trading Forexes and doing zero tradings at all. Sort out the relevant information that only affects your currency pairs. It is also advisable to have reliable sites to get information from and not a lot of them or some bogus ones.

### *Sync Your Preferred Trading Time With Profitable Trading Windows*

In Forex trading, timing goes a long way. It is everything. A trader should, therefore, come up with a strategy that ensures that their available time is also a profitable window to trade-in. It is not always that the free time you get and available to trade in will result in profits. Choose the most appropriate window and execute a trade.

However, a trader should also be able to enjoy his or her free time and also, at the same time, make money through Forex trading. This cannot be reiterated enough. Sync your 'available time' with profitable trading windows.

## Money Management

Money management strategies are important to a Forex trader to ensure that the trades made are profitable and reduce the chance of a loss happening to the bare minimum. Forex can be a game of chance to the traders who are not so keen on learning about managing their money in this type of trade.

New traders lose their money when pairing the wrong currencies, and even made the correct currencies by the trading patterns but at the wrong time. The rules on money management reduce the chances of having a negative account balance when it could have been avoided.

***Avoid Overexcitement of the Forex Market***

This is mainly applicable to the new traders who get overexcited on the trading patterns and tend to trade currencies in a rush with no proper analysis of the currencies and the market, thereby leading to huge losses. This should be avoided where the habit can turn out to be more of a game of chance or betting rather than wise trading.

You don't have to make a new trade when an opening presents itself every hour. It can prove to a fateful and damning idea where the profits made and accumulated may be lost in an attempt to reach for more. Don't be afraid to lie low for days when waiting for an opportune time to make a good trade that may have huge profits.

Being antsy for quick money and chasing the Forex market will, most of the time, result in losses. Most assuredly, it will. Analyzing the market, an opening for a profitable trade will surely come. A trade made in an overexcitement of the market will not equate that made after a careful analysis of the trading patterns. Very few trades will be lost when this strategy is put into employ, especially to the new traders.

No opportunities to trade and make profits, then no trade at all, a philosophy that should be a guide in making decisions in the Forex market.

Overexcitement for the market can also be displayed by opening a lot of trades in a short period, which may work against you should the tables turned.

This habit, coupled with other equally poor money management strategies in Forex trading, has left traders' accounts on the negative balance, wiping off a lot of profits. Let several necessary trades work for you.

***Take Caution to Trade on Leverage***

Leverage might be a great way to make money, double money, as is the thought of many new traders. This is; however, not the way leverage tends to work. It may turn against your trade, wiping all your profits. While on the one hand, large leverage might increase your money when one pair of currency is making profits, it can also create losses in a very quick way.

A trader has to look into ways how they can protect their startup capital before making huge profits on the same capital. Leverage can either work for the good or work for the worst where your money in trading Forex is concerned. It is therefore advisable in choosing the level of leverage to trade in, putting in mind that it may go either way, and when it doesn't work, the losses are steep, especially on large levels of leverage.

Being a cautious trader, you'll look into the balance that you have in your account before making the decision on the level of leverage you'll have on your capital. Other factors to put into consideration are such as the risk per trade and the stop loss distance.

When considering the risk per trade, carefully analyze whether the trade you are about to make will profitable and whether it is worth your money, or whether there is a change of a loss occurring, especially when you have a high level of leverage on your money.

## CHAPTER 26:

# Step-by-Step Instructions to Your First Trade

A lot of retail traders operate from a small home office. Others work in regular offices but remain small traders with limited funds but sufficient trading equipment. As a day trader, there is basically no boss or supervisor to tell a trader what to do. Nobody watches over them or bosses them around. This means a trader has the freedom to organize and manage their trading days.

Because of this freedom, day traders need to exercise a lot of discipline. Traders need to wake up early and prepare for the trading day. Mental preparation is part of a trader's morning ritual before, during, or after breakfast. It is advisable to be up a couple of hours before the trading day begins and ensure everything is in place. There are a couple of things that generally need to be achieved.

1. As soon as breakfast is made, the trader should rehearse their strategies in their minds and probably on paper too. Sometimes it is necessary to run a strategy on a demo platform. Also, a good plan should be made and followed to the letter. This plan includes how much money to place on a trade, which points to exit a trade, when to take profits, and so on.

2. Traders need to check and confirm their trading accounts and the amounts therein. A trader must know the amount available for trading purposes so they know the amounts they can spend per trade. It is recommended that traders should not spend more than 2% of their trading capital on a single trade. The accepted range is between 1% and 2% of the account balance.

Beginners with no prior trading experience should not spend more than 1% of their trading balance per trade. Also, a trader should exit their positions three minutes before a major financial or economic announcement.

3. It is advisable to always or regularly check the financial calendar and note any major events. Any such events should be clearly marked onto the calendar and remind initiated. These events have major implications for stocks and activity at the markets. It is crucial that day traders learn how to select the best stocks to trade. This is because the stocks chosen for day trading will pretty much determine the outcome of your trading ventures. As such, choosing the correct stocks ensures that you fare better at the markets and maximize profitability.

## Identifying Stocks for Day Trading

### *Funds Available*

The first instance is to take cognizance of a trader's financial position. Depending on the number of funds available, you can determine the stocks to choose from. There is a wide variety of stocks to choose from; however, you can only choose as much as your funds allow you. You need to consider the quantity of risk you can tolerate. Generally, the amount of risk a trader is willing to take, the more they stand to win. Traders also need to consider buying a security in a field or industry that they are familiar with. For instance, an accountant may be happy trading financial stocks while an engineer will be at home with tech stocks, and so on. Such considerations will ensure you understand what is going on in the industry, and this will boost trading ventures.

### *Liquidity*

Traders also need to find highly liquid securities and trade in large volumes. There is a reason for this. When a security is trading in high volumes, then it is easy to enter and exit positions. Also, highly liquid securities make it easy to get paid upon exiting a position.

Some of the best financial securities that have large volumes and are liquid are blue-chip stocks. These are stocks of highly valued companies that are constantly making large profits, are stable, and are considered very valuable.

Highly liquid stocks tend to be more easily traded and are easier to discount compared to many others. Also, stocks and securities from firms with large volumes of shares traded tend to be more favorable.

Traders should take the time to conduct analysis to find which stocks are most suitable. A good stock is one from a large-cap company rather than a low cap firm. This is because it is easier to find buyers of large volume stocks compared with buyers for low volume stocks.

***Volatility***

Some of the best instruments are highly volatile ones. Volatile stocks and securities provide day traders a chance to capitalize on the rapid and numerous price changes. Remember that day. Traders make most of their money due to rapid or frequent price changes. As such, stocks that are constantly moving up and down or are volatile are much better and preferable compared to less volatile ones.

We have what is known as the TVI or trade volume index. This is a measure of the volumes of a particular stock that is trading at the market. Using this index, traders can determine whether or not to choose the particular stock. TVI indicates the total amount of cash that is following into and out of stock. The volume gives a clear indication of the stock's activity at the markets.

***Industry***

Another crucial aspect to consider when selecting a stock is the industry. One of the best industries for day traders should be the financial services sector. This sector is excellent because it features most of the above factors like large volumes and volatility.

A great example is Microsoft Corp. This is a well-established company with a large global market, growing income, and a positive reputation.

Microsoft Corp. also happens to be among the most highly traded stocks. This is why it is among the most preferred stock by most day traders. It is definitely an excellent choice for day trading forays as it exhibits all the desired characteristics. Bank of America is a large corporation, it trades a large volume of shares each day, its stock is volatile, yet the bank remains stable and profitable through the years.

### *Emotions*

One best point worth mentioning is that a day trader should never let emotions take charge of trading activities. When a trading strategy is formulated, it should be implemented to the letter. All too often, traders either become greedy or despair and then begin trading guided by their emotions.

For instance, they refuse to exit a winning trade instead of collecting profits first. In other cases, traders choose to continue incurring losses beyond the stop-loss point. These are dangerous attributes and are common among new and novice traders. It is a practice that should be shunned at all costs for successful and profitable day trading.

### *Summary*

Day traders execute various intraday strategies to benefit from the volatility at the markets. To be effective, the first step should be the identification of suitable stocks to trade.

There are different stocks available in the market. A good trader will conduct an analysis using tools and charts to find the most appropriate stocks. These are stocks with high volumes from stable companies that showcase a fair amount of volatility.

It does not have to be stock only. Day traders can also deal with other commodities such as bonds, currencies, futures, and options. Once the trading instrument has been determined, the only other step is to develop a strategy and begin implementing it.

A major challenge that numerous traders experience, especially novice and beginners, is that they let their emotions interfere with their trading. This means that traders take their time to conduct research and come up with a trading strategy only to discard it at the last moment.

Emotional stability is crucial because it is the only way for a trader to successfully execute a strategy and make profits along the way. When emotions take charge, a trader will keep holding on to a falling position beyond the stop-loss point. They will lose money using this approach. However, when winning, they do not take profits as was intended, but instead, they tend to keep at trade and risk losing all their winnings.

CHAPTER 27:

# Forex Trading Vs. Stocks

One of the questions a new trader faces is what markets to invest in. Stocks remain one of the most popular ways to invest and grow wealth—and with good reason. The fact is, despite the frequent ups and downs of the markets, over time, stocks are proven to be a good way to generate large amounts of wealth.

We will look at the question of Forex vs. stocks and address the issue of picking one or the other. Of course, they are not necessarily mutually exclusive. If you have the time and ability to learn, follow, and manage two completely different markets, it's certainly possible to do so. However, for beginning traders, it's probably better to stick with one type of trading at least for six months. After you have developed a reasonable level of mastery, then you may find branching out a little easier.

## Forex Is Easier for Beginners

Forex has a reputation for being a high risk. In fact, from the perspective of many financial experts, Forex might even seem like its nothing more than a gambling casino. However, the reality is much different. Forex is actually easier for most beginning traders once they understand the concepts of currency pairs. There is far less information to worry about and less you have to manage. You can also use the volatility of the Forex markets to your advantage more easily than you can with stocks. With stocks, you have to be closely following different companies and keeping track of a large amount of information. You'll have to know how to read balance sheets and what everything means in financial statements.

You'll have to keep close tabs on company management and product releases, as well as any news about a company coming out day-to-day that could have a large impact on stock prices. And you'll have to keep track of macroeconomic and political news.

Of course, the economy can impact currency trading, but overall, the total amount of information you have to keep track of and learn about is much smaller with Forex. You'll need to keep up with basic financial news, and most importantly, with the international economic and political situations. But there are no financial statements to pour over, and with currency, there is always the possibility of just holding on until things reverse and go your way.

The skills that you learn trading Forex are easily translatable to other markets. So, you can learn a great deal about candlestick charts, price movements, and technical indicators in the simpler world of Forex – and you'll be able to translate this information to the world of stocks or options trading, or even commodities and precious metals.

## Forex Is 24-Hours-a-Day Trading

With stocks, you can trade during the "trading day," which is roughly 9:30 AM until 4 PM eastern time. Forex is not constrained to New York City; it's a global market. That means that you can trade any time of day or night during the business week, and that business week does the stretch from Sunday through Friday afternoon, so you basically have six days a week, 24 hours a day to trade. The markets are truly global, and so the markets are highly liquid and flexible. You can get in and out of trades at an opportune moment.

The 24-hour nature of the Forex market removes many of the constraints faced by day traders on the stock market. Because of the sensitivity of their positions, a day trader can get wiped out if they were to hold their positions overnight. The first minutes of trading at the next opening can cause them to lose thousands of dollars in the blink of an eye.

In Forex, you are not worried about a frantic activity like that over the "opening" because strictly speaking, other than the opening of the markets on Sunday afternoon New York time in New Zealand, there is no opening bell. You can hold out if a position is not working out for you, provided that holding out is the reasonable thing to do. The point is that the 24-hours-a-day nature of the truly global Forex markets means that you have a lot more flexibility on Forex as compared to the stock markets.

And the 24-hours-a-day markets mean something else – basic flexibility. If you are trading stocks, you might have a "day job," and you won't be able to follow the markets that closely. But with Forex, the situation is totally different. You can trade whenever it's convenient for you. The fact that the markets are open 24 hours a day means that you can even engage in activities like day trading while still working a full-time job during the day. For this reason alone, many people opt for Forex trading.

## Liquidity and Trading Volume

Two of the leading reasons that Forex is preferred by many traders as compared to stocks are liquidity and trading volume. This compares to around $220 billion per day on the NY Stock Exchange, and $100 billion per day on the NASDAQ.

What this entails in practical terms, is it's very easy to find buyers and sellers to help you get in and out of your positions quickly. The high liquidity of Forex markets makes day trading easier, and it even permits trading on very short time intervals using a method called "scalping."

Even if you are not into the idea of day trading or scalping, the increased liquidity of the Forex markets is a definite advantage for any trader. Prices on financial markets can move fast, and so it's reassuring knowing that with Forex, you will be able to find a buyer pretty quickly.

## Limited Options Makes Forex Easier

This might look counter-intuitive, but one of the advantages of Forex over the stock market is that there are a limited number of trading opportunities. In fact, the vast majority of trading is centered around a few major currencies like the euro, U.S. dollar, and Japanese yen.

As a trader, this makes life a lot simpler from your perspective. Rather than having to pour through hundreds of stocks looking for the right trade to get into, there are a small handful of possibilities on the Forex markets. This can help by just keeping your mind from being overwhelmed. Of course, this cut both ways. A large number of available stocks (there are 2,800 companies on the New York Stock Exchange and 3,300 companies on NASDAQ) means that it's easier to find investments that are personally tailored to your needs and interests. But the fact is most people that have that kind of interest in stocks and companies are more likely to be long-term investors, rather than traders who are looking to make short-term profits.

Traders are not the type to care about the details of what they are trading. They are only interested in short-term profit potential. So a volatile stock is going to be preferred over a stock that has a product they like or management team that they admire. If you are interested in the products some company is producing, then you're probably going to want to sink your money in that company for ten years. Many people invest in companies like Apple or Amazon for this reason.

But if you are only interested in price movements, the company is not all that relevant. So why even worry about companies themselves at all. With Forex, there are a limited number of major currencies that you can trade and make profits with; in fact, as we'll see, the vast majority of the trading volume is centered on a rather small number of currencies. That means that you can find the trades you want to get into rather easily, by only looking at a few different currency pairs instead of pouring through hundreds of stocks trying to find the right one.

It's not fair to say that one way is better than another. It comes down to sole taste, and the reality is that some people actually prefer the huge variety on the stock market, and even if they are only attempting to make profits from price movements, they still find finance, business, and corporations to be of interest. For others, the specific nature of the underlying financial asset is not all that important. Instead, the focus for them is simply the price movements and the potential for making profits in a risky environment.

You don't have to be some kind of math or financial whiz to trade Forex, but many people who are interested in Forex or even day trading stocks enjoy pouring overpricing charts and studying price movements of financial instruments. Forex provides ample opportunity to do this, and in fact, it comes with the territory. A Forex trader has to have at least some familiarity with candlestick charts, moving averages, and technical indicators. These tools are used by traders when they study charts so that they can estimate trends in pricing and coming price changes. The tools can be used with any financial instrument; in fact, candlestick charts were developed in Japan a couple of centuries ago to track changes in rice prices on the markets.

## Massive Leverage Is Possible with Forex

One of the major advantages of Forex on stock and even options trading is the ability to use massive leverage. If you are a day or swing trader on the stock market, you can use 2:1 leverage. That means you can basically borrow from the broker to make larger trades than you would be able to make using your own money. If you have access to 2:1 leverage, the broker will lend you enough money to double it, so if you put up $5,000, you can make a $10,000 trade. Of course, when you sell the shares, you have to pay the broker back the $5,000 you borrowed.

As you might imagine, leverage allows you to make a lot more profits than you could otherwise. Let's say that you were able to enter a trade on a certain stock that made a $2 a share gain in a single day. If you had $5,000 cash, and the stock was trading at $40 a share, you would be able to buy 125 shares. So, your total profit would be $2 x 125 = $250. Not bad for a day's work, but consider using leverage.

CHAPTER 28:

# Forex Trading on a Budget

If you have just started in Forex trading, you must have been wondering whether you need to have a huge amount of money to start trading. So, is it possible for you to trade the Forex market with little money?

The fact is that you can trade with little money, but your profits will be limited. With a few tips, though, you can successfully trade the markets without having to put down thousands of dollars on the line.

## Educate Yourself

Before you can place your money on the line, you need to be educated about what to do before you jump in. Make sure you understand the basics of trading the Forex market and know whether your limited funds will give you profit.

Understand the risk management processes as well as other concepts before you put any money on the line. If you have put some money on the line, then you should withdraw part of it and put it in a course. It will give you concepts that you can use to turn your money regardless of how much you have.

Learning resources also introduce you to analysis techniques that give you an idea of what trade to place and when to do it.

## Start Small

As a new trader, it is prudent that you start off with a small amount compared to putting all your money into the trade. Remember that you can't have the success you desire trading dollars when you cannot trade for pennies. To do this, you need to find the right broker that gives you a low limit trading account.

## Patience is Key

Forex trading is all about having patience. When you start small, you might see it be frustrating and slow, but it keeps you disciplined. Make sure that you start small and grow your account step by step.

Profitable Forex investing takes time and patience. All those traders that you see making money on the market were novices on their first day. Some were even worse than you. However, most of them started small and grew step by step to become the pro traders that they are right now.

## Do It Regularly

As you refine the craft, make sure you make trading your habit. To do this, start investing regularly as you learn the ropes. Add funds to your account several times a week, and you will see the account grow. The good thing is that you won't lose too much in any trade compared to putting up a lot of your money for trading.

## How to Earn With Forex

There are a few steps to make money with forex. Let us look at what you can do:

### *Grow Your Skills*

When you have the right skill, you will make money with forex trading. The forex market is dynamic, and you have to keep up with the changes. As you trade, you get more and more knowledgeable about the things that happen in forex trading. Take time to learn new techniques and engage with other traders to understand what they do to be successful.

The best way to learn about Forex trading is to make sure you look at the various reasons the market is moving in a specific direction. For instance, you might look at the analysis methods that are used by top traders and why they use them. You also need to understand what triggers make the prices to move in a given direction as opposed to another.

### *Learn to Perform Analysis*

The analysis is all about using charts and other visual tools to come up with a decision. Forex trading gives you two major types of tools to use – fundamental and technical analysis. Fundamental analysis focuses on events that will change the performance of a currency pair. On the other hand, technical analysis involves looking at price action and its effect on the market – including trends, momentum, and reversal patterns.

We shall look at these analysis methods in detail later, but at the moment, just know that you have a chance to make more profit when you perform the right analysis before placing a trade.

### *Work with the Right Broker*

A Forex broker makes it possible for you to execute transactions. This is just one of the major functions – a broker handles various other tasks that are vital to trading.

If you come across fraud alerts or issues with the withdrawing of funds, then look for another broker.

So, making money on Forex is all about buying a currency pair at a low price and then selling it off at a higher price to make profits. The profit, which represents your income, is the difference between the price you buy the price of buying and selling the currency pair. You pay the broker a commission from the trade called the spread.

If you believe that you can't place trades with your money, then you can use a feature given by the broker called the leverage. This is money that you follow from the broker to make your deposit higher.

Remember that the higher the deposit, the more the risk.

CHAPTER 29:

# Online Forex Trading

I will provide you with tips, tricks, and strategies that you can use to benefit from the values of foreign currencies.

## How Does a Foreign Exchange System Work?

When you trade forex online, your orders will be fulfilled immediately. Exchange rates change every second. Thus, the accuracy of the quotes you see on the screen is severely limited. When you run a transaction and maybe lock in an exchange rate, the online trading system will process your request at that same moment.

### *Updated Exchange Rates*

Because of the reason outlined above, you should use a forex computer program that shows the latest exchange rates. This kind of software continuously communicates with a server. The server, meanwhile, sends out the most updated exchange rates at any given time. Unlike the exchange rates you'll get from banks, the online data you will receive from the software is tradable. You can "lock-in" (or utilize) a rate while it is on your screen.

### *Online Trading Platforms*

Forex trading also benefits from the latest advances in technology. Many years ago, Forex traders sent their orders over the phone. This setup limited the options and potential profits of Forex traders.

Because of modern technology, you can now trade currencies anytime you want and fund your orders using your credit card.

## How to Use an Online Platform

To trade online, you should do the following:

- Sign up for an account in a trading platform
- Deposit money to fund your transactions

Trading platforms vary when it comes to their requirements and registration processes. However, the major steps are:

1. **Registration.** You need to do this online. Launch your favorite web browser and search for a trading platform. Once you have found one, click on "Register" or "Sign up."

    a. Registration forms vary in terms of length and complexity. You have to enter personal information because governments and other authorities require it.

    b. Here are the most requested pieces of information during the registration process: the name of the trader, phone number, email address, residential address, the number of a government-issued ID, and the annual income of the trader.

    c. It is rare for forex platforms to conduct thorough background checks on their new members. In most cases, they assume that each user-provided correct information while setting up an account.

Important Note: Your chosen Forex platform will likely ask you about the source of your funds. You must declare that your funds are unquestionable. Anti-money laundering campaigns are being enforced globally, and Forex platforms are active participants. It would be best if you'll do your own research regarding money laundering before trading currencies.

2. **Fund Transfer.** You should put funds into your trading account before submitting an order. Aside from the money that you'll use for your transactions, however, most trading platforms are requiring a specific amount.
   This "extra money" will add more security to your trading activities. You don't have to worry since you still own the money. In fact, you might get some interest payments from the required amount.

3. **Order Submission**. Trading platforms are in sync with international Forex markets. Thus, the said platforms run 24 hours each day. But many platforms require their members to use specific computer programs. That means you have to use the required programs if you want to trade currencies.

It would be best if you'll look for a trading platform that offers browser-based access. Here, you won't have to download any program. You can also submit orders using various devices (e.g., tablets, smartphones, laptops, etc.).

## Real-Time Software

Important Note: To keep things simple, this book will assume that you are using "Easy-Forex." Easy-Forex is one of the most popular platforms today. This book will give you universal information, so you don't have to worry if you are using a different platform.

Modern trading systems give up-to-date information. You won't have to refresh the page —the screen will communicate with the platform's remote server automatically.

Whenever you submit an order, the trading system will transfer the related information securely. This information will go to the platform's server, where it will be stored.

Platforms guarantee data integrity by storing copies of the information in backup servers. These things happen quickly and automatically. Thus, you just have to focus on finding profitable transactions.

CHAPTER 30:

# 3 Terms Trading

You need to understand that you have numerous ways to engage with your trade. Not all of them might be suited for you. What you need to do is practice with various techniques. After that, narrow down the trading style that best fits your requirement. Once you are able to do that, you can ensure that you are reading data before making any decision.

## Short-Term Trading

There is a fundamental difference in the way we trade in currencies in the short term as opposed to other forms of securities. If you have ever been in the stock market, then you know that you cannot simply buy and sell a stock at a time of your convenience. This means that you cannot purchase a stock and then decide to sell it at the end of the day.

But with the currency market, the situation is completely different. This is because you get to deal with a market that fluctuates in small increments quite frequently. When you are dealing with pips, you are dealing with an extremely small point change (imagine 0.0001 jumps or dive in a currency).

This is why, in a short-term Forex trading, you can strategize your sale in such a way that you do not have to keep your trades with you for longer than an hour. That could benefit those who do not have a lot of time to spend on their trades on a given day or those who prefer quick trades and small gains over time.

However, the time factor is not the most appealing of all factors in short-term trading. The thing that really attracts traders to this style of trading is the small pip changes. Traders who indulge in short-term trading create profits by frequently opening and closing positions after seeing an increase in just a few pips, sometimes even as little as 1 or 2 pips.

An interbank market is a network where financial institutions interact with each other to trade in currencies. In their world, when someone (or an entity) deals with extremely short-term trades, where they are opening and closing positions quickly, then that particular trading is called "jobbing" the market.

Online currency traders, on the other hand, have another name for it—scalping. You can call it whatever you like, either jobbing or scalping, both terms can work. Traders who engage in this style of trading are considered to be some of the most attentive and focused traders. This is because they have to make quick-second decisions for their trade.

If you want to be a successful scalper, then do not stick to a particular position. You should not worry about the up and down movement of the currency. What you are focused on is the pips. That is what will get you the returns you seek. If the position you have chosen is not working for you, then make a quick exit. Look for volatility and liquidity of the currency as your prime factors.

Here are a few tips for short-term trading:

**Make Sure You Are Focusing on High Liquid Pairs**. Such as USD/JPY, EUR/USD, EUR/JPY, EUR/GBP, and EUR/CHF.

And what exactly is a spread? Well, in the world of Forex trading, you have to deal with two terms, "ask" and "bid." The price that is quoted for selling a particular currency pair is termed as "ask," while the price that is quoted to a trader for the purchase of a currency pair is called "bid." The difference between them is called a spread. So, in this case, you do not want to have a big gap with the ASK and BID, or you might not make a lot of profits.

**Trade With Just One Currency Pair at a Time.** Dealing with multiple currencies means having to deal with the risks, trends, and quick fluctuations of those currencies. When you are dealing with the price movements of currencies that happen every second or minute, you do not want to be distracted easily by different pairs. You might not only end up making mistakes but also not make a profit at all. Additionally, you also get to feel comfortable with the pair that you are dealing with.

**Make Sure You Manage Your Risk and Reward Expectations.** As each spread you receive will be different, you need to know that what you can earn from those spreads will be unique. Most major pairs have close to 2- to 5-pip spread, and you should be aiming to get a hold of 3 to 10 pips per trade to negate any losses that the market might suddenly have.

**Do Not Trade Around the Time That Data Releases.** When the market releases some data, then there is usually a gap in the prices. This happens because the data is being added into the systems, and you might notice after a little while. This level of unpredictability might not suit the short-term trade strategy that you have set up. When you deal with currencies, you might notice that the markets receive price adjustments almost 15 to 20 minutes before the release of any major date. This could cause a sudden shift against your position that may not be solved before the data comes out.

## Medium-Term Trading

In medium-term trading, you are holding a position for a period that extends from a few minutes to a few hours. Some people might extend that to more than just a few hours, but traders rarely hold the position for more than a day. Because of the short periods involved in medium-term trading, you do not concern yourself with the length of time but the pips you are working with. And yes, this is quite similar to short-term trading as well. However, short-term trading does not deal with the overall position of the market. Its main concern is the profit that it can make from small price fluctuations. On the other hand, medium-term trading wants to focus on getting the general direction of the trade correct and make a profit from major currency movements.

Here are some tips for when you are using medium-term trading:

**Keep Your Eyes Attached to the News.** You are going to need it! This is because you need to have at least a basic idea on the direction in which a currency pair is likely to shift. This means that while you are performing minute changes, you are vaguely aware of the overall situation, making use of the knowledge to your advantage.

**You Need to Rely on Technical Analysis.** This is important because you should base your market expectations on chart readings, trend lines, support and resistance levels, and momentum studies. When you utilize technical analysis, you may be able to locate an opportunity somewhere on your charts, but by empowering yourself with global events, you might be able to make informed decisions. This, in turn, helps you open positions comfortably. When you know about events, you become informed about factors such as central bank events, interest rates, unemployment rate, and more. These factors help you predict the outcome of the position you are about to open, and they give you some ideas on when to make a closing.

## Long-Term or Macroeconomic Trading

This form of trading is for those with deep pockets and plenty of moolah to spend. We are talking about hedge funds and multimillion-dollar (and even multi-billion) corporations. When traders and institutions deal with long-term strategies, they open positions for weeks, sometimes even months. In some cases, the trade is held on to for years because the returns from those positions are incredibly massive. However, that does not mean long-term trading does not have its own set of flaws. For example, it has a high degree of probability of facing numerous short-term volatile situations.

## Carry Trade Strategies

In a carry trade, you invest in currencies that generate high returns and then sell currencies that have a lower yield than the currency you bought. Traders can benefit from this strategy in a couple of ways:

By having a long position in a high-yielding currency and a short position in a low-yielding currency, you can earn the difference in the interest rates between the two currencies. This interest is commonly referred to as "carry."

However, if you end up in the opposite position (when you have a long position in a low-yielding currency and a short position in a high-yielding currency), the rate of interest ends up working against you, and you end up in a loss that is termed as the "cost of carrying." A carry trade, in short, is simply making use of the difference between currencies of two different yields.

Now one of the most important features to consider is that you should jump in on a trade when you hear or see news about central banks working on their interest rates. This is because more traders end up taking advantage of the margin between the two currencies to make a profit out of it.

Let us take an example to explain this point. Let us assume that a particular trader spots the fact that interest rates in Japan are currently set at 0.5%. In the United States, the interest rate is close to 5%. What does this mean? The trader is hoping to make a profit of 4.5%, which is the difference between the two rates. He will first borrow yen and change them to dollars.

Next, he will search for securities to invest in that will pay him using the US rate. With that, he will be able to pay back what he borrowed and make a cool profit out of his transaction. Pretty neat, huh?

Of course, there is always a downside. In this case, you can chalk it out to market volatility. If the price of the yen improves, then the trader might end up getting lower profits. If the value keeps increasing, then the trader can effectively kiss his or her original plan goodbye.

However, many traders take into account this risk and place their expected profits at a rate that is adjusted for any changes in the market. However, once again, you cannot always predict that the trader's plan will work. What if the market suddenly shifts even further?

Carry trades are best focused on when the market has low volatility. This is because you can expect the financial markets to remain stable and avoid massive shifts. Another thing to keep in mind is that you need to have a big-enough interest rate between the two currencies to make a significant amount of money. Ideally, I would recommend looking for at least an interest rate of 2%.

CHAPTER 31:

# Tools for Mastering Forex Trading

In any business, the tools are really crucial to how the business operates. In forex trading, this is as well as a similar situation. The new traders or the experienced traders need the tools to master their trade and also make the right decisions to reach their goals.

Nowadays, the trading tools can be with a fee or without a fee. Many platforms offer free trading tools for traders to use at the basic level. Some platforms offer the subscription. Traders become the members and pay the services monthly or yearly.

## Economic Calendar

The economic calendar is helping the traders get fresh and updated news such as what happens in the future of the market, important related to trading economic data, new policies from the central bank, the elections and monetary policies updated around the world, and much more. These are really important for trading, especially the forex market.

You can get the economic calendar from brokers or financial websites. It will provide the big picture of the economy, such as the events that impact the economy at what level, the unemployment rate, expecting the market conditions. Traders will have to keep close eyes on these things because trading currencies will be effective.

The level of impact in each event will be effective for the economy. The currency pair will get effective, as well. The market volatility of forex trade will be either low or medium or high, depending on the events.

## Pip Calculator

Pip is the measuring unit, and it is the most popular and smallest measure unit in forex trading, especially between the currency pair. The pip calculation is convenient to use. Many traders use this forex trading tool to easy in exchange for the pair currency. The users just have to enter the detail of their position, the amount of the currency, size of the trade, currency pair, and also leverage.

## Time Zone Converter

The forex market has three biggest markets around the world. One market closes, then another market opens. That is why some traders can trade 24 hours. Besides that, the market also overlaps with each other, so the traders can also trade two markets at the same time.

With the right strategies, traders can get double profit. The time zone converter helps traders know exactly which market is opening at exactly what time. The experienced traders often trade around 3 or 4-morning Eastern times because they can trade in the London market, which is the biggest forex market. It also overlaps with the Asia forex market.

## Volatility Calculator

Traders should focus and always keep eyes on the market volatility. It can help you have a good view of which is a good currency pair to choose for trading. You do not want the currency pairs with a limited scope of volatility because it will not the best trade.

The volatility calculator will give the general the history exchange of these currency pairs and give you the overall of how much volatility the pairs will be. You will decide if you want to trade on those pairs or not. The history exchange can help the user pick what the time frame in which they want to focus on the week, month, quarter, or even years is. The more market volatility is, the better chance for traders to make the profit.

The traders can see the time frame with the currency pairs yield the most return, and they can start to trade on that time frame when it comes. It is working both ways that high returns will also be high risk included. The traders can manage to diversify the trading to protect the money by risk management strategies.

## Currency Correlation

Forex trading is all about currency pairs. Traders are sure not to ignore the correlation between currency pairs. The easy way to signal the currency pairs correlation is to mark them positive or negative correlation.

The correlations range from -1.0 to 0.0 to +1.0. These are easy to understand: -1.0 is the perfect negative or inverse that is often marked with color red color, 0.0 is no correlation, +1.0 is the perfect positive that is often marked with blue.

The correlations between currency pairs are calculating based on the historical data between them. One of the popular currency correlation tools that many traders are known of is Mataf. Besides, You can also search and will see a lot of online websites offering this tool for free.

## Trading Platform

Many trading platforms are available nowadays. The most used platform by the experienced trader is MetaTrader 4. The feature of this platform is one of the best and comprehensive in the market. MetaTrader 4 has strong analysis functions. The chart is really clear and easy to understand. Traders can put in currency pairs directly to the chart to comparing the up and down of the market.

MetaTrader 4 has a lot of advantages. Many traders use it, so if you run into problems, you can easily find the right answer quickly. MetaTrader 4 can operate and link with other software. Users can run automated trading with this platform smoothly.

MetaTrader 4 is not only used for forex trade but also used for different types of trading such as stocks, bonds, gold, and much more. Traders can download MetaTrader 4 on its online website. They can try, test their data. This platform is really for serious traders.

CHAPTER 32:

# Important Forex Terms

I've been gradually introducing more and more terminology within the text, and now it is time to come face-to-face with the glossary of forex terms you will need to know. Well, 'glossary' is a strong word. Think of it more as a primer on the important terms you will need to learn and understand well.

## What Are Pips?

The dictionary tells us that a pip is a hard seed contained within a fruit. Well, as useful as that is to know, it has nothing to do with forex trading, unfortunately. A pip is simply the smallest value by which a forex instrument's price will change. Usually, a pip runs up to four decimal places, but in the JPY denominated pairs, this is usually the second decimal point.

So, if you see a price quote for EURUSD as being 1.3678, the last digit represents a pip. Thus, it is eight pips, and the number seven to its left represents seventy pips, the six in front of the seven represents six hundred pips, the three represent three thousand, and the one represents ten thousand.

Some traders often confuse a pip for a basis point. While a basis point is 0.01%, this is not always the case with a pip since the smallest movement need not be 0.0001 at all times. The yen pairs are a good example of this. In addition to pips, there are also things called pipettes that you will see pop up on your screen.

Pipettes are the fifth or third digit in the price quote and are a tenth of a pip. Usually, brokers offer them as a means of displaying how accurate their execution is, but practically speaking, there isn't much of an advantage to be gained with a few pipettes either way.

The big question is: How do you calculate profit and loss and the value of a single pip's worth of movement in a forex pair?

## Pip Value

In the stock market, the value of a single movement of price and the calculation of profit and loss is quite straightforward. Everything is priced in one currency, and calculating P/L is just a question of subtracting the buying price from the selling price. In FX, though, it isn't as straight forward.

Since you're dealing with an exchange rate between two currencies and not the currencies themselves, you need to follow more steps than usual. The first step is to figure out how much a pip is worth in P/L. This is done in the following manner.

Let's say you decide to trade some USDCHF at 1.0234. Remember, from the discussion on base and quote currencies, this price quote can be read as one USD equals 1.0234 CHF. To get the value of a pip, we divide the smallest possible movement in the quote currency by the exchange rate, which is just the price quote itself.

Pip value= (.0001 CHF)/(1.0234)= 0.0000977 USD/unit

Thus, if we bought a standard lot of USDCHF, which is equal to 100,000 units, the value of a single pip's worth of movement would be $9.77. Now, you will have noticed that we used the price of the instrument to calculate pip value. However, with the price always changing, pip value changes as well. Thus, the value calculated is an approximate one.

If you happen to be trading across, then you will receive the pip value in a currency other than USD.

To convert this number back to USD, simply multiply it or divide it by the exchange rate currently prevalent. Let's look at an example.

EURJPY at 113.45

Pip value/unit= (.01)/(113.45)= 0.00008814 EUR/unit

Unit size= 100,000

Pip value= EUR 8.81

EURUSD at 1.1234

Pip value in USD= (8.81)/(1.1234) = $7.84

Here, we have two exchange rates involved, and thus the values are approximate since these will keep changing. The big question is, given how much of a pain all of this is, should you have a supercomputer nearby to do all of this yourself? Well, your broker will do everything for you.

However, when it comes to making decisions about position sizing, as I'll discuss later, you will need to do this yourself. Don't worry, though, and there are many calculators online that will give you the exact profit and loss numbers and the correct position size you need to enter a trade.

Despite the existence of calculators, it still pays to understand these calculations on a basic level. After all, you're trading them, so it follows that you should know how to calculate profit and loss. Aside from pips, there are other things to take into account when calculating profit and loss.

## What Are Spreads and Swaps?

I've already covered what the price spread is and how this works. To recap, the spread is the difference between the ask and the bid, and the price you pay to sell the instrument is called the bid, and the price you pay to buy it is the ask. Beginner traders often get confused when the price seemingly hits their profit targets, but the trade doesn't closeout.

For example, if you set your profit target at X, and you see that overnight the price seemingly hit X but turned back upward, now your trade is in a loss. Well, the reason your trade didn't close is that the spread didn't cross your profit target. Let's say you bought a lot of GBPUSD, and your profit target is 1.2345. In order to realize a profit, the bid has to hit 1.2345.

If the ask hits 1.2345, but the bid remains at 1.2344, your trade will not close at a profit and will remain open. Always remember to take the spread into account when placing a trade. This is why you want to trade in pairs that have low spreads. In our above example, if the spread is 1.2339/1.2345, the bid needs to travel an additional six pips before your target is hit.

In some exotic pairs, spreads can be up to thirty pips during off-peak times. This makes it almost impossible to realize a profit easily. Generally speaking, price charts always show bid values. This makes it easy to get confused when going short in the market, that is, when selling first and buying back later at a lower price.

In such cases, remember that the ask has to hit the price target. You will see the price chart hit the level, but this is just the bid. Often, you may see the bid on your price chart hitting the target, but your broker's spread will not hit it. You're pretty much powerless in this situation to do anything.

Your broker will honor the price spread and not the values on the chart when it comes to discrepancies.

There is another quirk to forex that stock markets don't have. This is called the swap rate, and it is this rate that was at the root of the famous carry trade.

## Positive Carry

Positive carry is perhaps the one thing that traders everywhere love the most. It is free money, quite literally. When you buy a forex pair, you're buying one and selling another currency at the same time. In order to facilitate this transaction, your broker has to borrow one currency and lend another.

Each currency has a certain interest rate associated with it, as is set by the central bank that governs the currency. Thus, if you own the currency that pays a higher interest rate and sell the currency that pays the lower one, you make money on the difference between the interest rates. This is what positive carry is. The interest rates on the currencies are called the swap rates.

For example, if you decided to buy the USDJPY back in the early 2000s, the interest rate in the United States was around 4-5%, which doesn't sound like much but remember that this is the rate at which institutions can borrow from the government. In turn, banks would then lend this money to businesses and others at rates of 7-9%.

Meanwhile, a deflating economy in Japan had pushed interest rates as close to zero as possible and thus created a large interest rate differential in the market. Now, differentials larger than this existed at the time, and they still do; however, these existed mostly with exotic pairs. The USDJPY was a major pair, and liquidity was guaranteed, as was low volatility.

Thus, emerged the carry trade. If you held a long position at 11:59 PM, you would be paid a swap amount at 12:01 AM in accordance with the size of your position. Often, these positions were large. The carry you earned was over and above your profit and loss on the trade and was so large that the carrying amount often wiped out and placed losing trades well into profit. Thus, trades didn't care what their positions did; they just bought and held.

Every position you hold will have the carry effect applied to it the longer you hold. Thus, trades that have a negative carry will eat into any profit and increase the size of your loss the longer you hold onto them. Positive carry trades will reduce your loss and increase your profit.

How much does the carry really affect your results? Well, between the major pairs, not very much at all, unless you hold on for something like years on end. These days, even the minor pairs don't have much of a differential. However, you should always check with your broker what the overnight swap rates are and plan accordingly.

While the effects themselves are small, over time, they add up, and you should take them into account as much as you would broker commissions.

CHAPTER 33:

# What Are the Risks of Forex Trading?

When learning to trade forex, it is imperative that you understand what the risks involved are.

There is some basic math involved with this, and once you understand how this works, you will see that making money with forex is really about getting the math right and not just about picking the right strategy.

## Types of Risk

There are roughly four risks you should be well aware of before you begin to trade:

1. Leverage risk
2. Transaction risk
3. Interest rate risk
4. Counterparty risk

These risks aren't inherent to just forex trading but really exist with every form of trading. Let's take a look at these one-by-one to understand them better.

### *Leverage Risk*

This is the most obvious one here. The more leveraged you are, the less the breathing room you have in case things go against you. While the upsides of leverage are huge, they're nothing compared to the downsides of it. Leveraged accounts are particularly vulnerable during times of huge volatility.

During those times, spreads widen and move dramatically. Often, the price jumps violently, and you will find that your margin limits will burst wide open, and you will be asked to post more margin, often far more than what you might have been planning for. During the aforementioned SNB incident, for example, traders incurred losses of close to $250,000 within a few minutes.

### *Transaction Risk*

Exchange rates keep fluctuating all the time, and there is a chance that if you're trading during particularly volatile times, the rate that you see on the screen isn't the true market rate. Thus, the prices you receive may be far worse than what you bargained for, and your risk limits will be violated, putting you in close proximity to a margin call.

This often happens with exotics and sometimes even with minor pairs during times of huge volatility. The key to avoiding this sort of risk is to steer clear of periods of huge volatility and to make sensible decisions with existing positions when riding out such periods.

### *Interest Rate Risk*

Interest rates are intricately tied to the forex market, and a slight change in the base rates of a currency can send its pairs running from one end of your chart to the other. Interest rate announcements are often waited for with bated breath and understandably so.

Managing your interest rate exposure is also simpler than it looks and will be explained shortly.

### *Counterparty Risk*

Lastly, we have counterparty risk. This is a type of risk that not enough traders worry about. While the stock market and its brokers are heavily regulated institutions, FX brokers aren't subject to the same level of scrutiny. This doesn't mean they're dishonest but just that the rules applying to them aren't as stringent, and there are a few bad apples who poison the reputation of the bunch.

The SNB decision caught several brokers napping because the sudden and violent price movements in all CHF pairs broke the market. A lot of brokers simply didn't receive quotes from the counterparties because, for a while, say five minutes or so, no one in the world knew how to price the new Swiss franc's exchange rate to other currencies.

Once the quotes started coming in, prices were driven mad by the rush of trades that needed to be closed out, and this put further strain on the system. Given the huge jump, naturally, a large number of traders were in margin call zones, but the brokers didn't have time to collect since the number of these accounts went from an acceptable number to unacceptable levels within a few seconds literally.

Thus, brokers found themselves having to pay their counterparties before they could collect from their clients. They couldn't realistically hope for collection, either. I mean, someone who opens a $2,000 account is unlikely to respect a margin call of $100,000 despite the threat of bankruptcy.

Evaluating your broker is a very important thing to do, and you should conduct thorough due diligence on them. For the time being, now that you know the inherent risks in forex trading, let's look at how you can manage these risks successfully.

To do this, we need to step aside for a second and visit a casino.

CHAPTER 34:

# Forex Market Hours and Trading Sessions

In general, the forex market is considered to be accessible 24 hours a day, seven days a week. Global Forex competition is theoretically accessible 24 hours a day, seven days a week, but the hours you can trade are still limited. Compared to other regulated markets, such as the stock market, the forex market consists of a network of financial and retail institutions that allows them to determine their opening hours. Forex trading hours are according to your time zone. Most institutions trade between 8 a.m. At 4:00 pm. The local time zone is comparative.

The currency market is registered 24 hours a day and five and a half days a week accessible for trading. It should also be noted that more experienced day traders realize that when business participation is strong during business hours, profitable deals emerge. In other words, you can operate every day, early in the evening, but due to regular exercise, it may not be the best time.

Many experts suggest focusing on the top three money businesses, such as London, New York, and Tokyo. You can use the highest business mode and the greatest chances of success in your usual Forex business, attacking these three main economies. Market professionals also demonstrate that when these important market centers are also accessible, the more serious forex traders specifically target and do their business. This small gap in business time zones leads to the most efficient business times.

With weekly volumes of around $ 23 trillion, the forex market is the largest financial market in the world. You have to closely research all the important elements of the stock market to become a good Forex trader. These include trading hours and Forex (FX) trading. When we refer to the currency exchange schedule, what do we mean? They are the respondents of the time in FX who can buy, trade, and speculate in various currencies.

The forex industry is available every day, five days a week. There is no mystery. In fact, global currency markets include loans, various corporations, central banks, hedge funds, investment management companies, and retail Forex brokers, as well as global shareholders. Most of the major global companies have many stores around the world in the interbank foreign exchange market, so they can transfer foreign exchange instructions to their local clients at any time during 24 hours at an affiliated office.

This method is generally successful at any time of the week unless the holidays are interrupted. Banks operated out of each national office during normal business hours, and the accessible list of transactions is generally transmitted to another national office in the next period.

During Forex sessions, the session will be titled during city business hours with the major financial center in the relevant time zone. If you are trying to figure out the best time to trade currency pairs, it is important to know what currencies or prices are during these trading hours and which Forex meetings are the most fluid.

As this industry operates in different time zones, it is available at almost any time of the day. Furthermore, the international money industry is not dominated by a single market, but by a global network of markets and brokers. Trading hours in each nation involved are focused when trading is available.

The main sessions are:

- Meeting in London
- Session in the USA
- Overlap London/USA
- Session in Tokyo

The small sessions are:

- Wellington/Auckland
- Sydney
- Frankfurt
- Hong Kong
- Singapore

When a major currency industry ends, another industry begins. The trend continues. Sometimes—and it's important to keep a record—they get more involved. For example, New York is 8 p.m. until 5 pm. ETE, Tokyo is starting at 7 p.m. Until 4 pm. EST, Sydney from 8 a.m. until 2 p.m. EST, London starting at 3 pm until 12 p.m. ITS T. Sometimes, the greatest amount of trade takes place when economies intersect.

## Use the Demo Account

Traders with a demo account can also trade with a demo account without risk. This means that traders cannot risk their assets and choose to move into private economies. The Admiral Markets Trading Demo Account allows a trader to have links to the latest industry information in real-time, to trade simulated currencies and the latest trading ideas from specialist traders.

## Trade Sessions

One of the most important characteristics of the foreign exchange industry, as described above, is that it is available 24 hours a day. Investors around the world can do business during normal business hours, after work, and even in the afternoon. However, it is not always produced in a completely equivalent way. There are times in global currency trading when price action is constantly fluctuating, and there are also times when it is completely silent.

Due to the general demographics of these trading respondents buying at that particular time, many currency pairs exhibit different behavior at different times of the trading day. This leads us to recognize that important Forex trading sessions are directly related to the time of purchase.

Although a 24-hour industry provides many personal and corporate traders with a significant benefit, as it guarantees liquidity and a great possibility to trade within the fixed hours of Forex trading at all times, it has no drawbacks. While different currencies can be exchanged whenever you want over such long periods, a trader cannot monitor a situation.

This means that Forex trading sessions will be available when there is a missed opportunity, or worse still, when changes in price volatility lead to the rejection of a defined position if the trader is not around. A trader must be aware of the most volatile industry, thus determining what times are appropriate for his personal trading strategy and type of operation, in an effort to reduce this risk.

The industry is usually divided into three business meetings at its pinnacle: Asian, European, and North American. More frequently, Forex is also called the Tokyo, London, and New York meetings for these three trading hours.

The designations of these three towns are used interchangeably simply as they constitute the main economic centers for each region. When those three power companies operate —because, most companies and companies conduct regular operations —the economies are most involved. An increased density of speculators is also available internet.

## European Trading Session

Later in the trading day, just before the end of Asian hours of trading, a European session will continue to keep currency markets active. European trading session or London session, this Forex time zone for trading is very thick, covering a range of important financial markets. London is honored to identify the European meeting parameters.

London's Official hours of a company operate from 07:30 to 15:30 GMT. Due to other capital markets, including Germany and France, this trading duration is extended before formal opening in the United Kingdom, while volatility is repressed as long as London is closed after the trading meeting. Consequently, the European Forex GMT trading time between 07:00–16:00 GMT is generally noted.

## North American Trading Session

The Asian markets were already closed for a couple of hours as North America's trading session or New York session. But for the traders in the European FX, the day is halfway through. The Western part-session is affected by exercise in the United States, with some additions from Canada, Mexico, and other South American nations. Not amazingly, New York activities are highly volatile, as well as attendance at the meeting on the GMT business hours of North American Forex.

Given premature business operation in the financial markets, stock trading, and noticeable accumulation of economic launches, the official beginning of North American hours at 12:00 GMT is unofficial. The liquidity interval is established at the conclusion of New York's trading at 20:00 GMT with a considerable break between the closing of US banks and the closing hours of the Asian Forex market, as the North American meeting ends.

## Forex Hours and Meetings Overlaps

The European/Asian meeting will result in a much larger reaction of monetary pairs that are most active during European and Asian Forex hours (such as GBP / JPY and EUR / JPY) and thus a reduced rise in cost intervention during the EU-North American meeting. Nevertheless, irrespective of whether the couple or the components' corresponding meetings have a substantive impact on the operation of each currency.

Asian/European overlapping is shown in pairs traded strongly over Asian and European forex hours. During pair effective business hours, long-term or basic FX traders who try to find a place could contribute to a low admission cost, missed access, or trading that is contrary to the strategy. On the other side, volatility is certainly crucial for short-term traders who have no place tonight or even forever.

## Non-Trading Risky Business Hours

There is significant trade danger during poor liquidity, generally when a stock starts and around 12 AM. In the ordinary course of trading hours, lower liquidity could result in higher volatility. The trade traders do not suggest anywhere between 12-2 AM starting locations. Most of these high threat moments might jeopardize a trader's account.

Risk variables include:

**A Volatility Spike:** Low liquidity can quickly trigger volatility peaks to your halt, lose or slow

**Liquidity:** This has to do with the size of the forex market and has to do with the capacity to manage big operations efficiently.

**Dealing Spreads:** Spreads typically extend at approximately 12 am.

## The Best Time to Trade Market

Traders then strive to discover the finest trading options. The TOTH (Top of The Hour) will generally provide volatility and spicy stock activities the first and last five hours of each hour.

In Forex, a market participant must first determine whether their personal trading approach works finest with elevated or low volatile volatility. If price action is more essential, it could be preferable to exchange business, overlap with the meeting, or just normal financial moments. The next stage is to decide on the finest Forex trading hours or moments, considering the volatility preference. Those who wish to be highly volatile must define the most effective timeframe for the currency pair to be traded on.

The European/North America Crossover Session will discover the most motion when assessing the EUR/USD couple. There are generally options, and an FX dealer should combine physical well-being with the need for good business circumstances. For example, if a US market participant prefers to trade the active Forex open hours, for GBP/JPY, it needs to wake up very early in the morning to stay on the market.

This could result in significant exhaustion and errors in judgment when trading if this individual also has periodic work. The European/North American border, which still has elevated volatility, could provide a much larger option for this trader. Moreover, a good agreement of knowledge of the Forex finest trading hours can provide a benefit in aspects of trade currencies, combined with an overall understanding of FX Trading Sessions.

# Conclusion

If you are reading this, congratulations on going through the book. At the end of this book, you have been able to get in-depth knowledge of the craft of day trading. You no longer have to question what day trading is and how to go about it.

If you are a newbie day trader, the book has given you numerous tips and guidelines to become a successful trader. Probably at the start, you did not know what instrument to trade-in. However, now you know about day trading in stocks, forex, or cryptocurrencies. The details in this book should be able to help you improve as a newbie trader or give you the motivation and information to start day trading.

Maybe you have always wondered if you can do a profitable business out of day trading. If this has been your dilemma, it doesn't need to be anymore. You now know it is possible to do business in day trading and earn your daily living.

Having all the equipment you need to trade is important. The book emphasized these things, and now you know where to begin. You don't have to procrastinate anymore but take a chance now and begin your day trading career.

Have your personal goals and strategies that you tie together with your day trading strategies and take the risk. Just like any other venture in life, day trading takes a risk, and, in most cases, it pays off handsomely.

Forex trading is not for everyone. You should never trade what you cannot afford to lose. Besides, you should be committed to keeping your emotions out of your trading decisions while making smart decisions based on facts.

If Forex trading is for you, then it is important to set realistic expectations. Even the very best traders like Warren Buffet only increased their portfolio by 20 percent a year, while most hedge fund managers are thrilled to grow their portfolios by 10 percent a year.

There are many approaches to Forex trading. Your personality, your available time, and your ability to read market indicators all play important factors in determining the best approach for you. Regardless of your approach, however, it is important to think before you trade as statistics show that the best way to lose money in Forex trading is to trade too often.

If you wanted to learn how you could make money efficiently and make huge profits by investing only small amounts of money, we have shown you that you should choose to invest in the stock market. There are only some people who know how to invest in the stock market because they have learned how to do so. If you follow the information in this book, you can learn how to do this too. You will gather plenty of information about stocks and the different types of stocks you can invest in. This book also sheds some light on the different techniques you can use to invest in stocks.

As a beginner, you may make mistakes when you start investing in stocks. This is absolutely fine because you will start off with a small amount of money. But you cannot do this in the future because you will tend to invest larger amounts of money. It is important that you always learn from the mistakes that you make. Remember, every experienced trader also made mistakes at the start, but they always learned from their mistakes. It is this experience that will help you do well in the market.

All the best!

# SWING TRADING FOR BEGINNERS

A Complete Guide
to Swing Trading for Beginners,
how to Create Passive Income
for a living. The Best Strategies
to Increase your Income, Discover
the Psychology of Investing

MARK P. ANDERSON

# Introduction

This book comprises how you can take control over your life and have success in managing your trades and investments in the stock market. You will need the right tools, and you will need to be motivated, work hard, and actively manage your positions and risk. If you can learn and master these techniques, you have the potential to manage some or all of your financial assets successfully.

In this book, I start by describing what makes the market "tick" and the basics of charting. Understanding charting techniques are critical for a trader because it helps them to get a read on the psychology of the market at any particular time. I have written the first part of this book with the novice in mind and have attempted to make it concise, practical, and easy to understand. It is written for everyone because I both share a passion for helping others better understand the stock markets and to assist them in taking control of their financial situation.

Intermediate traders will benefit from this book's overview of some of the classic strategies that many professionals and other Retail traders (they're the ones like us who trade for themselves and not for a firm) use effectively to swing trade.

The techniques that you will learn should allow you to see opportunities when they arise, and that will allow you to grow your portfolio over time. One important aspect of swing trading that you must understand and always keep in mind is that this is not a way to "get rich quick." It is a very common misconception that it is easy to make money trading stocks or other securities. Novice traders believe it is as simple as buying low and selling high. It sounds deceptively easy, but it is not. If it were that simple, everyone would be trading and making money.

There are lots of trading strategies and styles used by traders around the world. These are often used based mostly on preference. We can define swing trading as an approach whose primary purpose is to gain and make profits in the course of a few days to a few weeks. It is a form of trading where traders endeavor to benefit from small market movements, which can have a massive range in comparison. The average swing trading plan lasts between a single day and five days. However, it is common to see trade plans last a couple of weeks or even months.

Swing traders enjoy the potential of earning from breakouts within a relatively brief time. Part-time traders who have other things to do, such as employment, can benefit greatly from this method. It is easy to enter trades and then proceed to attend to other matters. Therefore, if you are a busy individual without the time and focus needed for short day-trades, then swing trading is probably the most appropriate strategy for you.

There are many distinct ways in which a swing trader can conveniently position his/her trades, and this is also in the context of the current theme. The popular and helpful strategy is to wait for the price level to be restored, and you will need to reach the trade before it continues to flow. The entry is usually made based on market reverberation of support or resistance rates, trend lines, or, in some instances, indicator verification may be required.

CHAPTER 1:

# Swing Trading Basics

There are different trading styles and strategies used by traders around the world. These are often used based mostly on preference. We can define swing trading as an approach whose primary purpose is to gain and make profits in a few days to a few weeks. It is a form of trading where traders endeavor to benefit from small market movements, which can have a massive range in comparison. The average swing trading plan lasts between a single day and five days. However, it is common to see trade plans last a couple of weeks or even months.

Swing traders enjoy the potential of earning from breakouts within a relatively brief time. Part-time traders who have other things to do, such as employment, can benefit greatly from this method. It is easy to enter trades and then proceed to attend to other matters. Therefore, if you are a busy individual without the time and focus needed for short day-trades, then swing trading is probably the most appropriate strategy for you.

Swing traders generally use technical analysis to guide them in their trades. Technical analysis involves studying a particular stock's history and using the information obtained to predict future movements. The reason is that past performance is a great indicator of future price movements in the markets.

## Technical Analysis

Technical analysis is very popular with swing traders. As such, they are least concerned about fundamental analysis and its implications. They do not care about a company's performance or its fundamentals.

Whether a company is doing well or performing poorly is none of their business. Even the thoughts of analysts, stockbrokers, finance experts, and others do not matter. The only important factor as far as day traders are concerned is the performance of the company's stock at the markets.

Swing traders often search for stocks with potential. Not any stock traded at the markets qualifies to be traded. A good stock is one with a positive market outlook, one that has plenty of volatility, high volumes, and possibly a blue-chip. Blue chips are valuable companies that are very successful and generate a lot of income.

The search, once relevant stocks are identified, focuses on definite risk versus reward ratios. Swing traders are aware that a suitable stock, once identified, is likely to make a move. It is crucial, therefore, to be there ready and waiting to capitalize on the movements. Swing traders need to be very fast and jump into a trade then begin to ride it.

## Market Speculation

Swing trading can be viewed as a form of market speculation for the short term. In this fundamental type of speculation, traders hold positions for at least one day but usually for longer. Numerous securities can be traded this way, including currencies, options, stocks, futures, cryptocurrencies, and even ETFs.

A trader will endeavor to make gains by entering a position and maintaining it for a day or longer in the hope of making some explosive gains. The period ranges from one day to a couple of weeks. When this period extends to months, then the trader is said to be an investor. The main distinction between traders and investors is the amount of time spent holding positions.

As a swing trader, you will use technical analysis most of the time to determine the trend and take advantage of its movement. Most of the time, there will be no bullish or bearish movement in the markets.

However, sometimes stocks or other values can move in a predictable trend, especially between support and resistance areas.

Even so, owning one is still out of reach for the average person. As a trader, you should take a small position near the resistance area or an extended position. Sometimes it takes a few weeks or even months to take advantage of the expected price change.

It is important to note that swing trading can expose you to risk on the weekend or overnight. What happens is that you can enter a position during the day. Still, unforeseen events happen at night or on the weekend. These events could affect the evolution of prices and significantly affect its position in the markets.

There is a well-established and reliable risk-reward ratio used by swing traders to profit. This ratio is primarily based on target profit as well as predetermined and defined stop-loss levels. The system can be set to profit when a certain profit level is reached or when a guaranteed loss level is reached.

## Why Swing Trading?

Trading transactions has proven to be one of the preferred forms of trading and generates money. It's important to make sure your technical analysis skills are zero if you want to trade consistently and be profitable. It will also evaluate the transactions based on the risk/reward ratio. This is done using graphics. Graphical analysis will help you determine where to enter a trade, when to exit, and where to profit. As a swing trader, you will rely primarily on 15 minute or 1-hour charts to determine the most appropriate stop and loss points.

In addition to technical analysis, you must also ensure that your fundamental analysis skills are zero. For example, you may notice that the stock is on the rise, and you want to take advantage of its move. Before doing so, you must confirm that its essential elements are healthy and safe.

As a trader, you can risk around $ 1 to win $ 3. This is considered a reasonable and favorable level of reward risk. However, the risk of $ 1 to win, maybe $ 1 or less, is considered unfavorable.

***The Uptrend Is Favored by Bullish Traders***

The movement of stocks in the markets follows almost a straight line. Instead, the movement forms a staggered pattern. For example, stocks or other instruments may trend upward for a few days and then fall for a time before continuing their uptrend. When you look closely at these patterns for a while and see that all the movement continues to go up, we can say that the stock is in an uptrend.

Bullish traders should first determine the initial uptrend of the stock before the expected pullback or reversal of the trend. This reversal is also known as the opposite trend.

***Profit From the Uptrend***

It is wise to wait for the uptrend to repeat before entering a trade as we have no idea how long a downtrend will last. So, always watch the uptrend, wait for the slowdown, and then watch the trend continue to make a move. This is true and applies to a bottom-up situation.

To do this effectively, you must be able to determine the most appropriate entry point. In most cases, this usually happens as soon as the uptrend continues immediately after the reverse trend. However, you must confirm this through a risk analysis. The point of entry must be tested to determine the target and assess any potential hazards.

You must also specify the exit point. This is where it will stop operating in the event of a recession. It is also known as a breakpoint. This approach is essential if you want to cut your losses. Also, determine the peak or highest point of the new uptrend. This pin should be considered as your benefit. Once you get to this point, you should have at least some profit, because there could be another opposite trend.

If the uptrend continues, then you need to determine the best possible exit point or profit point to build momentum even while blocking some of the gains. This is a great approach and one of the easiest ways to make money as a swing trader. The reward for each transaction is equal to the difference between the entry point and the profit point.

***Trading the Downward Trend***

Some traders prefer to enter a bull market and implement swing trade strategies. Entering such a trade requires the use of a marginal order, separately the buy-stop order. Most traders prefer to trade stocks or options. Call options are preferred in a bear market, as traders profit in these market conditions. Trading options in a bear market can be quite complicated, but it is an art that many experienced traders practice and prefer.

Stocks and options in a bear market tend to follow a zigzag or step by step. In such a case, the stock will lose value for several days, and then a rally will occur before the downtrend resumes. With close observation and time, the general trend can be considered the same way as the uptrend.

***Profits From the Downtrend***

First of all, you should only enter a bearish trade after carefully evaluating the risk-return ratio. We can compare the entry point, in this case, with the stop-loss point. If the security selection or stocks reach the lowest price level of the most recent downtrend, this point will be considered the profit point. Therefore, it is recommended to take profit and exit the trade.

***Transactions Against Markets***

As a swing trader, you will mostly follow the trend determined by the actions in the market. Following the trend is recommended, and this is what most traders do. You have to be extremely talented or experienced to resist the trend. However, some merchants do. These traders are said to "weaken."

Fading is just another term for trading against the market trend. There are other terms that are used to mean the same thing. These include the fading trade, counterfeiting, and offsetting trade. Sometimes swing traders choose to fade. This is where they take a bearish position during an uptrend and a bullish position during a downtrend.

As a trader, you want to exit blurred trades before the end of reverse trends. This is because the trend will continue to move normally, and your positions could start to lose ground.

CHAPTER 2:

# Swing Trading Techniques

Trading is not rocket science, and there is no secret formula. The market can behave differently, and it might work with a specific strategy. And after some time, the market can change and shift to a new trading pattern, which can last for a shorter term or longer. So what works today might not work the following day. The main question is, what are the techniques you can use, which will work for a long time and can adapt to different market conditions? Three techniques can work best.

***Breakout Trading***

The technique is to look for a new high or low in the market. The high can be for some minutes or even for days. This technique focuses on using intra-day or daily time. This technique is best suitable for markets with lots of movement and good liquidity. A technique can work for years but can stop working due to market changes. An example, this technique has worked for over 8 years for a stock like Apple, but the stock stopped rising, and breakout was not able to work well with the stocks and the market.

***Retracement Trading***

Retracement is also a commonly used technique when the market moves fast in one direction, and it stops and corrects, and then begins a new leg of the direction the same way it was moving to. This technique is best for strong trending stock. The downside can lead to reversals, which make the stock to move further from the main trend. Few swing trading uses this technique.

### *Reversal Trading*

This technique is popular with swing traders since it offers a good risk to reward ratio. The most essential is to have a method that has a good risk to reward ratio, and it works well with tough conditions where there is less market trending. The best method to choose is the one with high reward and low-risk profile.

These technique does not work well with options trading; however, it works well with stock trading.

All these techniques depend on the market environment you are in.

## Swing Charting

Swing trading is becoming a popular type of trading, and the technique used to recognize trends in the swing charting. In this chapter, we will look at how to use the charts to make a profit.

### *Importance of Swing Charting*

For better technical analysis, use the swing chart. This tool is widespread, and this is the reason why:

- You can simplify the process of locating trends by using this tool, and as you now know, the primary way to make a profit in the market is by using trends.

- This chart demonstrates less market noise; this way, you can accurately see other technical analysis that is not time-consuming.

- The swing charts show less market noise, helping you to be more alert and to apply other ways of technical analysis that aren't short term.

Different variations of the methods, for example, the Kagi the Gann charts, are very effective in locating trends. With this technique, you can make actual changes to help you improve your abilities in finding trends.

### *How to Use Swing Charting*

This can be used in various ways:

- Swing charting can be used to view a market trend. You can identify the patterns by looking for the highs and lows.

- You can use this technique to stop a loss and make a profit. And these trends can be applying in the moving stop-loss points.

- It can be applied to analysis that is not time scheduled. Fibonacci levels can be estimated, and you can use the Elliott waves. By doing this, you can monitor the shifting of prices.

- You can create price channels by connecting the highs and lows, thus helping you estimate the prices, profits, and stop-loss and liquidating positions at the right time. The price movement can be achieved by connecting highs to high lines and also connecting lows to lows.

## Swing Trading Commandments

By gaining skills in technical analysis, you become more efficient, and this increases how profitable you will be in swing trading. There are many techniques available which a trader can use, but the essential tool is the simple trendline. A swing trader can gain a lot of profit within a short time by using this tool.

By using these tactics when trading, you will have a winning swing trades. Here are some commandments of swing trading:

### *Align Your Trade With the Overall Direction of the Market*

Traders should make short-term trading decisions. The trends could hold themselves if the trade were successful for a short time since your focus was on the short-term stocks. However, you can pick the long-term trend and go with the flow and not against it. When having significant trends, there is the possibility of surprises such as upgrades and downgrades and hits and misses.

### *Enter the Trade at the Beginning of the Trend, Not Near the End*

Quickly identifying a pattern when it begins, you will assume less risk and add more profits. Noticing a change in trend can give you higher profits and fewer risks. By paying attention to the overall market averages, you will see when a trend is overbought or oversold and when it's prone to a reversal. Various indicators can be used to monitor when the market is likely to a reversal. Industrial stocks are consistent with the overall market direction; thus, they turn when the market shifts as well. Some of the early warning lights are indicators like candlestick and momentum, and they anticipate when stock will become. Crossovers and trendlines are the lagging indicators, and they only confirm messages of the early warning signs. You can choose to trade with either lagging or a leading, depending on your willingness to risk.

### *Never Trade Only on the Short-Term Chart*

Synthesize the messages from the charts. Use a two-year chart to analyze a stock to monitor the long term moving average and the overall trend. Synthesize the complete analysis, and here you will be able to have information about the stock: Is the stock breaking out? Is this information sufficient? Am I ready to trade in the short or long term to get a significant profit and fewer risks? Not all stocks allow you to know the information clearly, such as the asymmetrical triangle, which is challenging to estimate.

### *Stay Consistent*

It is not easy to monitor all the stocks, and the more natural way is having a group of stocks that you will be tracking daily and learn about those stocks. Another tip is to focus on financial news, use the internet to browse various trading websites to check and analyze the upgrades, earning reports, and any relevant trading information. You can also check the markets of other countries, the oil price, gold price, and the dollar trading. From the websites, you can check which stocks are active and save all the information collected. Besides, you can follow core groups of traders, pick a group with a broader sector, not just one specific group. Monitor their charts regularly and note their breakout levels, their stock prices, what they can make in a good trade, and many more. Always stay alert, track several stocks, their portfolio, check the charts regularly, stay updated with the latest financial news, and also analyze the company's trading stocks. By doing this, you will be confident in making better trade winning decisions. With all the information, treat a bad trade as an opportunity to learn more. Monitor your chart, stay to enter your trades early, set a stop-loss. The goal is to be able to improve and get better as time goes.

CHAPTER 3:

# Day Trading Strategies

Anyone who wishes to make money with the stock trading should have a better strategy on how to predict the trend in prices of the stock to maximize profits. The charts show the trends with different patterns that a new person in the trade cannot easily interpret. The patterns in the trend have meanings that give signals to the trader on when to make a move by either buying or selling stock.

## The ABCD Pattern

This is a harmonic pattern that is used to derive the other patterns of trade. This pattern is made up of three swings that are made up of the AB and CD lines, also known as the legs. The line BC is known as the correction line. The lines AB and CD are almost of the same size. The AB-CD pattern uses a downtrend that indicates that the reversal will be upward. On the other hand, the bearish pattern uses the uptrend than indicates a reversal downward at some point. When using this pattern for trade, you have to know the direction of the trend and the movement of the market. There are three types of ABCD pattern: the classic ABCD pattern, the AB=CD pattern, and the ABCD extension.

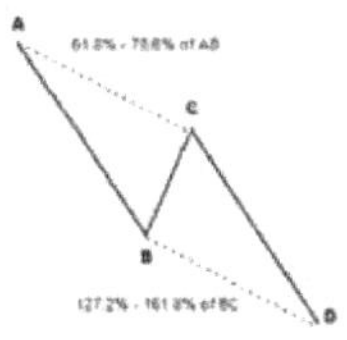


Classic ABCD Pattern

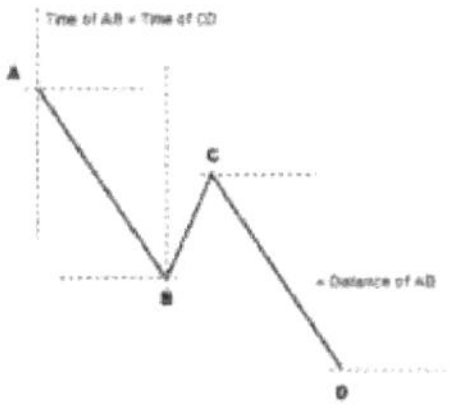


AB = CD Pattern

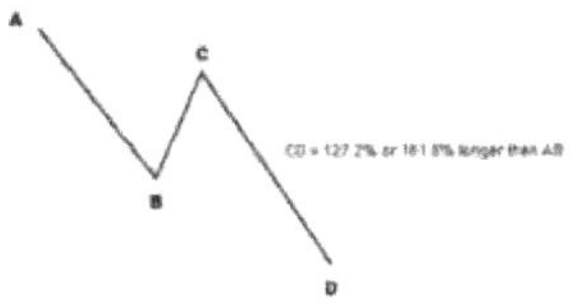


ABCD Extension

When using this pattern, remember that one can only enter the trade when the price has reached point D. Therefore, it is important to study the chart at the lows and highs; you can use the zigzag indicator, which marks the swings on the chart. As you study the chart, watch the price that forms AB and BC. In a bullish trade ABCD, C should be at the lower side of A. The point A, on the other hand, should be intermediate-high after B that is at a low point. D should be a new point that is lower than B. As mentioned earlier, the entry is at point D, but when the market reaches point D, you should not be too quick to enter the trade. Consider other techniques that would make sure that the reverse is up when it is a bullish trade, and down when it is a bearish trade.

## Flag Momentum

In a trading market, there are times when things are good, and the traders enjoy an upward trend, which gives a chart pattern that represents a bull flag pattern. It is named as such because when you look at the chart, it forms a pattern that resembles a flag on a pole. The trend in the market is an uptrend, and therefore the pattern is referred to as a bullish flag. The bull flag pattern is characterized by the following; when the stock makes a positive move with a relatively high volume, the pole is formed. When the stock consolidates on a lighter volume at the top, the flag is formed. The stock continues to move at a relatively high volume breaking through the consolidation pattern. The bull flag momentum is a trading strategy that can be used at any given time frame. When it is used to scalp the movements of price, the bull is used only on two instances of time frame: the second and the fifth minute time frames. The trading bull flags also work well when using daily charts to trade and can also be used effectively when swing trading.

It is simple to trade, but it is challenging to look for the exact bull pattern. This problem can be solved using scanners that help to look for stocks on the upward trend and wait for them to be in a consolidation position at the top. The best and free scanners that can be used to locate bull flags are Finviz and chart mill. Some tips can be used to indicate a bull flag: When there is an increase in stock volume that is influenced by news, and when the stock prices remain high, showing a clear pattern for a pullback. At this point, you can now check out when the prices break out above the consolidation pattern or on high volumes of stock. To make a move, place a stop order at the bottom of the consolidation. At this point, the ratio of risk to reward is 2:1, and it is the best time to target. The strongest part of the pattern is the volume of the stock, and it is a good sign that there will be a major move and a successful breakout. On the trend, it is also good to look at the descending trend as it gives a sign on the next breakout. This can be seen in the trend line that is found on at the topmost of the flag.

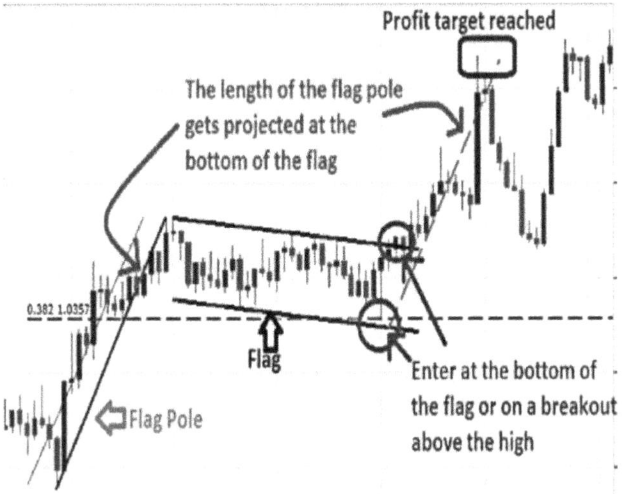


When used well for trading, the bull flags are effective tools of the trade; however, things can go wrong, and therefore one must be ready with an exit strategy. There are two strategies, one is placing a stop order at a point below the consolidation area, and the second method is using a moving average that is monitored for within 20 days. Within the 20 days, if the price of the stock is below the moving average, then it is time to close out the position and try out other trading routes.

## Reversal Trading

Reversal trading, also known as a trend reversal pattern, is a trading strategy that indicates the end of a trend and the start of a new one. This pattern is formed when the price level of stock in the current trend has reached a maximum. This pattern provides information on the possible change of trend and possible value of price movement. A pattern formed in the upwards trend signals that there will be a reversal in the trend, and the prices will go down soon. Conversely, a downward trend will indicate that there will be a movement of the prices, and it will be upwards. For you to recognize this pattern, you have to know where specific patterns form in the current trend. There are distribution patterns that occur at the top of the market; at this point, traders sell more than they buy. The patterns that occur at the bottom of the markets are referred to as accumulation patterns, and at this point, traders buy more than they sell.

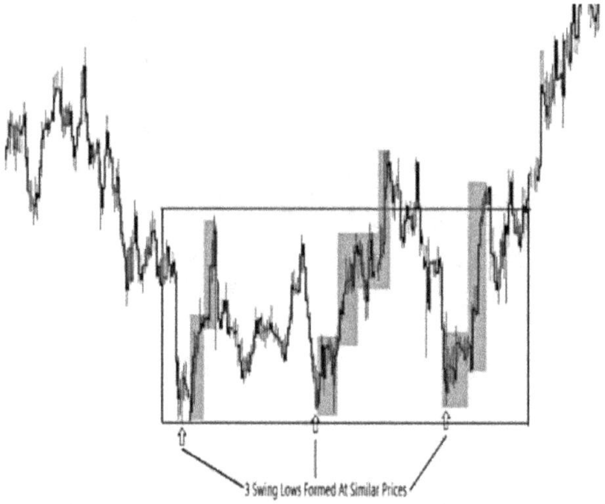


Reversal trends are formed at all time frames, and it is because the bank traders have either place trades and are taking profits off the trades. The trend can be detected when multiple up and down formations are fully formed, and they should be at least two upswings and two downswings, indicating a bearish pattern. The swing highs of lows on the trend line depend on which reversal pattern is formed.

The highs or lows form at a similar price because the bank traders want to appear as if they are causing a reversal in the market by getting all their trades places at the same time. In the real sense, that is not the case because they appear at different points of the trend. Therefore, as a trader, you should wait for a clear and steady trend upward for you to sell in the case of a bullish trade and a steady trend downward for the case of a bearish trade for you to buy.

There are different types of reversal patterns. The double top reversal pattern is a pattern that has two tops on the chart. It looks like "M." The double top has its reverse type, known as the double bottom pattern that resembles "W." The double bottom has two bottoms located either on the same support or at different supports.

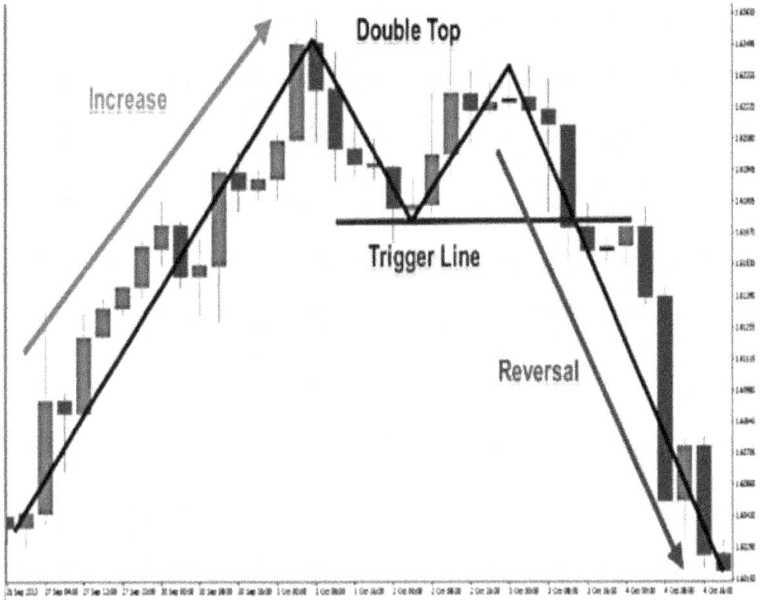


Another reversal pattern is the head and shoulders; this pattern resembled two shoulders and ahead. The two shoulders are tops that are slightly below the other top that is known as the head. The head and shoulders can also be represented in a descending pattern whereby the tops become bottoms.

## Moving Average Trend Trading

This strategy of trading is common among traders, and it uses technical indicators. A moving average helps to know which way the price is moving, if the moving average is inclined upwards, then the price is moving up, and if it is inclined downwards, then the price is going downwards. The moving average can also show resistance or support of the trend, but this depends on the amount of time of the moving average. Support is shown when the trend of the price is downward, and at this point, the selling pressure reduces, and buyers start to step in the market. Resistance is shown when the trend in the price of the stock is upward. At this point, buying of stock reduces, and sellers step in. It should be noted that the prices of trade stock do not always follow the moving average, but it is good to know that when the stock price is above the moving average of the trend, then the price trend is upward. Conversely, if the price is below the moving average, then the trend of the price of the stock is downwards.

Moving average is a powerful tool of the trade as it is easy to calculate, which makes it popular among traders. This tool of trade enables the trader to understand the current trend and identify any signs of a reversal. It also helps the trader to determine entry into the trade or an exit, depending on whether it offers support or resistance.

There are different types of moving averages. The simple moving average, which sums up five recent closing prices and calculates the average price, another one is the exponential moving average, whose calculation is a bit complex because it applies more weighting to the most recent data. When the simple moving average and the exponential moving averages are compared, the exponential moving average is affected more by the changes in prices that the simple moving average.

## VWAP Trading

VWAP is the volume-weighted average price. It is a trading strategy that is simple and highly effective when you are trading in a short time frame. For it to work for you, you must use different strategies, and the most common strategy is the waiting for a VWAP cross above and enter long. A VWAP that is across above gives signals to the traders that buyers would be entering the market, and there would be an upward movement of price. The bearish traders might short stock giving it a VWAP cross below, thus signaling the buyers to leave the market and take profits. VWAP can also be used as a resistance or support level for determining the risk of trade; when the stock trades above the VWAP, the VWAP is used as the support level, and when the trading is below the VWAP, the VWAP is used as a resistance level. In both cases, the trader is guided by the VWAP to know when to buy and sell.

CHAPTER 4:

# Advantages and Disadvantages of Day Trading

The first time I told my friends that I started day trading, I got two types of reactions: those who did not know anything about it thought that I was one of those big shots at Wall Street, earning thousands or even millions of dollars every year. Meanwhile, those who had some understanding about investing and trading, since they were doing similar things themselves, probably thought I was a nut case.

Day trading is controversial. Some traders believe that it is a get-rich-quick scheme, and you know how people feel and think about that: the faster you climb, the quicker and harder you fall. In other words, while you gain something faster than you think, you also lose a lot in return.

They were concerned that I was about to lose my money—let me correct that. I think they believed that I would go bankrupt. Of course, I lost capital, but I did not have to file for bankruptcy.

Perhaps these people also do not understand the simple fact that day trading is not for everyone.

## Advantages of Day Trading

You should probably consider day trading if:

**You Want to Earn Profits at the End of the Day.** The idea that it is a "get rich quick" scheme may be part truth since you do get to earn a profit after the market closes. For example, let us pretend that you invested $100 for 100 shares. The market fluctuation is in your favor, so when you sell it, you double your money, which means you now have revenue of $2 per share—not too shabby, right?

**You Want to Think Less About Your Investments.** This is because once the market closes, your trading also ends. Whether you win or lose, that is left to your skill and fate. The main point is that you will not have to think about whether your stock value will fall the next day or whether the US dollar will be strong in the following week. You think day by day, moment by moment.

**You Can Build Cash Inflow and Liquidity Very Quickly.** This can be related to the first point. Because you can earn revenues and profits by the end of the day, you can also boost your assets, which then means you can buy more securities and increase your chance of earning more money in a short period. I highly encourage that you diversify your portfolio even if they belong to the same class (e.g., class of stocks) to protect yourself in deep market fluctuations, which are not that common anyway.

**You Are Better Protected Against Market Fluctuations.** Okay, I mentioned just a while ago that diversification could help shield you from deep fluctuations in the market. But here is something to be happy about: the likelihood that it is going to dip extremely low is very small. As expected, market prices can change very fast in the blink of an eye, but the movements are often small.

**You Can Be Your Boss.** As a retail trader, you call the shots. You decide how much to invest, where to put your money, when to buy or sell, how much you like to earn, the securities you like to trade, etc.

**You Have Help**. You may be a beginner, but the learning curve is not as difficult as other securities or types of investing or trading. A variety of materials are available to make sure you do not have to trade blindly.

## Disadvantages of Day Trading

If day trading is not as bad as others say, now why should I say it is not meant for everyone?

**It Requires a Lot of Time.** Okay, all types of work or endeavor need it. I still have to find one that does not, and if it is legal and good, then I am definitely in. But when I say a lot, I truly mean it. You see, although there are specific hours of the day when you trade best, you still have to be alert as long as the market stays open because you will never really know what is going to happen. Stock prices could plunge, which gives you the perfect moment to buy blue chips or those that you can't afford before. If the European forex session is bad, there is a good chance US session will suffer the same fate as well. It is almost the same scenario when we talk about other securities like bonds, hedge contracts, futures, or commodities.

Let us not forget too that you would have to do your research after or in between trading!

**It Is Risky**. To be honest, life is all about and related to risk. You are surrounded by it. When you cross the road or drive the car, you run the risk of meeting an accident. When you sleep, there is still a good chance you will never wake up! Have you heard of the term idiopathic? In science, it means a disease or a condition happens with no known or determined cause. It is simply saying it occurred just because it can.

The levels of risks we face on a daily basis, however, can vary. In the world of day trading, it can be on opposite ends, depending on how you trade and how much you put in. The bigger the money, the bigger the possible loss. The higher the returns, the higher the chance of falling hard. Losing is all part of the game. The problem comes in if you lose everything—that is a possibility, you know.

**It Can Make You Emotional**. What has emotion got to do with day trading or any kind of trading for that matter? A whole lot than you can imagine. I remember the first time I earned a profit in day trading. It was not much, for someone who is just beginning, it meant something. I was so ecstatic I tried to trade more. Sadly, I lost the next day what I gained and traded. On the other hand, I know of friends who turn into monsters—angry, bitter, resentful, and irritable—once they begin trading. You can blame it on pressure, sense of competition, pride, or whatever. Whether you like it or not, day trading can get to you, and in many days, it is not a pleasant activity to do.

The relationship between emotions and commerce is strong. Many studies have already shown that customers are more likely to buy items on impulse and buy products that capture their emotions. The theory or concept of scarcity to sell something is also based on emotion. By instilling fear—the idea that if they do not act fast, they can no longer take advantage of the offer—is what has earned several businesspeople millions or even billions of dollars. You can, therefore, not avoid being emotional, whether it is positive or negative, when you are trading. However, you should learn how to control it and decrease its influence and impact on your decisions.

**It Can Make You Complacent.** These days it is so easy to get confident or even cocky with day trading. After all, you have more tools and resources compared to many years ago. You even have auto programs that can do the trading for you just in case you want to have some me-time in the middle of the day. But complacency can be one of your biggest mistakes. As you relax, that is when you become least prepared for the uncertainties. Your software can bog down, the analyses it provides you can be wrong, markets go down quickly without you knowing it—these things you could have resolved to minimize the effect on you only if you have paid attention and be more proactive or do your part.

**There Are Fees.** A lot of people think that they can just trade for free. Of course, it does not work that way. You have different expenses and fees to pay, including commissions for every execution (e.g., buying or selling). And there are tax implications! Yup, you still have to pay your taxes because you are getting some profit from the transaction. In fact, taxes are higher for short-term investments such as those of day trading than those held for a long time, which is at least a year. But the good news is there are caps set. Also, if you have a loss, you can write it off up to the number of your capital gains. In cases where you have more losses than gains in a year, you can go beyond the number of your capital gains and carry it over the succeeding year. For instance, last year, you have 10,000 capital gains and a $15,000 loss. You can zero your capital gains liability, leaving you with $5,000 more loss. You can then further reduce your tax liability by $3,000 and offset the next capital gains this year with $2,000. If you declare $18,000 capital gains this year, then your total liability is only $16,000.

## Can You Do It for a Living?

Now that you know the advantage and negative parts of day trading, it's time that you answer the question: Can you do it for a living? By this, I mean you trade not just as a hobby or a one-time thing or an occasional gig. I mean, you do it every day for as long as you can.

To help you answer that question, I have some more questions to ask:

- Are you willing to invest money? I am not just talking about hundreds or a couple of dollars. I am talking about thousands of them. As you go along the way, or as you trade for many years, you'll realize that you may be trading already a million dollars!

- Are you ready to lose? Between winning and losing, we definitely know what's a lot harder to take and get over with.

- Are you ready to win? The surprising question, isn't it? Why is it vital for you to be ready for it? The answer is simple: I don't want you to be complacent. Haven't you noticed that when everything in your life is going well, you tend to forget about what's happening around you? You pay less attention to them because you think your life is so good it doesn't matter what is occurring around you anymore.

- Are you willing to learn? Many of my friends can attest that one of the beauties of day trading is a huge opportunity to earn and learn at the same time. I, for one, believe that you can't put a price tag on education even if it means committing mistakes first before you learn your lessons. You also need to learn, too, as the market is dynamic, and you need to change and grow along with it.

- Are you ready to take risks? If you don't, then the immediate answer to the main question is a big NO.

CHAPTER 5:

# Choose Between Day Trading and Swing Trading

## What Is Day Trading?

Day trading means buying and selling shares on the same trading day. Trading positions are generally but not always closed before the market closes before the trading day.

Day trading is different from trading outside office hours when trading activity continues, even after regular trading hours when the exchange closes.

The buyers and sellers who partake in day trading are called day traders. While day trading suggests the picture of hectic trading activity during the trading day, it may not be in practice. You can make multiple trades, say a dozen, on one trading day, or you can limit yourself to just one trade.

In some cases, you can just buy a stock one day and sell it the next day if you don't think it would be profitable the same day. There are no legal restrictions that require you to end your trading activity on the same day. You may have to pay a brokerage if you delay your trade until the next day.

Generally, traders tend to close their trading positions during the day. However, your trading depends on the strategy you decide to use at a given time and the objectives set for that particular trade.

Some traders focus on short term trading. They complete their transactions in minutes, even seconds. These traders sell and buy several times a day, and their trades usually consist of high volumes.

They are the favorites of brokers who reward them with significant discounts on commissions.

However, some traders do not go bankrupt after a reduction in brokerage. They focus on momentum or trends in the stock market movement. They are very patient in anticipation of a strong move, which can happen during the trading day. These day traders are only making a few trades.

Some traders prefer to sell their shares before the end of the market day to avoid the risks associated with price differences between the closing price on the day they bought a share and the opening price the next day. They see this practice as a precious rule and follow it almost religiously.

Other traders believe that profits should be able to function to remain in position even after the market closes.

## Profit and Risk In Day Trading

Day traders make both quick gains and quick losses in minutes or at the end of the trading day. Day trading can evoke the vision of players who play in casinos. However, there is a clear difference between day trading and gambling.

While you can't make calculated moves or develop intelligent strategies in the game, except when you cheat on others, day trading involves a firm understanding of the trading process.

You study general market developments and the movement of shares. You perform fundamental and technical analysis and keep up to date with the newest news about the stocks of the companies you trade-in and much more.

Day trading is not about playing a blind buff or just rolling a dice. You should be very alert and careful before any movement.

Experienced and intuitive traders generate a considerable percentage of the day trading returns. Some stock traders manage to make millions per year on the trading day. Many people have successfully created day trading, the only way to make a living.

## Profit Expectations per Company

### *Day Trading*

Day trading is much shorter. You usually trade charts of 1 minute, 3 minutes, 5 minutes, or 15 minutes.

Due to the use of shorter deadlines, your profit expectations should be aligned with this approach.

I am convinced that if you want to succeed in the long run, you have to earn more than a few cents per transaction. Of course, there are high-frequency trading systems that carry out thousands of trades per day just looking for pennies each way.

I understand, but I remember that the Tradingsim blog is for the average person who wants to start daily transactions and does not have access to MIT engineers.

The only thing I want to make clear about day trading is that you must have a goal in mind. With the amount of market price recovery due to automated systems, you should record your earnings when your goals are reached. The probability that a fuse has a problematic trend in one direction for 3-4 hours in a row can occur 20% of the time. You should try to return the remaining 80% to a penny.

Here's an example of a day trading chart:

Below is a table from Apple. Watch the stock bounce off the top of the valley. There are times when stocks will trend very hard, but it will likely be the morning after a reaction to a news event. For me, the morning is my favorite time to trade just for that reason.

However, if you are going to trade daily throughout the day, the price at Apple below is your likely scenario. So don't be cute, book your earnings consistently, and don't worry about the trades you make.

### *Swing Trading*

Swing trading offers a much higher profit than day trading. On average, you can cut down for a few percentage points up to 20% and more.

Because your trading time is longer, your income targets are also higher. It is where the trading starts getting interesting. For example, you may have a specific income target, but because your holding time is much more extended than that of day trading, you can even increase your profit.

Below is a graph from FSLR over a five-day trading period. The stock has increased by almost 100%. As you can see from the graph, if you did day trading, you would have tried to time your swing points at A, B, C, D, and E. Most cases like this, the profit potential of swing trading is also sweet.

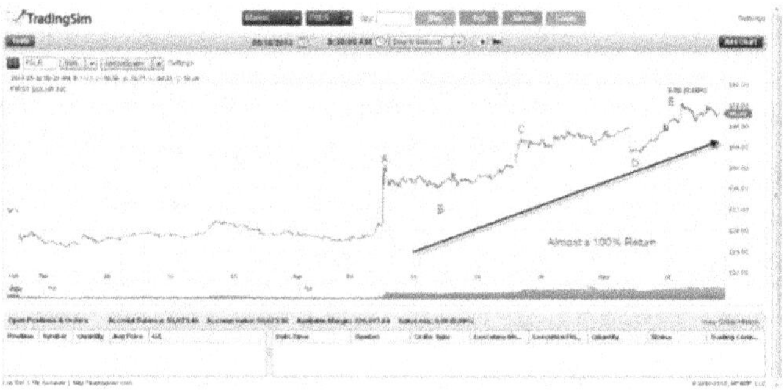

## Number of Transactions per Day

### *Day Trading*

Day trading shows that you can open and close deals on the same day. You can only trade up to a hundred trades or more once a day. I believe that if you trade manually, the more you trade, and the more likely you are to damage money over time. That is why I like to place 3 to 5 transactions per day.

How many transactions do you want to execute on a given day?

### *Swing Trading*

Swing Trading does not require you to trade daily. Typically, trades are placed every 2 to 3 weeks. The longer duration is because the stock must offer the possibility to "kitchen" from one price to another. Now there are times when a stock just has an outbreak gap, and of course, you hold onto the 2 to the 3-week timeframe and just let the stock run.

CHAPTER 6:

# Differences Between Day Trading and Swing Trading

As you are looking through these two options, you may notice that swing trading seems very similar to working with day trading. While there are some similarities between these two, and there are many times that they will use some of the same strategies, in the same way, they are two very different forms of investing. In many cases, investors tend to favor working with swing trading because it gives them more time to make decisions and can help them to earn more profit on each trade. These are just a few of the benefits that you can get when you decide to get started with swing trading rather than relying on day trading. Let's take a closer look at each of these reasons to get a better understanding of why swing trading may be the strategy that you need.

***Temperament***

If you are someone who doesn't really like to make snap decisions, then day trading is often not the best idea, and swing trading can work better for you. One advantage of this kind of trading is that you have more time luxury than others. You can take some more time to consider the trades that you want to take before you make a trade. You can use a variety of tools and analyze the trade a bit before using the strategy. You also have more time to determine your rewards and your risks, which can be very important when you want to be a successful trader.

Swing trading is a much better option for those who see themselves as methodical thinkers, the ones who like to plan out trade in advance, the ones who like to determine the best entry points, analyze the upside and the downside, and the ones who want to settle on an exit strategy. Moreover, they want to have plenty of time to do all of this before they push to either purchase or sell the security they want to trade.

To keep it simple, if you are someone who likes to have some time to figure out if a specific approach is the best for you, then swing trading is the best option. In some cases, you may find that you are well adapted to doing both swing trading and day trading. But, for those who want to have more time to think through their decisions and those who want to enjoy the trading a bit more, then swing trading is the better option.

***Availability***

The next thing that you need to look at is your availability. All of the exchanges in North America are going to open up at 9:30 am Eastern Time and then will go until 4 pm Eastern Time as well. The chances that you get to trade outside of these hours are known as pre-market and after-market. Still, trading during these periods is usually not recommended because there are less predictability and higher volatility.

The amount of time you have to trade the market during certain times of the day can depend on a few factors but mostly on where you live or your specific time zone. If you live on the west coast, for example, you would have to trade between 6:30 and 1:00 each day. This may work a bit for you because you could get a few hours of trading in before heading to work.

But, if you live on the east coast and you have to be at work by 9:00 in the morning, you may find that there aren't many hours in which you can trade. In this case, swing trading may be the best option for you. You will have the luxury of trading in the evening or even during your lunch break. You can use this time to check your stocks, view the market action, and then get back to work.

With day trading, you would have to watch the market all day. But, with swing trading, you could just check in on occasion and see how the market is doing when it works for you, just make sure that you put in the correct entry and exit orders. If you do this, then the price movements of the securities will come to you and fill your orders during the day, even when you are doing other obligations during the day.

***Lifestyle Balance***

Now, we will spend some time looking at how swing trading is better for a lifestyle balance. Everyone is different when it comes down to how much time they want to set aside for work and how much they want to set aside for play. Some like to work all of the time, but most people like to have at least a little time for fun activities in their days. You also have to figure out how much time you need to devote to your family and other commitments on top of the work that you want to do with trading.

Again, one of the advantages of doing swing trading is that there is a lot of flexibility for the trader to enjoy. You don't have to sit in front of the computer all day, so you get some freedom to come and go. Yes, you do need to sit down each day and check your position, look for some new opportunities to take care of, and pay attention to what the market is doing. But you don't have a requirement for what time to sit and watch the market, and you don't have to stay there all day long.

***Financial Demands***

With swing trading, you won't need to have as much money ready to get started. Ideally, you will start at about $5000 in your account. If you can, it is better to start with more, but it is possible to start with less depending on the trades that you want to do. Just remember that the less capital you put into your trading account to start, the more limited number of choices you will have when it comes to stocks you can trade with.

If you want to open up a margin account, the amount of capital that you need to start can be a little bit less. Government regulations state that these margin accounts need to have a minimum of $2000 in them. The deposit can be made in cash or in other negotiable securities, like bonds or stocks that you hold onto. You will have to talk with your broker about using those first.

Compared to doing day trading, the US requires that you deposit a minimum of $25,000 in the account before you can even take a look at trading. This amount is pretty high, and it is going to be more than what most people are able to do. This alone can be a significant advantage when it comes to trading with swing trading.

***Less Idle Time***

Most people have better things to do than just sit around and wait to see something happen. You have other obligations, work, chores, family, and more that you want to spend your time on. But, when you are a day trader, you will have to spend a lot of time sitting, watching, and waiting in between all of your tradable opportunities, and this can be a lot of wasted time, which most people don't want. When it comes to swing trading, though, you can still monitor your positions while doing some of your other responsibilities and duties for the day. You don't have to keep yourself tied to a computer screen, waiting to see an alert from your scanning program, or waiting for a big market event to take place that will help you see that security is going to move in one direction or another. This can free up a lot of your time compared to what day traders have to deal with to make any profits.

As you can see, there are a lot of benefits that come with swing trading. It is a short-term strategy, so you don't have to stay in the market for too long, but it still provides you with the benefits that you are looking for when you want to earn a good profit in the process. You still get more time to make the trades, you don't have to stay connected to a computer all day, and swing trading is usually seen as an easier option compared to other trading strategies.

CHAPTER 7:

# Risk Management for Swing Trading

Discipline is one of the hardest things to ace. In the meantime, it is the most significant component of effective exchanging. It is dependent upon each merchant to set up a pre-showcase routine and construct solid exchanging propensities.

You ought to endeavor to accomplish discipline on the off chance you ever would like to accomplish any degree of exchanging achievement. Exchanging control is polished most of the time, in each exchange, every single day.

Along these lines, to give you a hand, this blog entry goes for uncovering the ten brilliant guidelines of exchanging discipline. You should consistently condition yourself to be restrained. On the off chance that you need to be a genuine broker, then read through the standards consistently before the exchanging session starts. It shouldn't take over three minutes to peruse them. Think about the activity as reminding you how to behave all through the exchanging session.

### *1. Adhere to a Proven Trading Method*

Furthermore, do not transform it. If you have a demonstrated technique, however it does not appear to work in a given exchanging session, do not return home that night, and attempt to devise another. If your strategy works for more than one portion of the exchanging sessions, at that point, stay with it. Keep in mind, the Holy Grail of exchanging is cash the executives.

2. ***Effectively Trade the First Three Hours of Each Major Session***

It is the basic information that the Forex market exchanges 24 hours every day. In any case, not all of those hours are practical for day exchanging. In the event that you are an informal investor, you need to focus on the accompanying exchanging perspectives: unpredictability, force, bearing, pattern, and difference.

Also, you have to settle on positional exchanging and scalping. Take positions that appear to be the most self-evident, on the grounds that these are the ideal approach to amplify your benefits. You can figure out how to recognize easy decision arrangements utilizing our investigation and online courses. Additionally, focus on your exchanging plan. The initial three hours of each significant session are typically the best for force, pattern, and retracement. It is then that we brokers will, in general, locate the best exchanging potential outcomes.

3. ***The Market Rewards You for Your Discipline***

Exchanging with control should (all being great) compensate you with a positive cash stream. The purpose of exchanging with control is to have more pips in your record and fewer pips out. The one consistent truth concerning the business sectors is that exchanging with control ought to furnish you with greater benefit potential.

4. ***Consistency Is Confidence***

How great does it feel to have the option to turn on your exchanging stage, realizing that, if you play by the guidelines, the likelihood of a fruitful exchanging day is generally high? The appropriate response? Great! Keep in mind: If you make somewhat consistently, at that point, you have earned the privilege to exchange greater.

5. ***Try not to Let a Winner Become a Loser***

We have all abused this standard every once in a while. Be that as it may, it ought to be our objective to invest more energy, not to abuse it later on. What I am discussing here is the voracity factor. The market has compensated you by moving toward your position. Be that as it may, you are not happy with a little victor. Along these lines, you clutch the exchange of the desire for a bigger increase, just to watch the market turn and move against you. Obviously, you presently falter unavoidably, and the exchange further weakens into a misfortune now and then considerably.

The brilliant standard I use is – benefit taking. When we exchange on an intraday premise, we have to utilize benefit stops. When we are in benefit, we have to move our stop-loss into an advantage in this manner, verifying benefits. That way, we ought to ensure our benefits. To perceive how this is done for all intents and purposes, I propose you visit my life exchanging online courses.

### *6. Try Not to Chase the Markets*

You ought to abstain from bouncing on a cargo train. This may suck you into a winding of fate as you understand the business sectors may betray you. Quietly sit tight for the arrangement. The business sectors resemble a shadow. On the off chance that you pursue it, you'll never get it. In the event that you stop, it will grasp you.

Proficient merchants that pick Admiral Markets will be satisfied to realize that they can exchange totally chance free with a FREE demo exchanging account. Rather than going to the live markets and putting your capital in danger, you can dodge the hazard out and out and essentially practice until you are prepared to change to live to exchange.

### *7. Remember EOD – End of Day Trading*

At the point when the London session is going to end, regardless, you have roughly a few extra hours to adventure advertised developments. In the event that you neglect to utilize this time, your exchanging may stop in its tracks until the Tokyo session opens. EOD exchanging is extraordinary, as you more often than not have to exchange against the pattern. Why?

Since when most day exchanging market movers take benefits, the cost follows. Each end of a purchase position is a programmed sell again into the market. The enormous bit of leeway of EOD exchanging is that it doesn't require consistent observing which, thusly, makes it perfect for dealers with normal everyday employment.

### *8. You Are a Long-Distance Runner*

Have you at any point wanted to exchange while not having the option to do as such because the value in your record is excessively low, and your specialist probably will not enable you to exchange except if you submit more assets? That occurs on the off chance that you go out on a limb. Huge misfortunes hurt, and they hurt excessively. Use influence keenly. Try not to hazard over 4% per exchange. Keep in mind. You need to have the option to exchange one more day.

### *9. Pursue Your Trading Routine*

Your exchanging routine should comprise of a significant market hours trading, pre-advertise investigation, and end of day (EOD) hours.

Never attempt to break your exchanging schedule. Pursue real markets and exchange just during the significant markets. These include New York, London, and Tokyo markets.

The value moves all the more detectably during significant market sessions, so you can disregard minor markets. Significant markets furnish you with an incredible number of arrangements as well.

Truth be told, you can, as of now, check the day's monetary schedule for any solid financial reports that may impact your arrangements; at that point, move to value activity investigation to check whether the costs have gotten through significant help or opposition levels. My recommendation is to exchange drifting markets.

### *10. It is a Step-by-Step Process*

Attempt to utilize exacerbating. Aggravating is an incredible method to add benefits to your benefits. It is entirely appropriate for littler estimated accounts. At last, you may even have the option to assemble a six-make sense of the whole of a two-figure account.

By following these ten brilliant principles of exchanging discipline, those gainful days may before long become increasingly visit. This is because you will have adopted perfect, risk-averse techniques for swing trading.

CHAPTER 8:

# Understanding Swing Trading

A few years ago, popular trader Melvin Pasternak established what he called the 11 commandments of swing trading. Today, beginners are learning more about swing trading because of this information. While Pasternak usually discusses these commandments in his class, he shares them through his website. Like most traders, he wants to do what he can to help you reach your full potential.

1. ***You Need to Have Long Strengths and Short Weaknesses***

The first commandment focuses on bear and bull markets. When you are in a bull market, you want to focus on longer trades because the market is strong. When you are in a bear market, you need to focus on shorter trades because the market is weaker.

2. ***The Direction of the Market and Your Trade Need to Align***

When you are analyzing your potential stock's trend line, pay close attention to the direction it is going. If the trend line is moving upward, the conditions of the market should be moving upward. If the trend line is moving downward, the market's conditions should be doing the same.

3. ***Always Take a Look at Long-Term Charts***

As a swing trader, you are not going to hold your stocks for a long time. At most, you will hold them for a couple of weeks. Because of this, traders believe they don't need to look at charts beyond a two-week mark. However, many experienced traders feel you need to pay attention to the trend line over the last few months, even if you are a day trader or scalper.

Doing this will help you get the best idea of the trend line. Moreover, it is helpful for beginners, as they will learn more about trend lines with various stocks.

### *4. Don't Enter a Trade Near the End of the Day*

While this isn't always possible, you want to do your best to make sure you don't enter a trade at the end of the day. Many people feel that once the stock market picks up between 2:00 and 3:00 in the afternoon, it's time to find a stock to trade in a few days. The fact is, the market is so busy an hour or so before it closes because people are trying to close out their stocks. Day traders need to ensure all their stocks are traded before they close out for the day, or they acquire high overnight risk. Because stocks are being sold, their prices are going to decline. While this is a pull for many people as the stock's prices are lower, it doesn't mean that you will receive a higher profit. Allow the day traders to sell their stocks and focus on your end of the day activities.

### *5. Don't Jump from One Stock to the Other*

Do your best to make sure you are consistent when it comes to your stocks. While you want diversification since this can increase your success rate, focusing on different types of stocks can be stressful for beginners. You need to learn about the stock market slowly. In fact, even if you have been a trader for a while and find yourself struggling, you can take a step back and become more consistent with your stocks. This often helps people who are losing money on their trades.

When you are consistent with your stocks, you find that you are using the same strategy. This will help you become a master of your strategy. From there, you will become a master of the stock market. Consistency will help you learn all the details within swing trading. Because you aren't focusing on different types of stocks and strategies, you will learn how to analyze charts easily. Stress is a factor that can come with the territory of swing trading. When you are inconsistent with your stocks, you can find yourself feeling stressed as you struggle to keep up with your stocks and strategies. With less stress, you will be able to think more clearly and keep your focus.

### *6. Have a Clear Plan and Follow It*

As stated before, you will want to ensure you have a clear trading plan and that you follow it. This will take a lot of self-discipline, but this is necessary if you want to beat the market on swing trading stocks. Take your time to write down your plan before you officially enter the trade. As you go through your day, re-read your trading plan, as this will keep it fresh in your mind. If you find yourself struggling to hold the stock or sell it, look at your plan and remind yourself of the best moment to trade your stock.

### *7. Use Both Fundamental and Technical Analysis*

By now, you have a good understanding of fundamental and technical analysis. While people generally turn to one or the other, you should try to use both as a swing trader. The reason why both are important is that you hold your stocks for longer than a day.

### *8. Don't Forget About the Psychological Side of Swing Trading*

There is a lot of psychology that goes into trading. First, you can use psychology to help you control your emotions so you can always make clear decisions as a trader. Second, psychology can help you keep the right mindset. The right mindset focuses on having confidence, self-worth, and the belief that you will succeed as a swing trader. These are factors that you can psychologically build-up through meditation, breathing exercises when you become anxious, or other mindset building strategies. While you don't need to learn the basics of psychology and how your mind works, you will want to have a general understanding. This will help you reach your full potential as a swing trader. If you do find yourself struggling with the psychology of trading, you want to start focusing on the positives. You can do this by writing down what is positive in your life. For example, you might make a list of all the people you love and cherish and who feel the same way about you. You also want to ensure that you are getting enough sleep and eating healthily. Both of these factors can cause you to feel negative, which will start reflecting on your mindset.

### *9. Put the Odds in Your Favor*

There will be times where you will ask yourself, "Can I make a profit off of this stock?" You will find yourself stumped as you continuously analyze the charts to try to find your answer. You know you need to do your best to limit the amount of risk you have, but sometimes you feel that this is keeping you from making a larger profit on a stock. You can be right about this. Sometimes traders do become so focused on limiting their risk as much as possible that they forget to put the odds in their favor.

If you feel that you can handle a stock, but the risk is higher than what you are used to, you can look at setting a target price. This will become part of your trading plan and will decide for you. Your target price will tell you when to buy and sell. It is important to remember to set a stop-loss price along with a target price. However, you want to ensure you follow your target price no matter what the stock market's conditions do.

### *10. Be in Harmony With Your Trends and Time Frames*

In trading, there are three separate time frames:

1. The longest time frame - a year

2. The immediate time frame - three months

3. The shortest time frame - a month

The basis of this commandment is the further you look back on your stock's charts, the better idea you will get. This will help you know when you should enter and trade. If you look at the first couple of weeks and struggle to understand the trend line, go back a month. If you are still unsure, go back three months. While swing traders will rarely have to go back to the longest time frame, it is an option if you feel you need more guidance with the trend lines.

### *11. Don't Create Isolation*

There are a lot of tools to use in the stock market world—put them to use. While consistency can be key, you never want to become so consistent that you are only using one tool or strategy the whole time. If you are a beginner, you might feel more comfortable doing this, and that is fine. Work with your broker to get comfortable using a variety of tools, so you don't create isolation. After all, the more tools you use, whether it's a strategy, chart, and trend lines, the less risk you will have attached to your trade.

CHAPTER 9:

# Common Mistakes to Avoid in Swing Trading

Mistakes are always part of the game in any trading. Traders in swing trading make mistakes, too, that make them not succeed. Others commit the mistakes due to ignorance of the different rules and strategies used in swing trading.

## Mistakes That Swing Traders Make

Below are the various mistakes swing traders commit while trading:

### *Lacking a Trading Plan*

Most of the traders starting off on swing trading lack a well-defined plan. What do you normally think of when you do this? Swing trading is a risky arena. You need to be well-armed and prepared before entering into trading. Lacking a proper trading plan makes you misbehave in your trading, which is a very bad idea.

You normally lack a trading routine when you fail to have a plan. You find yourself lacking the objectives and goals for your trading. A trading plan enables you to stick to it and work hard for your objectives. Failing to have a plan makes you do things when you feel like it, which is very risky in the swing trading environment.

A plan is basically composed of objectives and strategies. Without it, it is like going for a war with no weapons with you. Prepare yourself with a good plan to know the risks involved in the market since it enables you to formulate your own trading strategies.

### *Lacking a Time Horizon for Your Trading*

Always know as a swing trader the duration you have for investment reasons. It enables you to be aware of the time duration you have before expiry. When you select your time horizon to be until retirement, it tells that you have to invest for a while before the time of retirement.

***Failing to Utilize the Stop-Loss Orders***

Stop-loss orders are very crucial for all kinds of traders. You need to implement it for safety reasons during trading. A trader who fails to utilize stop-loss orders strategies ends up with huge losses on their trading. You find yourself making big losses that could be controlled.

Losses all times turn down the success of any business. Failing to arm yourself so well in trading is just a total failure for your swing trading. You need to be alert with the crucial strategies in swing trading to survive and succeed.

***Lacking Control Over the Trading Losses***

Losses will normally occur in most businesses, but does that mean you should have no control over them? You need to make fast and efficient actions when losses occur in your swing trading, even the smaller losses. Ignoring the smaller losses will make them accumulate so hard, and time will reach, you will have no control over them.

You need to be serious about the losses that come up and be able to handle them before they shut down your trading. Losses promote no growth in swing trading. You need to have policies with you on how to handle losses. Most of the traders neglect this mistake, which makes them fail in swing trading tremendously.

***Putting Many Trusts in Financial News***

Watching and following up on the news is not a bad thing; however, you need to be extra careful with what you hear or come across online. Some bloggers mislead the novice traders a lot on how to handle their trading. You should be alert with all the information. Some people just want to see you fail. Do not apply all the information you hear from other people. Have your own ways of how to handle things in swing trading. You do not need to copy what others are doing. People have different abilities. Rely only on the trusted sources and swing trading forums. Consult the experts in swing trading for any information you have heard and are not sure about it. Have trust in yourself that your ways will also succeed in swing trading.

### *Working on Too Many Markets at Once*

A high number of swing traders fail in their trading due to being over-occupied with too many markets at once. You are not like a robot machine. You need to decide on a reasonable amount of markets that you can handle. Do not be greedy for money; you need to calm down and at least focus on a few and perfect your skills rather than being involved with too many markets.

This will make you get out of control. Concentrating on many markets is even not healthy for your body and mind. You do need to select every market. You should choose the ones you are highly interested in, perfect your skills on them, and ace swing trading.

### *Being Overconfident*

Being a confident swing trader is a good thing, but being extra than that is really a poor thing to do. Overconfidence has killed the dream of many swing traders. Traders are normally too confident with what they are doing and fail to list down even the risks that may be involved in their trading. You need to remember both the worst-case and the best-case scenarios in swing trading while planning. Consult others when you need help with your strategies. You may learn a few things that will help you in your trading. Do not be that kind of a bold trader who does things alone with no trainer or some sort of master in swing trading. Do not trust yourself that much. You might be doing things the wrong way.

### *Lack of Patience*

Good things take time. This saying is also relevant in our case here. Most traders have no patience in waiting for huge profits. They only want money to be accumulated in the first days after joining swing trading.

That is not possible unless all you want to accumulate are huge losses. You need to give yourself more time before you begin to earn more money.

The kind of traders who rush in trading for their greed for money end up nowhere. You need to be realistic sometimes to succeed in swing trading. Do not rush when trading. The money will still come. Do the right thing at the right speed. Do not implement many strategies on your trading and get confused. Work at least with one successful trading strategy and be relaxed.

***Indiscipline***

Being undisciplined in swing trading is not advised. Success is directly related to discipline. When you are disciplined in your trading, you can handle your trade with caution and the right mindset. Traders who mix their trading procedures and activities with other things end up mixing everything up. You need to be aware of all of your strategies and objectives at your fingertips to be able to know what you want to achieve. Not being disciplined makes you even forget your targets and your policies. This, of course, leads to total failure in your trading.

***Too Much Focus on Profit***

Profit-making is one of the main objectives of all businesses, but why focus too much on profit and forget about other crucial factors in swing trading? Factors like risk management and loss handling losses also need attention. Do not be the kind of traders who just think of making a profit and end up making big losses in their trading. You need to have a balance on how you handle your trading activities. Do not allow to accumulate high profits, which have the same amount as losses. There will no earn since the losses made will decline both your trading capital and your profits.

***Failing to Trust Your Abilities***

You need to have trust in your capabilities. As a beginner, you should not compare yourself with the expert successful traders. This will make your esteem to decline. You need to be yourself and remind yourself that you will succeed. All you need to do is to comply with the strategies and objectives that you wrote down. You also need to learn a lot and do much research in swing trading in order to succeed.

***Using Much Money on the Investment***

The amount of money you are dedicating for investment should be a good amount of your disposable income that you can quickly or easily refund. Utilize a little money at the beginning to avoid huge losses. The higher the amount of money you use for swing trading, the higher the number of losses that can come up due to the many risks that are involved in swing trading. Most traders boast around with a huge amount of cash for trading and, unfortunately, end up making huge losses. Also, do not trade with your school fees or rent. You will have issues with your school finance.

***Being Emotional on the Money Lost***

Catching feelings in trading are not advised for any swing traders. Some traders give up when losses occur and decide to quit. Do not be a faint-hearted trader; you need to be strong that the money lost will get refunded. Stand strong and wish yourself good luck.

***Being Too Much Aggressive***

Most unsuccessful swing traders failed to succeed because of their aggressive behavior. Being aggressive makes you lose a lot of money, which leads to the failure of swing trading. This normally happens on a bullish type of market. Relax, and everything will work out.

***Laziness and Being Irresponsible***

All types of trading are tough. You need to put much effort into your swing trading in order to widen your knowledge. Failing to do much research will not keep you informed and updated. You need to go with the trend. Do not be left behind. Failing to go through different newsfeeds on swing trading will enable you to be outdated.

Irresponsible swing traders who lack trading plans and strategies get confused and finally decide to quit swing trading. You need to be responsible and make decisions even during the worst-case scenarios. Do not fail to work even on the small losses that occur during swing trading. Trade responsibly, bearing in mind all of the risks involved in swing trading.

***Ignoring Risk Management Trading Strategies***

What do you expect when you fail to implement the few strategies needed for risk management? Swing traders who fail to implement the risk management strategies, of course, end up being involved with too many risks. You need to check on the different swing trading strategies that exist and choose the best handling risks in swing trading. This will protect your trading capital and also the amount of profit accumulated. Failing to arm yourself well enough will bring failure to your trading.

***Implementing Many Small Moves***

This mistake is normally committed by the novice traders who make moves on any small change in the market. You find yourself making trades even on your weakest points. There are high chances of big losses during this time, and that's why you need to be extra cautious and only make sure moves when relevant changes occur in the market. Small moves contribute to huge losses, so you should always trade at the right time according to your trading plan. Avoid this mistake in order to succeed in swing trading.

CHAPTER 10:

# Time Management for Swing Trading

Swing trading and time are relatives. You cannot mention swing trading and fail to mention time. Right from the definition, swing trading is the holding of a given instrument over some time, usually from overnight to a fortnight. You see, it's all about time.

So, time management is very crucial in swing trading because it is one of the limiting as well as determining factors to the trade.

The objective of holding on an instrument is to observe the shifting in price levels as opposed to the days' trading. Because of the following greater price shifts and ranges, you must calculate the positions and their sizes in order to limit the downtrend risks. For you to achieve all these, you are supposed to do a technical analysis to recognize instruments that have short term price force. This trade, in most cases, is done by individuals who have much time to follow up with trends. Large institutions, however, do trade mostly in large-sized securities that do not call for easy entry and exit.

## Swing Trading Risks

There are various risks associated with swing trading. These are stepping stones that need to be revisited for better returns to be achieved.

### *Market Risks*

It is easy to lose money. Even if some people or traders have taken it so lightly, it hurts most where your finances are involved. In every speculation of markets, lessons are ever learned the hardest way possible. On the other hand, margin trading and leverage are some of the profound causes of money loss. It digs deep into your initial capital.

### *Time*

In swing trading, time is a very crucial factor. As for longer-term trading strategies, you can measure your trade over some factors that can only work with time.

But as for swing trading, you need consistent monitoring due to its nature of the short term.

It takes up much of your time to monitor the movement of the trend as you weigh it against other factors like price changes. Therefore, it is not easy to mix swing trading with other day jobs.

### *Taxes*

As a swing trader, you need to pay taxes as well. If you do not pay your taxes, especially in the United States, you will be caught up by the trading laws. Always ensure that you meet all your financial obligations and liabilities.

### *Risk Management*

It doesn't matter if your interest is in penny stocks or algorithmic services when you do not observe money and risk management strategies, you could suffer losses.

Risk must be respected. If you ignore risks, they will take you by surprise.

### *Psychology*

If you are ever in love with fast-moving trades and most dynamic, or are you so intolerant with a requirement to know your fate of being right or wrong immediately, then you possess the right mindset required to be a rich man and swing trade master.

Sometimes, you may employ a strategy that isn't working for you; what do you do? These are the tips to consider solving that question.

The above mentioned are the major rules which govern swing trading. It is upon these rules that you can weigh your objectives to see if your vision is still true.

### *Plan and Stick To Your Plan*

As the nature of the markets, you expect high and lows. It is better if you allowed the pen and paper to evaluate those ups and downs instead of extending it to your emotions. S

ometimes you may be so quick in reacting, especially to sell off your stock, supposing they do not trend well across then week.

Therefore, it is better if there was some well-set plan to guide you in running your business.

### *Fight Fear by Limiting Risks*

People react to fear or risk in different ways. It is good, therefore to define risk parameter which suits your situation. At times you may not be willing, to begin with, a capital of more than 2 percent of your trading account on just one trade.

You cannot wait for a mentor to educate you on this issue. It is easy to get to know this with time.

### *Think About Long-Term Trades*

Many traders are usually obsessed with the last or the upcoming trades. It is, however, good to take it easy if you lost it on your first trial. You need to focus on long-term goals or future expectations. It was once said that: if you personalize losses, you won't trade.

There are survival tips that every swing trader needs to know in order to avoid unnecessary losses and further mistakes.

### *Make Good Use of the News*

As a swing trader, you need enough information on ways on how to limit risks and losses in order to maximize profits.

News events are moving markets today. There are many sites that do the analysis of the markets and general finances by use of price actions, volumes, and charting materials.

If you like information, you could easily tap into such prospective options and perhaps dividend stocks. You can easily organize your entries and exits appropriately.

***Make Learning Part of You***

If you wish to excel in trading, you should yearn for more knowledge and information. Trading information is available all over for those who need it to make diversifies strategies from it.

There is trading information on the internet, and even other sites offer interactive platforms just to provide more information on trading strategies and potential plans. The information ranges from written literature to video tutorials for you to study.

You can easily go through the MT4 indicators platform and possible daily alert settings.

***Establish the Best and Right Broker***

Not all traders have common needs and priorities. Different platforms are available for different traders by other brokers. You need to do research on which broker best will suit your personal needs. There are also various places where you can get quotes and exchange your securities, so its the work of the brokers to find for you the right place to do so.

***You Need a Journal***

Perhaps an excel journal will do for you. Things like prices, market rates, dates, positions or sizes, entry and exit reasons, etc. are some of the issues that require a warm record for future reference. Furthermore, it could help you to view your plans for pairs of currencies which do not work on given plans like weekly, etc.

***Money Management for Stocks Traders***

As a swing trader, you need to have a strong yet flexible money management strategy to help govern your finances. It is not so easy to control the market; however, you can only control your finances and the potential risks that come with your trades.

It was said by William O'Neill that secrete to win for a stock market is to lose the very least amount possible when you are not right.

If you have a well-established money management strategy, it will be able to respond to such queries as:

- What is the right amount of money that needs to be risked on a given trade?
- How many shares are supposed to be bought?

A firm trading strategy will remain invalid as long as it has no money management plan. If you admire trading stocks or would like to gain much from the markets, then you need to embrace a smart money management plan.

The most important aspect as a swing trader is to maintain your capital for long a long time and watch other winners cover your costs of losing trades to make some profits. This can only be achieved through a reasonable money management strategy.

***The Two Percent Rule***

It is true to most swing traders that you do not need to risk more than two percent of your capital one trade. As you know, the stock market is usually random in nature, and this is the plain truth.

Whatever the case, even as for good charts, chances are that the stock won't go in your expected direction; hence you will end up losing money on such a trade. Ask yourself how much money you would lose.

Confirm the total amount of money on your accounts every first or a new month. Assume you have a total of say $10,000 on your account. Two percent of this amount will be $200. Now this will be the amount you stand to lose on a trade.

***Position-Sizing***

Assume you are working with a stock that has pulled, thus trading at $20.00. Because it looks like it may reverse, you, therefore, decide to go for it. It is wise to speculate where your stop shall be placed. You need to think about how much of your money you may lose rather than imagine making profits.

Assume that your stop is resting at $19.00. When you buy stocks at $20.00, when your stop-loss is placed at $19.00, it means that your risk is $1.00/share. You can purchase the number of shares equivalent to the risk amount like, in this case, $200.

The reason is if you do not purchase this amount, then you risk losing the $200 of your shares, which is actually the most amounts you are eligible to lose. In this instance, the real number of shares that you need to purchase should be less due to commissions and slippages that you need to account for.

When you manage your money well on all trades, it is easy to refresh because all losses incurred as a result may remain insignificant to your accounts. It also gives many traders some rest from emotional stresses.

In case you get a loss once, you will breathe in and out and continue with other trades, but if you have a series of losses, then sit down, reevaluate the possible causes and even reduce the size of the position to 1 percent.

***You Need a Money Management Calculator***

This is a written program that helps you to calculate your finances to determine how best you would wish to invest. If everything sounds funny, what you need here is a money management calculator. You need to establish the right calculator that suits your needs.

***Establishment of Trading Mindset***

When you do not have the right trading mindset, the chances are that you might fail terribly. This is the greatest aspect that any trader possesses. You need to work on your trading mindset long before you even think about beginning the real business or its strategies.

If you have a positive mindset, it is an asset; you should work on maintaining and preserving it at all times as long you are still a trader.

Mindset is a well-established attitude that is held by any individual. This tells us that we need to have a set of attitudes that will govern the way we trade for us to be successful.

Successful trading is not very easy because the development of the right attitude is also the way of developing habits and necessary skills for profitable trades.

CHAPTER 11:

# How to Become a Successful Swing Trader

There are different ways of becoming successful in swing trading. These can be implemented by the use of different swing trading strategies.

## Strategies Used to Be a Successful Swing Trader

Strategies are a set of guidelines that assist their traders on how to run their swing trading. Strategies are there to guide you on your journey by minimizing losses and protecting your trading capital. Below are some of the detailed strategies to be implemented in swing trading in order to be successful.

### *Breakout Strategies*

This is a type of strategy used by most traders in the swing market. The trader selects the best trade by checking on the behavior of a stock monitoring its volatility and fluctuations of its price. Most of the market trades selected are the ones that break their own level of resistance and level of support.

### *Breakdown Strategy*

This is another type of swing trading strategy used for monitoring the best market trade that does not break out its level of resistance and support. It normally focuses on trade securities with lower prices in the market.

### *Options Strategy*

Combining options with your swing trading enables you to decide whether to sell or purchase an option at a certain price within a specified period. When the time of expiry reaches, without exercising on the option, you lose the initial amount of money you paid for.

### *Stuck in a Box*

This swing trading strategy is all about identifying all the various market ranges, which are lower than the level of support. It leads to the setting of the stop-loss order, which enables the maximization of the trading capital.

### *Catch the Wave*

This type of swing trading strategy identifies any move that comes up in the market. It basically monitors any trend that takes place in the market—mostly concerned with the market trade with the 50 moving average having a bullish rejection price.

### *Fading the Moves*

This is a type of swing trading strategy that enables you to do your things against what is supposed to be in the market. Monitor the prices and select the better price in the market.

### *Aligning Trade With the Market Direction*

The behavior in the market varies a lot. You need to observe the different market trends happening in the market and go with the trends.

Most of the traders select the long-term market trends for the maximum amount of capital.

You can decide to form your own policies of trading based on the current changes in the market. This will enable you to do much research and be keen on all kinds of news feeds related to the type of trading you handling.

### *Be Stronger Than Your Weakness*

This strategy enables you to be wise when selecting the type of trades. It assists you in selecting the trades with the long term in bullish markets and trades with the short term in bearish markets.

This enables you to have a high potential for high profits and minimize losses in your swing trading.

### *Get Advantage of the Long-Term Swing Trading Charts*

This strategy enables you to not only monitor the short-term trends happening in the market but also the long-term trends with a duration such as weekly and monthly trading charts.

### *Be Alert with the Market Trends*

This strategy helps in handling the trends taking place in the market. It considers both long-term trends and short-term trends. It alerts you in case of any market trends that take place.

### *Have a Trading Plan When Beginning Trading*

A trading plan is a simple swing trading strategy that all swing traders need to select. Having a trading plan strategy when starting off swing trading is the best strategy for any trader. A trading plan enables you to note down all your trading objectives and goals of your trading. It provides you with guidelines and organizes you. You can come up with even a time routine for making your trades.

A trader is able to know the trading estimates, thereby offering protection to your trading capital. A trading plan also outlines all the tips and tricks for swing trading. It is a simple strategy that most traders are advised to implement. It assists in risks and loss management. Why shouldn't you select a simple strategy like this? Be awake and implement the simple strategies in your swing trading in order to be successful.

### *Have a Positive Attitude*

Your attitude determines your performance at all times. You need to have a strategy of possessing a positive attitude when you are trading. A positive attitude in swing trading contributes to good spirit, psyche, and even happiness while trading. You need to be excited and feel motivated.

Do not begin your morning trading with a sad face. You will not even be able to spot any trend on the market. Be joyful and positive that your trading will work out.

A positive attitude will also enable you to be alert and keen on market trends. You will have the psyche to make trades and make good decisions even on your worst-case scenarios in the market. Put a smile on your face and wish yourself the best in swing trading by possessing a good attitude.

## How to Use Moving Averages

Moving averages are basically trading tools commonly used by most swing traders in various trading activities in the market. Moving strategies cannot really be described as simple as they sound. Moving strategies require much learning before implementing them because they are quite complicated and need sufficient mastering for them to be fully utilized by a trader.

Various mistakes are normally committed by most traders when they are trying to implement the various moving tools as one of their strategies in getting large amounts of profits in swing trading activities. There exist two major kinds of moving averages tools in the swing trading market; the exponential moving average and the simplified moving average. A trader is encouraged to select the kind of moving average he or she would like to engage with in advance before commencing any swing trading activities.

This is much expected because different tools normally bear different ways of operations that a particular should master and utilize in every kind of strategy that is likely to be involved. Let us venture into some of the factors which a potential trader should consider when choosing the preferred moving averages tools to implement in his or her swing trading activities:

## The Difference Between the Exponential Moving Average and the Simplified Moving Average

There exists a common difference between the two moving averages, which is the rate of speed in which they operate. The exponential moving average is quite faster as compared to the simplified moving average in swing trading and changes its direction much drastically as compared with the simplified moving average.

The exponential moving average highlights its immediate changes faster and much boldly rather than the simplified moving average, which really takes some time to highlight some of its recent market updates and the general changes that have been experienced in the swing trading market.

Quite a number of traders have engaged themselves in the exponential moving average because they claim to consider it much reliable, and the trader is able to spot out the latest market feeds concerning the market. Updated market feeds depicted from the market inform the trader of the actual status of activities that are happening in the market. The trader gets to remain informed of the market volatility rates.

***The Advantages and Disadvantages of the Moving Averages***

The potential trader ought to pick the kind of moving average that totally seems to work out for a particular kind of trader. This can be achieved if he or she gets to highlight the various advantages and disadvantages of each kind of moving average in swing trading and confirming the specific kind of moving average that seems to work well for a specific kind of swing trader.

The exponential moving average seems to be quite faster in pronouncing the changes that have been made in the swing trading market as compared to the simplified moving average. This justifies that the exponential moving average is quite vulnerable in giving out the wrong signs at a very early stage during trading.

Wrong signals that have been pronounced at such occurrences may cause the inconsistent trader to make wrong decisions just based on the current market trends and, therefore, to cause large amounts of losses to be made that may eventually lead to a great financial breakdown.

On the other hand, the simplified market average, which is much slower as compared to the exponential market average, may take quite a while in the market when there exist market price movements that have been short-lived. However, the simplified moving average gets a trader involved in swing trading much later as compared to the exponential moving average; hence a trader is able to discover the changes later in the market, an event which may cause the trader to miss out on the good opportunities present in the market that might get grasped earlier by the other traders.

***Weighing and Confirming the Right Kind of Moving Average***

Noting down the various advantages and disadvantages of the moving averages help a particular trader to decide on what he or she really wants. We have concluded that the simplified moving average spotlights the market trends at a later period, therefore outputting a lot of late results that may be so wrong when compared with the current actual market happenings. This case is normally an effect caused by the volatility of the market.

On the other hand, the exponential moving average is usually depicted at a quite faster rate since the signs are normally expressed immediately, and the trader gets to spot on the actual status of the market happenings. However, the signals said to be much vulnerable, an occurrence that can lead to wrong results due to the day market volatility that has been affecting the market. As a trader, try your best to pick out the best one that totally works for you, that is, much efficient and one that can easily be implemented to acquire larger amounts of profits.

## CHAPTER 12:

# Goals and Routine of a Swing Trader

Swing trading goals are, in many ways, different from other forms of trading. Day trading, for instance, is often a trader's sole occupation and so the goals include living needs. Swing traders often have another occupation elsewhere and only trade occasionally.

For most swing traders, cash is often not a problem because they have additional sources of income, such as employment, investments, or business. To make really big money, traders need to be well prepared.

## Why Swing Trading?

Swing trading constitutes a trading strategy where traders enter positions and exit only after a certain period. This period ranges from at least two trading sessions to a couple of months. While swing trading gains may be smaller, they can add up to significant amounts over time.

Swing traders target profit margins of between 5% and 10% rather than the 20% to 25% margins. While such margins may not be impressive to some, they do add up over time. Traders are searching for 20% - 25%, and higher gains often invest more time into their trades, sometimes running into many months. They are often considered to be investors rather than traders because of the time factor. Basically, it is a lot more attractive to make 10% gains each week than 25% each month. Swing traders take on average between 5 and 10 days. As such, it is possible to make lots of small money amounts, which then add up the course of a trading month. Swing traders, therefore, tend to make more money in the 5 to 10 days trading sessions compared to investors and other traders as well.

## Factor in Both Profits and Losses

Most traders set out believing they will win all trades. Sadly, this is not how things are in the real world. Traders actually lose out on some trades. Not even the most brilliant and most successful traders win all their trades. The important factor to keep in mind is to keep the losses to a minimum while maximizing profitability.

Prudent money management techniques, as well as a proper state of mind, are essential ingredients in keeping losses at a minimum. Small gains are great over a certain period of time, but this can only be maintained if the losses are adequately managed. For instance, if you are to have stop-loss points, then position these at 2% to 3% rather than the usual 7% to 8%. This way, you will limit your losses and enhance your winnings. You will also manage the desirable trading ratios of 3 to 1 profit – loss ratios.

These are crucial points to note because it takes just one large loss, and an account could be wiped away. Major losses eat away at a trader's capital, which will affect subsequent trades. Swing trading can present excellent individual gains to a trader. Also, partial profits can be taken from a trade that is then allowed to continue its run. Swing traders use both fundamental analysis and technical analysis to determine stocks with an upward trend and with momentum. A swing trader's work includes identifying financial instruments such as stocks that have a well-defined trend. The aim of a swing trader is to purchase securities when the prices are low, hold the securities for a couple of days, and then exit when the prices are high. This way, they exit trades profitably, and it is the method that they use to earn their profits. It makes sense to enter trades when prices are low and then sell when the prices go up.

## Trading Techniques

Swing trading techniques are easy to learn. They are also straightforward and simple to demonstrate. After learning these techniques, it is advisable to practice for a couple of days until you get confident enough to trade live. If your practice trades were largely successful, then trading the real markets will also likely prove to be successful.

As a swing trader, you do not have to focus your energies using complicated formulas and learning complex techniques. You also do not need to buy and hold stocks or other financial instruments like currencies. Instead, you only need your trading charts.

## Retail versus Professional Traders

As a retail trader, you may be at a disadvantage compared to professional traders. Professional traders are generally more experienced, have a lot of leverage, access to more information, and pay lower commissions. However, you do have some advantages in some instances because you are not limited to the risks that you can take, the size of investment, and types of trades. As a retail swing trader, you need to ensure that you have all the knowledge necessary to take full advantage of the markets.

Day traders lack a regular paycheck, especially retail, self-employed traders. They have to practically work hard and sweat to earn a living. Swing traders can withstand not trading or being away from the markets. It is generally not a matter of life and death to them. This is another major difference between the two.

## How to Identify Potential Trades

So, how do you find trades that you'd be interested in? As a swing trader, you may want to find a catalyst. A fundamental catalyst will enable you to enter a trade with sufficient momentum. Then all you will need is technical analysis to confirm your exit and profit points.

1. **Special opportunities:** There are different ways of entering the market. One of these is to find a great opportunity with lots of potentials. Great opportunities can be found through companies planning an IPO, those ready to file for bankruptcy, situations of takeovers, buyouts, insider buying, mergers,

acquisitions, and restructuring. These and other similar events provide excellent trading opportunities, especially for swing traders.
To find these opportunities, you need to check out the SEC website or filings from companies. Certain forms, such as 13-D and S-4, contain all the relevant information that you need. While these opportunities carry some inherent risks, the possible rewards are too great to ignore.

2. **Sector or industry opportunities:** Apart from the rare opportunities, we also have options that are specific to a given sector. These are opportunities that you will find on certain websites regarding sectors whose performance is well above average. For instance, we can determine that sectors such as energy are doing exceptionally well by observing energy ETFs. There are certain sectors that pose a high risk but have high returns and can be very profitable.

3. **The chart breaks:** We can also rely on chart breaks to find opportunities. Chart breaks are especially suitable for swing traders. Chart breaks are really stocks or securities that have been traded so heavily, such that they are very close to major resistance or support levels. As a swing trader, you will search for opportunities out there by identifying patterns indicating breakdowns or breakouts.

These identifying patterns can be Gann or Fibonacci levels, Wolfe Waves, channels, and triangles.

However, please note that these chart breaks are only useful when there is a huge interest in the stock. This way, you can easily enter and exit trades. Therefore, whenever you note this chart breaks, you should also focus on factors such as price and volumes.

### *Have a Securities Watch List*

One of the things that you really should embark on is building a list of stocks or other securities to watch closely. The stocks that should constitute this list include those with a great chance at high volumes and upward price movement. It should also include stocks with a major catalyst.

### *Confirm Your Current Positions*

It is important to keep tabs on your current positions. You probably have other trades, so take a look at these and see if there is anything needed on your part. This is something that you should focus on early before the trading day begins.

Checking this out is pretty easy and straightforward. This will reveal plenty of essential information that you need to be successful. Should you come across any material information that can directly affect your trades, then consider what you should do, such as adjusting the different points like take profit and stop-loss.

### *Trading During Market Hours*

Now that the markets are open, it is time to get busy as a trader. During this time, you will mostly be trading and watching your screen. Check the market makers of the day and also be aware of any fake bids and asks. Find a viable trade and apply all the skills and knowledge you have acquired to identify entry and exit points. There are plenty of techniques you can apply to arrive at these points. Think about Fibonacci extensions, for example. These can help you identify entry and exit points. You can also use price by volume and resistance levels.

As the trading day proceeds, you may need to make certain adjustments to your positions. These adjustments will depend on a number of factors. However, it is not advisable to adjust positions once you enter a trade, especially if you plan to take on additional risks. If you have to make adjustments, then it is better to focus more on adjusting the take-profit points and stop-loss levels.

### *After Hours Trading*

Most swing traders are largely inactive after the normal trading day is over. At this point in time, the market is not liquid at all, and the available spread not suitable to enter any trades. Therefore, take this time to do some evaluation of your earlier trades and your positions. Examine your trades and see where you could do better. Focus on any open positions you may have and consider all material events that could affect your positions.

Also, remember to come with relevant alerts. Some traders prefer using multiple screens to monitor multiple developments at the same time. Instead of multiple screens, you can choose to create specific alerts so that should something relevant occur somewhere, then you will get to hear about it on time. Alerts are crucial and will ensure that you get to find out when there is a price movement, and so on.

CHAPTER 13:

# Risk and Money Management

## Taking Time off

Everyone has their good and bad months or times of the year. Recognizing these moments, when your mental state is likely to be disturbed and accordingly disconnecting from the market will ensure that you don't do too much damage to your account.

More than this, it pays to take some time away from the markets and refresh yourself. You don't need to trade every single market day or hour to make money. The market's always going to be there when you return. Take some time away to go on a vacation and run the statistics on your trading. You can also use this time to develop new trading systems in a slower, simulation environment and practice your existing skills.

## Journal and Check-ins

An important part of your trading journal is the psychological check you will run on yourself before you decide to trade. This involves simply taking stock of your mental state and checking in with yourself.

How refreshed do you feel? Is your mindset today particularly negative, or are you focusing on something that will distract you? Briefly, how good do you feel? If you feel less than seven out of 10, with 10 being the best you could feel, it is inadvisable to trade. You're better off working on whatever is bothering you and figuring out a solution to that problem before trying anything to do with the market.

As you work through the trading session, take the time to keep checking in with yourself. This will seem weird at first, but as your awareness builds and as you track your results and your mental state, you will see the correlation between the two. Taking up practices that increase your concentration levels as well as build awareness of your mental state is a great way to increase the efficiency with which you trade.

Meditation is a great tool for traders to use. Simply following and observing your breath for 15 minutes per day is a great way to build awareness and increase focus. It will refresh your mind, and you'll be able to tackle any issues with trading a lot better.

## Mindset

All of us have certain limiting beliefs we employ to restrict ourselves. The crazy thing is that we have no idea what these beliefs are, for the most part. This is because they lie beneath our conscious mind, in our subconscious. These beliefs are formed primarily thanks to our childhood experiences and the environment we grew up in.

Trading is an intense activity that deals with money. The only way to determine the success or failure of your trading business is to look at how much money you've made over time. Money happens to be a very emotional topic, and people have all kinds of ideas about it. Certain things you might have heard while growing up will influence how you feel and think about your results.

The fact is that all the things you've heard and learned about money when you were a kid will cause you to make decisions that could be detrimental to your trading success. For example, if you believe money is scarce, you'll end up creating situations that confirm this belief in your life. You may find that you have trouble keeping the money you make in trading intact and that your account's equity balance fluctuates massively.

Take some time to explore what your beliefs about money and success are. The easiest way of doing this is to ask yourself what your parents told you about money. Did you hear statements such as "Money needs to be saved and not spent" or "money doesn't grow on trees?" These are pretty common things one hears.

How good were your parents with money? Was it always a struggle to make ends meet? Or were they profligate with it? Almost everyone has issues with money that causes them to sabotage themselves. The key is to recognize these troublesome beliefs and then take action to rectify them. Beliefs are just thought patterns you have learned over time.

If you learned one thing, you could just as easily learn another. The way to change habits is to become aware of the existence of the troublesome belief and as it rears its head, practice the action that counteracts it. Let's take a look at an example of how this works.

A lot of traders beat themselves up a lot over their results. They take a look at their trades and realize that there were opportunities they missed at the moment due to being too nervous and due to an inability to pull the trigger. To counteract this, they go to the other extreme and begin taking trades that are less than perfect, as per their system. This, of course, leads to even more poor results, and a vicious circle is formed.

The thing to do is to understand that poor trading results over time (at least 100 trades) is a symptom and not the disease itself. If the major cause of poor results was missing out on trades due to fear of pulling the trigger, let's examine why could this be so? Is it because the trader is extremely nervous about the result of that trade? Why would they be nervous? Could it be because they believe that this result is all-important and that it's a referendum of how successful they are in life?

It seems a stretch to connect the result of a single trade to this point but remember that money is at the bottom of the issue here. An inability to make money will cause most people, especially men, to feel inadequate and like a failure. If you feel as if you're a failure, you're likely to avoid situations that might paint you as one or create situations that confirm this feeling. Avoiding a trade and then beating yourself up over an inability to get good results does both.

This is why trading is such a slog for so many people. They're constantly fighting the ups and downs of their emotions and think that finding a better system is the answer. The fact is that their problems have nothing to do with the trading system and everything to do with their mindset.

Write down your beliefs about money and success. What does success look like to you? Are your expectations of trading realistic? If you're expecting swing trading to be able to give you enough money to buy a Porsche within a year, it's safe to say your head is up in the clouds a bit. Trading can make you millions when done well. It's just that the way you think it will make you millions is not how it happens.

How much of a return on your money are you expecting? Before you answer, consider that the greatest stock market investor of all time, Warren Buffett, averages a 20% return over his lifetime. And he's considered to be pretty far ahead of his peers. The fact is that most institutions such as hedge funds and private equity firms will be very happy with a trader who earn anywhere from a 10-17% return on their money.

Yet, one often sees retail traders dream of turning $1,000 into a million within a year. If a professional trader could realistically achieve that sort of return, we'd have many more billionaires on this planet! What's more, every single wealthy person would liquidate the rest of their assets and invest it entirely into a trading venture. Such numbers are ludicrous.

Keep your expectations in check and don't dream of earning outsize returns with your trading capital.

## Risk per Trade

Given that R is your average loss, it stands to reason that this number represents the risk you encounter in every trade. You have no way of knowing whether a trade will go for a win or a loss, and thus it is in your interest to risk the average loss amount exactly, every single time you enter a trade.

The R amount is what determines your position size as well. A common practice is to designate R as being two percent of your account size. In other words, if your capital is $5,000, you'll risk $100 per trade. You've already seen how the size of the support or resistance zone determines the distance of the stop-loss from your entry point.

Thus, your position size will vary with every trade. Let's look at this via an example of a stock trade. Let's say your stop-loss is five points away (or five dollars), and you're risking $100 on this trade. This means your position size will have to be 20 shares (100/5). If you're targeting an average reward of 2R, your take profit level will be $10 or 10 points away from your entry point.

Calculating this in FX is a bit more complicated, and this is why you should use a calculator to find this out. There are online calculators and plugins that will spit out exact numbers where you need to place your stop-loss and reward levels.

If you were to vary your risk per trade, this would throw off your risk math, as you can see. If you risked two percent on one trade and then risked five percent on another, your average reward amount will change. If you were to lose the five percent trade, all of a sudden, your previous win will not compensate your loss even with a 2R multiple. Effectively, you've moved the goalposts.

This is why risk management is so important, and ignoring this is why most traders lose money. Trades that struggle tend to pick and choose their risk amounts based on how attractive they think the setup is.

They ignore the fact that there's no way of knowing in advance how a trade is going to turn out. The most terrible looking setup can go for a huge gain.

The reason is that price movements depend on opinions, and what is ugly to one might seem beautiful to another. You just don't know, and this is why you need to play the odds. The question at this point is, how do you know the odds of your system, and how should you plan to set up your trading business?

CHAPTER 14:

# The Mindset of Swing Trading

The mindset of swing trading starts as we face a daily reality such that the inability to accomplish something is accepted to be because of the activities of another. Another development rises consistently that takes the weight off your shoulders and says the issue lies outside of your control.

My view is that equivalent is unjustifiable because "equivalent" is utilized with general terms.

While opportunity and the capacity to look for circumstance ought to be reasonable, the results ought not. They cannot be equivalent as everybody will alternately approach opportunity giving various outcomes.

Life owes us only the opportunity to be as well as can be expected to be while we make the most of our brief timeframe here on earth.

Trading achievement is the same.

## Trading Is a Meritocracy

Trading, at the center, is a meritocracy. You gain your prosperity.

On an average day, markets will give you the chance to profit, and it is up to you what you do with those changes—neglecting to underwrite or, more regrettable, giving back all that you earned beginnings numerous on the way of rationalizing. Some seem to find a few things to blame for their failure:

1. They blame the representative for running stops (since they have zero thought how the markets work).

2. They accuse the framework ( the gleaming new article consistently gets a “traders” eye).
3. They accuse flawed guidance from a discussion, or they accuse the news.

We hear that brain research and overseeing risk has a significant impact on the life of a trader and their trading achievement.

At last, that implies that the trader is on the way to either getting eaten up and let out by the markets or beating the chances and profiting.

It is a truly enormous obligation trader's face.

There is no one that they can blame.

- Either you pursue your tried trade plan, or you don't.
- Either you pursue mindful risk conventions, or you don't.

Netpicks plans trading frameworks, and before discharging them to people in general, they are back tried, yet additionally forward tried in the live markets. They are not 100% mechanical, and there are rules to help explore the stones the happen every once in a while.

Some progressed toward becoming a trader, others used examples of overcoming adversity with them, and some were disappointed with them.

One of the shared factors is that those traders that discover achievement take the trade plans and make them their own. They remain near the primary structure of the framework since they comprehend there is no compelling reason to waste time when they have a decent one before them.

Those that bomb more often than not change the frameworks enough that it never again takes after the underlying framework.

- They overlook the trade plans and neglect to comprehend that any framework will present losing streaks.

- They disregard dependable risk parameters and inevitably granulate their accounts to a useless whole.

Some even go to the extent of questioning the cases made of the strategy for the one single explanation.

## Where Can You Find Trading Success?

The absolute first thing you will need to do is assume liability for your prosperity (and your disappointments).

Removing duty takes you from the unfortunate casualty segment and enables you to endeavor to fix things.

One of the primary spots you should begin is the way you think.

Give me a chance to ask you: have you, at some point, begun the day off in an undesirable manner, and as the day advanced, awful things "simply" continued happening?

What about going to capacity even though you hated going? You show up, and keeping in mind that every other person is having an extraordinary time, you can't ascend.

Your condition of being huge affects what comes to your path, and as a trader, you would do well to keep in line with your "state."

You are just going to execute just as you are feeling particular when your trading has an optional side to it. One thing learner traders experience serious difficulties with is quieting the feelings of dread and ravenousness.

Those two feelings will lead you down a flippant way as a trader, which will lead you further from the objective of achievement – whatever you characterize as "achievement."

Capitulating to these feelings can prompt a calamity when the loses heap up. They take a washout, and afterward, they wind up turning into a trading failure.

## Overlook Your Trade Plan and Perish

Delivering retribution type trades and hurling your trade plan out the window is what is genuinely unforgiving. Losing your trading account because of idiocy and an amateurish frame of mind is unforgiving.

If you fire out in trading and do some spirit looking, acknowledging it was your very own failings can be destroying.

It has been demonstrated that what you state to yourself affects how you perform throughout everyday life. It impacts how you feel.

## Your Trading Mantra

Make this a day by day mantra for yourself, and the objective is to carry center and clearness to all the beneficial things about you and what you have in your life. During your trading hours, have a duplicate taped over your screen.

Each time your musings turn negative, or your self-talk says how "idiotic" you are, rehash so anyone can hear what you have composed.

Keep in mind; trading is a meritocracy. It rewards the readied. Keep that in mind, trading and life, and you gain your prosperity.

CHAPTER 15:

# Advantages of Swing Trading

To see success with swing trading, you need to make sure that you are working on the right strategy. There are a lot of different strategies that you can work with when you are ready to join the market, and each of them has the potential to earn you a profit if you properly use them. But you have to know how each of them will work, and you need to stick with that strategy throughout your whole time trading.

Take a look at a few of them and see which one will work the best for your trading personality.

## Looking at Good Patterns

One thing that you can look at is the charts for a particular stock you would like to look through. There are a lot of different patterns that can come up all the time, and the way that they look will determine whether they are a good one to use for your trade or if you should go with another option. When you notice these patterns, you will be better able to predict how the stocks that you want to work with will behave in the future and use this to make a profit. Let's take a look at some of the successful swing trading patterns that you should look for when you get started.

**Triangle:** The triangle shape is a very successful pattern to look for, and if you see it in one of your stocks, you will be likely to see success. With the triangle pattern, you will notice that the trend is going either upwards or downwards, but the variations are getting smaller between the highs and the lows. When these start to get together on the right side of the triangle, you can see that a breakthrough trend is about to happen. This can go the opposite way as well. If you see a triangle that goes in the opposite way of the picture above, it means that the trend is about to go down, and you should not join in.

**Double Top:** This is another pattern that many swing traders will take a look at, and it can be really successful. This pattern is one that you want to look for when it comes to working with swing trading. The same pattern works even if it is turned around. For example, if you notice that this trend is upside down, you can use this information to help with going long in your stock.

**Channel Pattern:** Next on the list is the channel pattern. This is a great pattern even though it is not always as successful as some of the others. You will find this one repeating through various instruments that you may be moving. There are two ways that you can trade for this pattern. One is on the channel, and the other is to trade when there is a breakout. It often depends on which way you would like to trade with your swing trade and how the market is doing.

## The Moving Average

Another option to use is the moving average. Since swing trading can do really well with technical analysis and the moving average is considered one of these, it is a good option to go with it. The two options that you can use include the exponential moving average and the simple moving average. With the simple moving average, we will look at the average of a security over a specified number of periods, such as over fifteen minutes or another time frame. The exponential moving average will spend more time looking at recent prices. The point of both of these is to identify the direction of the trend and figure out where the resistance and support levels are to make the most money possible.

One thing to notice is that these moving averages will lag from the current prices because they base themselves on the prices that happened in the past. The longer the period you use for a moving average, the bigger lag you will deal with. This means that a 200-day MA will have a bigger lag compared to a 20-day MA because of how long of a period it covers.

The best bet is to use shorter moving averages since you are working with a short-term trading strategy. If you decide to make a longer-term investment, you can go with a longer moving average if you would like. Going with something near the 50-day MA is a good option because it gives you a good amount of average to work with and when breaks happen, either below or above this moving average, it can be an important signal for your trading.

You will find that moving averages are also important trading signals all on their own, but they can be important when there are two averages that will cross over. When there is a moving average that rises, it shows that the stock is going through an uptrend, but when the moving average is starting to decline, it means that the stock is starting to go on a downtrend.

Similarly, an upward momentum can be confirmed when you see a bullish crossover, which is something that happens when the short-term moving average starts to cross higher than the moving average for the long-term. The opposite will be true when you are looking at downward momentum with a bearish crossover.

## Other Strategies That You Can Use

So far, we have talked about some of the most common strategies that you may choose to work with when it comes to swing trading. These strategies can help you to pick out which charts you should work with to see results. There are a few other strategies that you can use to see success with swing trading, including:

**Use Technical Analysis and the Price Action**. These are techniques that most swing traders will use. This kind of analysis will make it easier to figure out which stock or option you should trade and for how long you should hold it.

**Don't Spend All the Time With a Company**. While most long-term investors will focus on the fundamentals of a stock compared to how well it is doing at a particular moment, this is not something that swing trading will worry about. You may want to pick a few stocks to stick with for your trades because this helps you to learn the history and make better predictions, but you don't need to worry about the particulars of the company. The intrinsic value, who runs the company, who owns the company, and what the company does is not all that important unless it will lead to a big increase in stock value over the next few weeks.

**Stick With the Trends**. Many swing traders will choose to look at the trends in the market and then use those to help them develop their own strategy. For example, they would use a bull trend bar when they are working with a bull market, and then they would do a bear trend bar any time they are in a downward market.

Work against the trend: It is more common for a swing trader to work with the current trend of their stock or the market they pick. However, some decide to work against the trend, something that is known as fading. For example, when the stock is swinging high, they will choose to work with a bearish position, but when there is a downtrend, they will take a bullish position.

**Japanese Candlesticks**. Some new traders like to work with candlestick charts because they are a bit easier to understand compared to a bar chart. You can use these charts to identify where there is pressure for buying and when there is pressure for selling. You can also use these charts to figure out how intense the pressure is at a particular time. If you can read these charts the proper way, it is easier to know which way the market is going, and you can make some smart investing choices.

**T-Line Strategy**. With this strategy, you will go look at your charts and identify where the T-line is located to help you make good trading decisions. If you see that a stock is closing above this line, there is a good probability that the price will keep rising. On the other hand, if the stock ends up closing below this line, it is likely that the stock price will keep falling down. In many investment trades, this strategy will prove successful.

Picking out the right strategy will be one of the most important decisions you will make when it comes to any investment, especially when you are dealing with swing trading. It will determine what information you are looking at for the market trends and will ensure that you catch the upward trends at the right time. If you can pick out a good strategy and stick with it for the long-term, you will see success with swing trading. Figuring out your risk to reward ratio and your profitability.

The profitability of the trades you work with will be the percentage of trades that you complete that end with a profit. So, if you earn a profit on sixty of your trades and you trade 100 times, your ratio will be sixty percent.

On the other hand, the risk to reward ratio will be the amount that you end up risking compared to the amount that you are working to gain. As a beginner, it is best to pick a risk to reward ratio that is no worse than 1 to 1. This means that if you risk about five percent on the trade, you will try to make five percent on that trade as well.

This ratio is not going to make you a ton of money, but it does help you form a base and will build up confidence as you go. Depending on the chart pattern that you work with, you may change the ratio around a bit, but this will vary based on the strategy that you want to use. As you become more of a professional trader, you can increase your risk to reward ratio so that you can earn more on each trade.

CHAPTER 16:

# The Entry and Exit

Volatility is likely to increase the moment the stock trades beyond specific price barriers, and the prices of stocks often trend in the direction of the breakout. Since they are the starting point for future volatility increases, major price trends, and huge price swings, breakouts are definitely a great trading strategy. While trading, you need to factor in the resistance and support levels of the underlying stock. The more the price of a particular stock has touched such areas, the more credible these levels will be, and this, in turn, increases their importance. Also, the longer the support and resistance levels stay relevant, the better the outcome will be when the price eventually breaks out. Several price patterns will appear on the price chart as the prices consolidate, and different formations like flags, triangles, and channels provide you with great indications of stocks to trade. Also, the consistency and duration a stock has maintained both resistance and support levels are great factors to consider in your quest to discover a good candidate to trade.

## Your Entry Points

After identifying a good instrument, you need to plan your trade, and this happens to be the easiest thing to do. When prices of stocks are set to close below the support, investors will assume a bearish position while a bullish position will be taken when the prices are set to close higher than the resistance level. You can wait for a confirmation in ascertaining the difference between a fake-out and a breakout. When traders enter too fast without having a confirmation, the possibility of the price getting into new territory isn't guaranteed. The above-average volume is often used by most traders as a confirmation, or they wait till the end of a trading period in order to determine if the price will sustain the levels that they have broken out of. If everything goes according to plan, the market should retrace back to the wave and start showing signs of going up, at which point you should place your buy order. The way you determine this is by looking to see if a bullish candlestick is forming. Once you see that, prepare to place your order. Once again, this can be determined by looking to see if a bullish candlestick is forming after a succession of bearish candlesticks. If you see one forming, you should get ready to place your orders, which brings us to the next step.

## Planning Your Exit Points

This is a market setup that allows you to profit in both situations. Either temporarily as the market reverses at the channel resistance line and goes up to the trend line or traditionally as the market bounces at the trend line. Having predetermined exits is necessary if you want to trade profitably. There are usually three exit plans that you need to arrange before taking a position:

### *Exit Point With a Profit*

You should determine a reasonable objective when planning your target prices, so look at the stock's recent behavior. You can calculate the recent price swings and get the average to get a relative price target. Setting a price target is your goal for each trade, and you can exit the position when the goal is achieved by exiting just a portion of your open position and let the remaining trade run. Also, you can lock in profits by raising the stop-loss order.

### *Point to Exit With a Loss*

Knowing when your trade setup has failed is important, and you can identify this fairly well with breakout trading. Old resistance levels usually become new support, while old support acts as new resistance, and this is an objective way to know when a trade has failed and where your stop-loss order should be. Since losses can accumulate, always when your stop-loss is hit (don't keep moving it and hoping!).

### *Point to Set Your Stop Order*

By doing this, you will protect your position without leaving the trade with much downside risk.

There are several swing strategies that you can adopt. What you need to know is that each strategy will work well for a different market environment. This brings us to the topic of market cycles. A market cycle is simply another term for the direction that a market will move.

This step should be obvious to you by now. Your entry points should be where future resistance will develop. That point will be denoted by where your trend line is. What you simply need to do is sit down and watch for the market to retrace and start showing signs of a U-turn anywhere near your downtrend line. Once you see that, then you should be ready to take action.

### *Don't Fail to Exit a Losing Trade*

It can't be said enough; all too often, people let emotions take over their judgment in the stock market. When you set up a big swing trade, you might get overconfident and excessively excited about it if you are new to the business. Moreover, if the stock starts moving the wrong way, you might hold onto the trade when you should simply exit and take your losses. Sometimes people can't believe it when a "sure thing" turns out to be a loss, and they hold on too long hoping things will turn around. Waiting too long can be costly –sometimes catastrophically so. We hate to beat a dead horse – but protect every trade you make with stop-loss orders rather than letting emotion take over.

### *Don't Exit Too Soon*

The right time to exit a trade can be a difficult thing to figure out. That's why it's best to plan ahead of time and set an exit point where you are going to be comfortable with profits. If you go into a swing trade without a definite plan, it's going to be too easy to fall prey to a situation where you might get out too soon, afraid that you aren't going to be able to make any profit and fearing possible losses. You can also get fooled by temporary downturns. Remember that there are always counter-trends on the way up. Don't be fooled by the counter-trends into exiting too early. Emotion can get heavy immediately after placing a big trade. Also, remember that you should set a time frame for your trade to work out. Swing traders are not day traders, so don't get the impulse to exit a trade two hours after you've entered the position.

CHAPTER 17:

# How Does Swing Trading Work?

Swing trading is one of the most used and common trading strategies used in almost every market, including forex, futures trading, stocks, and much more. Swing trading is about buying and selling the stock, buying it from the market, and selling it for gains. For this purpose, traders mostly rely on technical analysis to spot good selling and buying opportunities.

Subsequently, swing trading mostly relays on fundamental assets because of its great determent of significant price movements. Sometimes it will take days and even weeks. It also helps to improve trade analysis. Therefore, a trader can verify where the fundamental assets are favorable or not, or it could potentially improve instead of relying on the bearish patterns. Swing traders use the technical analysis indicator to identify the price of swing trade and determine whether a stock price will rise in the market or drop. By experiencing technical indicators, swing traders are not concerned about the long term value of the stock.

How to make swing trade with trends?

Swing trading is one of the best solid tradings, and it has one of the obvious trends in trading strategies. For beginners, it is necessary to understand its importance in the market that once you get to know how to invest your money, it will offer a lot of high possibility of trading opportunities with a high upside. For a beginner, it is obligatory to have enough knowledge about the market. The initial step that every beginner should take is to identify the market needs, and know about the market trends.

For getting a good position in the market, every trader should go with the best trends, any trend that goes on the top of the list that if you show them to a child, they would clearly choose the right one whose prices are getting higher or lower.

One of the most common mistakes that every beginner makes when looking to swing trade within a trend is not entering with the right swing point.

## Tips for Beginners

When you should choose Swing trading:

Swing trading is easier than day trading, but to see whether choosing swing trading is a good decision for you or not, you should enlist all the points and see which one will give you more profit.

Make sure that you are ready to spend your days, weeks, and months on this trading as swing trading contains a longer period for trading.

If you already have a job and want to invest your money for extra income, but you do not have enough time to sit in front of a computer, then swing trading is the best option for you.

- You do not need to do constant monitoring and keeping an eye on market activities.
- Swing trading will give you a less stressful life and will reduce the risk level.
- As a beginner, you should always have a plan and stick to it as it's the nature of buying and selling that there will be highs and lows, but you should stick to the plan.
- Before you start swing trading, you should practice it by watching markets. Having knowledge about pre-trading will help you in gaining the loss.
- Don't expect to have money on a quick note; just focus on your aim and let the process sink in.

- Having a good observation will help you in investing money in the right stock, so if you want to gain money on the first stock, then you should know how to use the technical analysis indicators.
- It is important for a beginner to keep in mind while trading the entrance and exit strategy. Before entering a market, we should check everything and keep ourselves updated with the study of the charts, noting the price the stock will likely reach in its current swing.
- Most of the traders (like partygoers) find it more favorable to choose how to exit before they have entered the trade.
- There will be more chances of losing money in the earlier stages of trading, but a good trader should stick to it, gather basic skills, polish those skills, learn new technical techniques, and improve your knowledge. It's important not to give up in a condition.
- They should read books and follow the swing trading tips for beginners.

## Trading Platforms

For successful swing trading, the trader should select the right stocks to profit in the market. Therefore, traders can also opt for stock with large market capitalization. The most active assets will be among beginners, and they will be the most actively traded ones on top exchange. If we talk about the platforms for swing trading, then, on the one hand, there is a bear market, and on the other is the bull market. Similarly, there is a stable market between both of them. Yet swing trading in a bear or bull market is pretty different from that stable one.

For example, stocks in the market might tend to spike and dump using various patterns in both markets, unlike a stable market where a similar pattern could have upheld for weeks or months. In the bear market and bull market, the momentum can cause stocks to trade in a specific way for a long time. In that situation, to gain the maximum profit, a trader should trade in the way of the long-term trend. And to experience that profit, a swing trader has to correctly regulate the current market, whether it is bearish or bullish.

## CHAPTER 18:

# Fundamental Analysis

It is a technique used by traders and investors to decide regarding the value of a stock or any other financial instrument by examining the factors that directly and indirectly affect a company's or industry's current and future business, financial, economic prospects.

At its most generic form, fundamental analysis endeavors to predict and learn the intrinsic value of securities such as stocks. An in-depth examination and analysis of certain financial, economic, quantitative, and qualitative factors will help in providing the solution.

Fundamental analysis is mostly performed on a company, so a trader can determine whether or not to deal with its stocks. However, it can also be performed on the general economy and particular industries such as the motor industry, energy sector, etc.

Most of the fundamental analysis is conducted at a company level because traders and investors are mostly interested in information that will enable them to decide on the markets. They want information that will guide them in selecting the most suitable stocks to trade at the markets. As such, traders and investors searching for stocks to trade will resort to examining the competition, a company's business concept, its management, and financial data.

For a proper forecast regarding future stock prices, a trader is required to take into consideration a company's analysis, industry analysis, and even the overall economic outlook. This way, a trader will be able to determine the latest stock price as well as predicted future stock prices. When the outcome of fundamental analysis is not equal to the current market price, then it means that the stock is overpriced or perhaps even undervalued.

When it comes to stocks and options, the fundamentals include profit margins, price to earnings ratios, cash flow, and other indicators that give a picture of the overall health and prospects of the company. You'll be wanting to take a look at quarterly earnings and reviewing earnings calls for companies that you are invested in. Fundamental analysis also means looking for stocks that are currently undervalued. The price of undervalued stocks is likely to increase at some point in the future, so spotting an undervalued stock could be useful for the swing trader.

Since swing traders have different time horizons as compared to buy and hold investors, short-term results like earnings calls are going to take on a larger role, as compared to looking at trends in revenue and profits over the course of years. It's also important to keep your eye on company news of a more general nature. Suppose a product fails or ends up creating legal trouble for a company, that can be an opportunity to short the stock or invest input options. Alternatively, the release of a new product that exceeds expectations can be an opportunity to go long on the stock.

## Fundamental Variables

There will be several questions that come to your mind immediately as you start to perform research on a company. For example, you might ask yourself how long the company has been successful. You might ask yourself if this is a company you believe will give you a good profit or if this company has a history of getting traders high returns. Whatever questions you ask yourself, you need to realize that you have to do more than just ask the basic questions. In fact, you have to make sure you take the time to look at the fundamental variables.

## Price to Earnings Ratio

In the trading world, there are people who are known as market analysts. These are people who will often analyze how well companies are doing and then give the companies a review or a forecast, which allows other people to notice where the company is sitting. Market reviewers are typically known as cautious people and don't tend to believe that companies will pass their forecast. However, this does happen, and when it does, it brings us into positive earnings adjustment.

Basically, this states that we need to look for stocks that have surprised the market analysts. This is because if companies pass their forecast, they will continue to succeed. Therefore, they become known as one of the best companies to gain a profit from, which is always a great thing for a trader to know. However, you will still want to make sure that you do your deep analysis before making any moves on a stock.

## Short Interest

This is the process that market analysts go through when they are evaluating how well a company is doing so they can give them a forecast. As stated above, these analysts are cautious and very careful to note where they think the company is going. Therefore, when the company goes farther than what they initially thought, they need to re-evaluate the company. Of course, admitting they are wrong is not an easy thing for analysts to do as it isn't easy for anyone. However, when they do need to admit this, people can quickly learn what companies they should start paying attention to.

## Earnings Momentum

While there are many important fundamental variables to look at when you are making an analysis, earnings momentum holds a special place. This variable is very important, especially when it comes to bull markets.

Earnings momentum is the variable that looks at the year to year growth of earnings. Therefore, this is what will often set the price for stocks.

## Hot Sector Manias

This is another fundamental variable that will tell you how much free cash a company has. This is a very important variable because it will let you know where a company financially sits after paying all of its bills and expenses. When you are getting into trading, you want to pay attention to the financially stable companies. You want to make sure that a company can grow because the more they grow, the more profit you can make. Think about it – if you put your money into a stock where the company could barely pay the electric bill, do you think that your money would be secure, if even for some time?

## Earnings Growth

Another variable you want to pay attention to is how much more money the company is making as the years go on. When you look at this variable, you will be looking at the earnings growth variable. This is another company that you would think of investing in because you know that they have seen considerable growth for a certain number of years. Therefore, you analyze that the company will only continue to grow.

If you want to be a successful stock trader, a swing trader, or an analyst, then you have to learn about fundamental analysis. It is the most crucial aspect of any investment or trading strategy. Many would claim that a trader is not really accomplished if they do not perform fundamental analysis.

The fact is that fundamental analysis is such a broad subject that what it entails sometimes differs depending on scope and strategy. It involves a lot of things such as regulatory filings, financial statements, valuation techniques, and so on.

## Total Revenue

A company's total revenue is important and can be easily understood even by investors with limited financial knowledge. This revenue number is a measure of a company's total sales of their products and/or services. It is often a good indicator that a company is doing well if its revenue grows at a steady pace year over year. If the revenue numbers are flat or dropping year over year, it shows that a company is probably having trouble growing its business and that profits will likely be flat or dropping as well. Falling profits usually translate to a falling stock price.

As a swing trader, you can check to see if the stock you are considering for a position has growing or declining revenues and determine if that is aligned with your trade. For example, are you going long on a stock with growing total revenue numbers?

## Earnings per Share

Earnings are calculated by taking the total revenue and subtracting the direct costs of production. Positive earnings are important in the long term for any business to continue operating. However, the name "earnings" should not be confused with profit or profitability. Profits are calculated by subtracting the additional costs of doing business, such as interest paid on debt. At some point in a company's history, it will need to start turning a profit, or investors will lose patience, funds will run out, and bankruptcy will follow.

## Debt to Equity

Most companies need funds to start up and operate their business. They need money to pay employees, to purchase inventory, to buy equipment and computers, etc. That money can come from 2 sources: 1) debt and 2) equity.

Debt is essentially borrowed money that the company usually pays interest for its use. The debt will also need to be repaid at some point in time. Equity is money invested in the company, and, in return, the investor is given shares. Those shares represent some percentage of ownership in the company. At some point, the investor hopes to sell their shares for a profit and/or collect dividends, which are payments that come from the company's profits.

Debt and equity represent different levels of risks for a company and its shareholders. Debt comes with obligations to pay interest and repay the outstanding loan at some point. Therefore, it is a higher risk to the company compared to equity, which has no such obligations. Equity has more risk for the shareholders because if the company goes bankrupt, the debt holders usually get first pick at whatever is left of value. The equity investors get what is leftover, and that is usually nothing.

CHAPTER 19:

# Technical Analysis

What is a crucial examination? In basic terms, it is an investigation of hard information on an organization, a product, a budgetary instrument, an area, and so on. That information can incorporate at least one of the accompanying:

- Earnings Per Share (EPS)
- Total Income
- Leverage: The Measure of Obligation to Value
- Price to Earning Proportion (P/E)
- Product Pipeline: Future Potential Development Driver
- Conditions That May Support or Impedimenta Specific Division/Product
- Upper Hands-On, an Organization May, Have Over Contenders
- Company Management
- Administrative Situation and Pending Changes
- Shared Correlations
- Short Interests
- Hot Sector Manias

The critical estimates recorded above are not a total rundown, but instead, they are a portion of the more typical ones utilized when performing a principal investigator. The test for many us is that we don't have the opportunity or the skill to, for instance, a profound plunge into budget summaries. We should leave that work and exertion to the bookkeepers and the examiners.

The critical investigation has noteworthy significance for a worthy speculator like Warren Buffett. Worth speculators usually take more prominent positions and search for moves over longer time frames because it frequently takes a year or more for different financial specialists to understand the future estimation of stock.

Some principal investigation can likewise be useful for a swing trader.

## Fundamental Analysis Factors

In any case, an essential comprehension of a portion of these critical components can be useful to a swing dealer. Specifically, you'll be better ready to perceive possibly wise venture openings in stocks. How about we grab a gander at a couple of these significant variables in more profundity and afterward look at the one you feel is the considerable champ.

Performing a major formal investigation can take a lot of time and exertion.

Genuine top to bottom investigation of an organization's fiscal summaries requires some mastery in bookkeeping, which most swing brokers don't have.

There are a couple of principal examination apparatuses that a swing trader with next to no bookkeeping experience can utilize while scanning for trading openings:

***Earnings per Share (EPS)***

Profit is determined by taking total income and taking away the immediate expenses of creation. A decisive advantage is significant in the long haul for any business to keep working. In any case, the name "income" ought not to be mistaken for benefit or productivity. Benefits are determined by deducting the extra expenses of working together, such as intrigue paid on obligation.

### *Total Revenue*

An organization's total income is significant and can be handily seen even by speculators with restricted monetary information. This income number is a proportion of an organization's complete deals of its items or potential benefits. It is frequently a decent marker that an organization is progressing admirably if its income is developing at a consistent pace year over year. On the off chance that the income numbers are level or dropping year over year, it shows that an organization is most likely experiencing difficulty developing its business and that benefits will probably be level or dropping too. Falling profits, for the most part, mean a falling stock cost.

### *Return on Equity (ROE)*

The advantage for value (ROE) is a measure, communicated as a rate, of how much benefit an organization produces with the cash investors have contributed. For instance, if a financial specialist puts $100.00 into an investment account that acquires 1% every year, they expect their $100.00 to be worth $101.00 in a year. Along these lines, speculators in an organization hope to see the organization make a decent profit for their venture. The proportion of ROE shows how well the organization is getting along as far as the contributed capital.

Organizations with higher and developing ROE numbers will, in general, be all the more profoundly esteemed by speculators. Making an inquiry that incorporates organizations with higher ROE numbers is another primary hunt alternative that you can try different things with as a swing trader while doing your outputs for trading openings.

This money related proportions recorded above can be utilized to help you whenever you're searching for swing trading openings.

The degree of short intrigue gives some understanding of the slant of traders toward a stock. An elevated level of short intrigue shows that brokers are anticipating that the cost of the capital should drop substantially. Be that as it may, if some uplifting news comes out on a stock that has an elevated level of short intrigue, it can go about as a substantial impetus to drive the stock cost higher with a quick press.

A short press happens when brokers purchase in mass when they see the cost of that stock begins to rise drastically.

The best essential examination factor for a swing broker is finding and putting resources into the hot part of insanity plays.

Hot sector manias oppose most major investigation standards – sound judgment contributing is disposed of.

Probably the best open door for good returns is to discover these division insanity plays at the point when they begin to happen, get in ahead of schedule, and afterward, get out before the inescapable pullback or breakdown.

***Debt to Equity***

Most organizations need funds to begin and operate their business. They need cash to pay representatives, to buy stock, to purchase gear and PCs, and so forth. That cash can emerge out of 2 sources:

- Debt
- Equity

The debt is borrowed cash that the organization pays enthusiasm typically on for its utilization. The bond will, likewise, should be reimbursed sooner or later. Value is cash put into the organization and, consequently, the financial specialist is given offers. Those offers speak to some level of possession in the organization. Eventually, the financial specialist wants to sell their proposals for a benefit or potentially gather profits, which are installments that originate from the organization's interests.

Obligation and value speak to various degrees of danger for an organization and its investors. Responsibility accompanies commitments to pay intrigue and reimburse the exceptional credit eventually. In this manner, it is a higher hazard to the organization contrasted with value, which has no such commitments. Benefit has more risk for the investors provided that the organization fails, the obligation holders typically get first pick at whatever is left of significant worth. The value financial specialists get what is left finished, and that usually is nothing.

***Price to Earnings Ratio (P/E)***

Price to earning proportion (P/E) is considered by numerous speculators to be the one crucial measure that beats the entirety of the others in deciding an organization's stock value development. The P/E gives you a perspective on how the market evaluates an organization's offers comparable to its income. It is determined by taking an organization's cost for every offer (P) and partitioning by its profit per share (E). For instance, if a stock is evaluated at $100.00 per provide and it has an EPS of $10.00 per share, at that point, the P/E proportion is 10 ($100.00 separated by $10.00). A higher P/E proportion implies financial specialists are eager to pay more for every dollar of yearly profit. You can utilize this number to look at how speculators esteem different organizations in a similar business division.

CHAPTER 20:

# Psychology of Swing Trading

The business world, just like any other world, requires a keen strategy when wanting to indulge. Various key factors make up the business world. Mastery and noting of these factors will see to it that you trade carefully and in the right way.

## How to Control Emotions

When engaging in business transactions, due to the complexity of the business world, you may find that you are falling prey to emotions. The challenges in the business world may come in many forms. Forgetting comes without saying when you are engaging in this complex form of trade.

It becomes easy to forget. It is true that whenever we channel our money into something, we are attached emotionally. This is because we always have the vision to succeed. This is normal for us, and we have to learn to embrace this fact to thrive. This will involve keeping the mind in a state where it does not experience much resistance.

What our mind focuses on the most is the public outlook. Separating our emotions from the decisions we make becomes subtle. People will often respond to how they feel.

The comprehension that emotions make part of us and that staying devoid of them is what will make you thrive. An individual needs to understand that clinging to a particular feeling will not be good when trading.

The various emotional challenges that an individual faces while trading includes:

### *The Challenges of Losing*

Before engaging in trade, traders often make sure that they have in place a well-cultivated strategy that is going to take them through the venture. No matter how much top-notch perfection it may accrue, there are always points of weakness. These are the points at which the plan may fail to succeed.

People will see the truth the way they want it to be. When stressed, the human body responds by releasing a hormone known as cortisol. This hormone interferes with the brain's process of thought and decoding.

With human beings, loosing is not on their bucket list, and thus it comes as an undesired act. When this happens, not only does it affect our decision-making but also our general morale. To counter this type of feeling effective, one needs to ensure that they cut this feeling at its onset to make sure that it has no basis. As a matter of fact, prevention is better than cure and so reducing the effects of this feeling at the beginning will work best for you rather than providing a remedy to an already formed perception.

To make sure that you maintain your physical health, you need to make sure that you avoid putting your emotions in an investment.

### *The Challenge of Ignoring the Price*

When we engage in a business, we have a vision that often works as a morale booster in making you succeed based on the price. The misconception that exists in trading is that those traders who are the most successful have some kind of value that makes them second-guess markets, which is a subtle venture for other people. This misconception is, however, not a reality because the most successful traders are those that stick to the market even through lean times with a vision that one day they will emerge. Their winning comes because of trying and testing the system that is in place.

The system has a means of working out returns on the input that has accrued over a specific period. The discrepancy that that lies between these two clusters is the fact that a professional trader trades with a long-term expectation. In contrast, an amateur focuses on the short-term outcome of every trade.

***Challenge of Taking Money From the Business***

To a trader, making a profit is the sweetest adventure. This is the sole purpose of engaging in the company in the first place. A trader will feel the need to use his or her profits because the tides in the market cannot be forecast. At one point, you may be making a profit, and the next minute, it all turns to loss. Research has it that human beings are most inclined to feel pain rather than joy. Distancing ourselves from this kind of emotion is not an easy adventure, as it tends to take a toll on you.

To beat this, a trader needs to understand that losses exist, and the way you respond to them is the most significant determinant on whether you will be able to move forward or stay stagnated. When you encounter your first win, joy and the temptations might surface, which makes you feel like you need to enjoy your earnings. This is not the case as using your first winnings may see to it that those are your last.

***Acknowledging Regret***

Various options are available in the business world. A trader may choose to settle on a particular option, which may work best for him or her. Usually, the choices that traders make do not automatically imply that there will be a success. There are various options that you may settle on and, in turn, occasion loss. This often brings about feelings of remorse whereby you regret your failure to settle on another option that has been successful. A trader's regret falls squarely on the emotions I should have, or I could have. Traders regret that they could have acquired a particular stock whose price graph is on a high. A trader is feeling this way because of the thoughts of missing profit. There is a feeling of anger that comes as a disappointment. The result of this is that this trader will sit back and curse the movements of the market.

This type of emotion is adequate to the extent that it affects various movements in the market. With regrets, traders only emphasize outcomes that repeat success. To achieve this, you need to develop a sense of self-acceptance; we have no power of insight into the future.

## Why Do Most Traders Lose Money?

In a bid to have a candid comprehension of why traders lose their money, we first have to establish a basis for the understanding of price movements. We have to first set a foundation on why a large number of traders get involved just when the price is about to take a turn. This is simply because most losses happen during this period. The most common problem is that the prices are in constant movement, and when another trader sees others buying, they pay attention. This is because they understand that if they act now and buy, others will follow their lead. The perception that people will buy after you do is often the drive that pushes you to buy because you are visualizing an instance where you are likely to make profits when others buy after you do.

The upturn of prices occurs because of many traders coming in to buy. The forecasts that we engage in analyze the movements of the cost and often show positive speculation that people will go in and buy. The analysis that we carry out is usually checking on patterns that have existed before. A trend upwards is the result of large numbers of people coming to buy. The only way that a price will go higher is through the willingness of the traders to pay.

A problem that arises when trading is that many traders will be concentrated at the top of the price. Take, for instance, a stock that has continuously been on the rise in the recent past. More and more traders keep on finding it as they buy in a bid to sell at a profit. This number is often limited only to those who are interested. Getting involved in trade at the points of turn makes it risky for many people to make profits, and thus they end up in losses.

As the market is on an upturn, you may find that some people are not in their right sense of wishing to buy. The situation changes when the improvement continues in that you will find many people coming in and buying. This is because they have already witnessed its success. Most professional traders find it tricky to earn more than ten percent of their total investment.

## The Trader Mindset

Several factors need to be put into consideration to succeed. This involves formulating several strategies that you will use when conquering the market. This will mean that a past failure will not be visualized as a loss but rather as a stepping-stone towards greater heights.

The business world is not a comfortable place to trade-in. This is because various people whose sole aim is to benefit them alone curtail it. In the business world, people suffer from losses only because they were not aware of a particular set of facts or misrepresented a specific set of circumstances. A positive mindset is what enables some people to win consistently in the game of trading. There are several factors when it comes to trading. Often these factors relate to the attitude and the beliefs of an individual.

The attitude concerning the market is an umbrella mindset. The mindset of a person involves his or her feelings towards that particular person or thing. There are personal traits that winners will often assume. Take, for instance, self-confidence - a value that plays a huge role when it comes to the success of a trader. This is usually because of a past mistake that they may have fallen prey to. With a sense of self-doubt, a trader would not be inclined to make the right choices that would see him or her succeeding in trade. Often you will find that these types of people procrastinate when it comes to making their move.

With traders who tend to win, they realize that, although their analysis might be the best, it may not be able to fit in the shifts of future prices. Having this mindset is what will determine how high you will rise. This is because when you fall, you have support so you can pull yourself back up.

## Stay Focused

Having focus entails that you are in pursuit of a goal and that you are not going to rest until you have achieved. Staying focused thus requires that you are watching the price until you are in a position to succeed. When trading, remaining focused is a crucial aspect because, at every stage of trade, you will be required to engage in decision-making that has an overall effect on your performance. It is key that when trading, short-term winnings carry less weight than when you are engaging in long-term goals. This is often because long-term goals have a short implication on the changes in the market.

Staying focused entails maintaining the vigil all through your venture. Most traders often begin on a high. You may find that the trader actively engages in various searches in a bid to make his investment better. The stage that follows is that you will find this particular trader has let go and is now letting everything take its course. When engaging in trade, your focus ought to have a complete understanding of when and where you are supposed to make a move.

CHAPTER 21:

# Do's and Don'ts of Successful Swing Trading

## DO'S

It does not matter what kind of trader you are; alike customs usually follow accomplishment. A strong schedule is a vital part of being dependable when you are using a swing-trading strategy. To achieve this aim, most successful futures traders do the subsequent things to ensure they retain a competitive edge:

***Premarket Preparation***

An important characteristic of specialized trading is to research the patterns of market movement as it relates to periodic instability and liquidity. Daily safeguarding of computers and software systems is also significant to productive trading.

***Game Plan for the Next Session***

Planning for the financial calendar of the day and probable market dynamics before the start of vigorous trading will help you to be familiar with opportunities while reducing risk. Breaking down appropriate technical levels and potential order entry/exit points ahead of time is a wonderful way to make sure that your plan is implemented on the live market faultlessly.

***Post-Market Performance Assessment***

Taking inventories of the day's victories and failures is a significant part of that as a trader. Trader construction is unlikely without the continuing success scrutiny.

But any experienced trader can tell you that it's not sufficient just to be ready for the opening bell to ring. Achievement in the markets depends on continuously building and executing solid plans with steadiness, as well as through past wins and losses. Across these three areas, the most active futures traders do extremely well on a customary basis.

## DON'T'S

There are factually hundreds of things not to do when it comes to guaranteeing success in the marketplace. The trail to success is comparatively straightforward – making more currency than you lose.

Okay, it is not that straightforward to trade active futures. Even if you have a feasible trading strategy and the promise to industriously executing it, outside factors will destroy effectiveness. Anyone who makes a living in the markets knows the following things:

***Trade Emotionally***

Emotional trading is the number one efficiency killer. Bad habits such as overtrading and taking ecstatic risks will easily blow out the equilibrium of accounts. The name of the game is to stay behind even-keeled.

***Lose Respect for Money***

This item seems understandable, but it can hurt a trader of the future. When audacious financial risk, it is significant to be somewhat disengaged from the actual real-world value of a currency. And when all regard for your resources is gone, taking wild, irresponsible risks is much simpler.

***Become Complacent***

You can get used to almost the whole thing in the human mind. Money making and losing is absolutely no exception in the markets. Many traders fall victim to this trend and become familiarized with taking losses and profits that are less important than expected. Both of these behaviors make arrangements risk difficult to reward, eliminating any likelihood of long-term success.

The human element can be a deceitful adversary, particularly if active trading is concerned. This reality is respected by most energetic futures traders who take action to diminish the harmful impacts of emotion-based trading and satisfaction.

CHAPTER 22:

# Swing Trading Rules

These are my general rules, which have evolved through experience and knowledge gained over the years. It is up to you to develop your own set of rules, which may include some or all of these.

The rules are based on 2 factors that I consider important for a trader to keep their capital and have a profitable business. These factors include the following:

- Risk of holding a security
- Over-the-counter stocks

## Risks of Holding a Security

As a swing trader, under the right conditions, you can see significant gains just by holding overnight or up to several weeks, which makes this type of trading attractive.

### *Earnings Reports*

Even if a company reports good total revenue and profit numbers, there can still be some negative comments made on "forward guidance" for earnings that the market did not expect. One negative comment could easily send the price heading lower even if all of the other results were very good. This would be great if you were short the stock, but not good if you were long and hoping to move higher after the report.

There are other ways to play earnings report events, such as using options to limit risk and potential losses. Options strategies are more advanced and are not covered in this book.

### *Announcements about a Product or Service*

Any positive or negative announcement about a product or service provided by the company has the potential to move the price significantly, either up or down. Pharmaceutical companies are a great example of this type of announcement. Events such as the results of a drug trial can cause a stock price to swing dramatically one way or another depending on the outcome. If the results are negative, look out below, because small pharmaceutical companies have been known to lose 75% or more of their value overnight. If you happen to have a long position in the stock, you will have a substantial loss. Just like earnings reports, the problem with this situation is that the trader does not know which side to take prior to the announcement.

Other events, such as a product recall that would negatively impact your position, can also take you by surprise. Alternatively, you might be holding shares in a small company that wins a contract with a large company. Singular events like these are harder to predict and can be primarily managed by limiting how much of your portfolio is invested in any one position.

### *Secondary Offerings*

Companies that need to raise money to sustain their operations while developing a product or service often do secondary offerings. Announcements about an offering are usually done after normal trading hours and might come as a surprise to many holders of the stock. These offerings are often done when their stock price is moving higher, which would have led you to think you're "on a good roll" with your long position.

The amount of the gap down will depend on how far below the current market price of the stock the offering was completed at. For example, if a stock ends the trading day at $30.00 per share, and the company announces a secondary offering at $23.00, that is probably going to be viewed by existing shareholders as very negative. Recent investors at around $30.00 are going to be really unhappy, and selling will likely follow.

If the secondary offering was made at $28.00 on the other hand, then that is not so bad because the new investors are paying much closer to the market price.

The offerings are not made public until they are completed, so there is no way to know when a company might make a secondary offering. This makes them hard to guard against as a swing trader. The best you can do is understand it is a risk, and companies that burn a lot of cash with little current incoming revenue are the most susceptible to this risk.

***Downgrades, Upgrades and Short Sellers Reports***

Brokerage firms and analysts are constantly upgrading and downgrading companies and modifying their performance expectations. Some brokers have specialists that follow only one stock, such as Apple. Other firms have specialists that research and report on a sector like semiconductors. A rating downgrade or upgrade by a brokerage research firm can cause a stock price to move one way or the other depending on the sentiment expressed in the report.

There are also a number of firms that specialize in looking for companies where they can make an argument that the business model is flawed or where there is the potential for fraud being committed. These firms focus on finding companies to be short and then release their arguments as to why they feel the company is overvalued. I recommend you watch "The China Hustle" (which is available on Netflix at the time of writing) if you have any doubts about how fraud can happen relatively easily in our regulated markets.

These analysts will normally release their reports outside of normal market trading hours. Therefore, unfortunately, for a swing trader, it is impossible to see these reports coming. Like many other unique events, the only way to protect yourself from a big loss is to practice your risk to reward strategies and limit how much of your total portfolio is invested in one position.

### *Other Announcements*

Any other negative announcement such as a data breach, an SEC investigation, or a new lawsuit can hurt your position if you're long. A positive announcement such as the introduction of a new product, a partnership with another company, or the resolution of a lawsuit can negatively impact your account if you are short.

Unanticipated events are one of the challenges a swing trader faces. As with all other unexpected occurrences, the best way to protect yourself from these is to practice your risk to reward plan. There is always the possibility that a singular event will work in your favor, such as being long a stock that announces a major partnership. You are there to capture the upside, but you need to follow your trading plan and your risk to reward plan to protect your account on the downside.

### *Changes in Market Sentiment*

Events and announcements can change market sentiment overnight. Regular reports such as the Institute of Supply Management's Manufacturing Purchasing Managers' Index (known as the PMI) are used as an indicator of the overall economic condition of the manufacturing sector. A release of an unexpected number can cause the overall market sentiment to become more positive or negative. With the PMI, a reading above 50 indicates that that particular sector of the economy is expanding, and a reading below 50 indicates it is generally contracting.

There are numerous other government and non-government reports regularly released, such as housing starts, non-farm payroll numbers, inflation numbers, and Federal Reserve announcements. Each has the ability to impact overall market sentiment. A swing trader should be aware of these coming events and whether or not the market participants are putting a lot of weight on the release of an upcoming number. These events are easily accessible on a variety of websites, including Estimate (under its Calendar tab).

### *Over-the-Counter or Penny Stocks*

Over-the-counter trading happens off regular exchanges like the NYSE, NASDAQ, and NYSE American (formerly known as AMEX). These transactions happen between dealers and can include stocks, bonds, currencies, and other financial instruments. The stocks traded can include both company shares that are listed on recognized exchanges like the NYSE and stocks that do not have a recognized listing on an exchange. These unlisted stocks are primarily referred to as over-the-counter (OTC) equities.

These unlisted equities are traded through dealers because they are too small to get a regular listing on a recognized exchange. Therefore, they are unlikely to meet an exchange's requirements for listing. Unlike listed companies that are required to make regular filings with the SEC, OTC equities may not file as often or with as much detail, which means there could be limited information available about the company.

OTC equities may also trade in just a small number of shares per day. This limited trading activity means that there is a greater potential for share price manipulation by insiders and that it could be difficult to exit a trade once you have a position.

I avoid trading any OTC equities for the reasons listed above. I also try to avoid trading penny stocks (stocks under $1.00 per share), as they can also be more easily manipulated by insiders and are therefore less predictable. On occasion, I may consider a stock trading under $1.00 if there is a strong case for going long, but it would be a rare exception to my rule.

There is no need for a retail trader to trade listed stocks OTC. If a stock is not listed on a regular exchange, then I do not trade those equities.

CHAPTER 23:

# When to Trade and When Not to Trade

The markets go through different phases. There will be times when you will feel like it is difficult to read the market or other times when there are low volumes and high hesitation from market participants, making the market evolve in a flat and boring momentum.

## DAX Future, 5 Minutes

For this example, I have used 5-minute candles in order to fit the whole day on one chart. As you can see, the market makes roughly 60 points between its lowest of the day and its highest of the day, which is not too bad. But how did that happen? A rapid 30 points drop in the morning, followed by a return to opening prices by the end of the morning, and then, 6 hours of long waiting until a little awakening again at 5 pm. Apart from doing mini range trading during these 6 hours, there is not much you can do.

It is difficult to predict how a day is going to be. I am not talking about trends here, but just about price volatility. Is it going to be an active day or a very quiet day? You can't really know in advance.

## DAX Future, One Hour

When the market is testing significant levels such as supports and resistances, you can expect some hesitation as no one is willing to buy at the highest and push the market further, until an event or something triggers the market to make a breakthrough or consolidate sharply. When reaching significant levels and testing them, expect the market to test that level before breaking it or reversing it.

Another hint to look for market activity can be found in the economic calendars and how the market reacts to the coming events or news to be announced. The market may enter into a quiet phase, with fewer participants willing to trade, waiting for the news to be released. Some participants will indeed decide to stay on the side, as I will advise you to do next. During this quiet phase, the volumes exchanged could be below, again due to the fact that many day traders don't want to have too many positions opened while facing the risk of high price volatility at the time of the news being released. You should get familiar with the average volume exchanged throughout the day for the product you are trading so that you can assess if the market is being pushed around in low volumes by fewer participants or if indeed there is increased interest.

When scalping, you may want to close all your positions before the news is released because the market might get very volatile after the news is being released. While volatility normally serves us, at the time of a news release, the market can move erratically in any direction, come back to where it was before the news went out or set up in a specific direction. What will happen is that you may have traded in the right direction, but the market went to hit your stop loss first due to price volatility. Now, you may say, let's not put a stop loss in this instance or place it further away, but what happens if the market goes against you and then doesn't reverse in your chosen direction? Placing orders just before the news is released, from my point of view, is just gambling. Don't try to apply logic to the market's reactions to the news either, thinking that if the news is positive, the market will certainly go up or the opposite, because it may not happen. The market may already have priced the news with some market participants starting to cash in their profits making the prices go in the opposite direction of where they should logically have gone. When news or a figure is released, you don't have all the information around it. For instance, if crude oil inventories are lower than forecast, is it due to higher oil consumption or lower oil production? What strategies do the market participants have in place? Many factors and many questions for which we don't have all the answers to analyze the news and predict how the market is going to digest the news. Sometimes, following a news publication, the market reacts strongly by going one way, but recovers in the next two hours and resumes its current activity. So, don't try to gamble on the news. With experience, however, you will get to know when important news is likely to have no impact on the market at particular times while they may be strongly scrutinized at other times.

The main macro-economic news that often impacts the markets are interest rates decisions from central banks and their press conferences, crude oil inventories, American employment, inflation figures, GDPs, and home sales. Depending on the context, they may trigger volatility when released.

You can find calendars with news release dates and times on many websites.

## Economic Calendar

As the week is finishing, I look at the following week's events and report them to my computer calendar and save reminders and alarms that go off one hour to 30 minutes before the news release. That way, it reminds me not to open any more positions just before a news release, and close existing positions while in positive territory.

Below is a list of additional times when I recommend not trading:

**The First Ten Minutes After the Stock Market Opening.** I am talking about the stock market opening and not the future market. During the first ten minutes, the market can move in different ways, not giving us useful readings. Other participants may open or close positions due to their option hedging work, and so on. Different traders with different agendas. The first ten minutes may create volatility that again may trigger scalpers' stop losses without giving any opportunity to the scalper.

**The Triple Witching Day**. This is the name given to the day when, every month, index futures contracts, stock index options contracts, and single stock options contracts expire; even quadruple witching day when single stock futures contracts add to this list quarterly. Triple witching day takes place on the third Friday of the month and quadruple witching day on the third Friday of the month every quarter-end. Volumes become artificially higher due to positions being rolled over to the next contract term. Volatility may also increase as market participants have different agendas, but it may not help the scalper, so I choose to take it easy these days.

**The Last Day of the Quarter.** Some market participants may be at work to improve their balance sheets and quarterly reporting. However, don't start thinking that it will trigger an uptrend because if rising prices may improve the balance sheet of institutional investors, it may have an adverse impact on those with short positions in their books.

**Holidays and Festive Seasons.** During those times, volumes are lower. The market may be in a free-spinning mode or move rapidly in low volumes. If you absolutely want to trade, do it on lower volumes because when institutional investors and big market movers are on holiday, the market may not give you the right opportunities to realize good trades.

**Trading After 10 PM**. Mini DAX and DAX futures are not tradable after 10 pm, but for the e-mini Dow, CME lets traders carry on their trading on an OTC system via its GLOBEX platform. So, if you really want to trade e-mini Dow non-stop, you can start at midnight on Monday until 11 pm on Friday (these hours can change slightly during the winter and summertime changes). However, trading after 10 pm is not recommended because the volumes are likely to be very low. Focus your energy instead on the US pre-market opening, which is at 14:30 CET.

## Trading the Mini-DAX and DAX Pre-Market Opening

Mini DAX and DAX futures markets open at 7:50 am one hour and 10 minutes before the stock market opening.

Most of the time, a pre-market opening is very quiet with low volume transactions. No need to rush to your screen and start trading at 8 am. However, when the market made a strong move the day before, there may be opportunities arising in the pre-market opening. We know that market participants have different agendas, but when the market reacts strongly in one direction, it can put speculators in difficult positions. For instance, if the market went down by 300 points in one day, some long traders may face margin calls meaning they will have to either put more cash in their account or close some of their positions. This will lead to more sales orders being put on the market. At the same time, some sellers may want to cash in and close winning trades. In the first minutes of pre-market opening, you won't know how the market will evolve, but you can certainly use the Heikin Ashi candles to perform some trades because after a strong move the day before, there is likely to be volatility in the pre-market opening.

CHAPTER 24:

# Swing Trading Plan

The swing market can be overwhelming if a person is new in the market. The best way an individual can be successful is that he or she has a trading plan. The major aim of developing a trading plan is to help an individual in swing trading to capture the track of huge money. There are several advantages it poses, such as making a swing trader making his or her trade with conviction.

An individual getting to write a swing trading plan has to understand who is in control of the prices of the financial instrument. There is a major need for this factor to be cleared by a swing trader. Institutions that deal with swing trading have the role of determining the reason for buying or selling of a certain financial instrument. There are often movements of huge chunks of money in these kinds of markets. There are two major reasons that make the phenomena come to surface. The reason might either be the presence of a single large fund or the existence of several big players who have a similar idea.

There are simple ways that a swing trader can be able to monitor the activity. It entails the usage of technical analysis rather than basing everything on fundamental analysis. Fundamental analysis subjects an individual to basing his or her speculative moves on interpreting cash flows and financial statements. At this point, an individual can have the mentality that it is an easy ride. That is not the case. The whole point is tracking the flow of cash makes the trading process to be easy and manageable.

The general trading plan used by big players in this sector focuses on accumulating a position for long-term moves. It is not an easy task as it sounds because it takes a person to build on several weeks and months to make these positions viable. There are several people who are lucky in the market of swing trading despite the huddle. The lucky group of people is known for using charts that inform them what they are doing. These charts help people to know moments swing trades are supposed to be considered.

A monthly candlestick chart has several potential that it possesses. Its first role entails informing swing traders if the huge amounts of money support the high prices in the financial markets. The second role it performs is giving information on whether to dump the financial instrument because of declining prices. This has seen several traders terming it as a master class tool because of its simple nature and yet powerful nature. These attributes by the candlestick are fully utilized in the event an individual is disciplined to read it closely.

The candlestick chat presence in the plan shows several relationships in swing trading markets. The relationship depicted involves low, high, close, and open positions during a specific moment in trading sessions. A swing trading plan that is effective entails an individual being able to know what green and red lights in a candlestick mean. The green light is present to portray that a person has closed above the market price he or she opened on. The red lights are used to signify an individual closed below market prices she or he opened on.

A swing trading plan is supposed to be as simple as possible. There are common mistakes that a person is likely to make in this form of active trading. It entails a trader reading the net change from the preceding close. The mistake is detrimental because a swing trader can know the current market's pressure exerted on buying or selling. A trader is supposed to know what he or she is supposed to change from the moment he or she is open to trading. The focal point is to know whether he or she will focus on the green or the red light.

There several people that might find the point above confusing because of several reasons. However, the candlestick can still be sticking with the red color. The depiction could be a good show on the pressure for a swing to sell his or her financial instruments. The common trader would wish to be a buyer of the financial instruments in the event the charts are green, signifying gains in the market. One is advised not to purchase any financial instruments unless this is the case being portrayed. The case is strongly advised for an individual who is making large capital investments.

## How to Write a Swing Trading Plan

Developing a swing trading plan involves a trader to write it down to make him or her successful. The development of a plan is critical irrespective of which kind of financial instrument and individual is planning to trade. The trading plan is helpful in strengthening the trading strategies an individual will settle for swing trading. The role played by a trading plan goes a notch higher to help a swing trader adhere to a well-developed trading system.

The details in the trading plan give a trader the bearing of entering and exiting the market. These entail following the subtle steps stated in it. Several misdoings are prone to occur in the event a trader does not follow the trading plan. The susceptible errors entail overtrading and making instant decisions in markets that are volatile. However, this is not supposed to be the case to discourage a swing trader since there are easy steps of writing a trading plan. They include:

### *Deciding on Which Financial Instrument to Trade*

There are several financial instruments that can be traded in swing trading markets. This includes futures, stocks, options, and bonds, to mention a few financial instruments. A person interested in or participating in swing trading is supposed to choose a financial instrument he or she is comfortable trading. One is encouraged to check on the volatility of the underlying asset prior to his or her investment. A trader is lucky if he or she finds an underlying asset that he or she is comfortable trading.

### *Determining If There Are Other Financial Instruments to Trade*

There are moments an individual can settle for an underlying asset that is another financial instrument. These moments are common when a swing trader is looking to diversify his or her trading portals. The major reason for this practice is always to minimize risks that can befall a single financial asset. Therefore, an individual needs to be able to keep this information on which financial instrument that diversifies his or her trading portal clear.

### *Identification of Perfect Market Indicators*

Trading indicators have the potential of making an individual be able to analyze the swing trading market. A swing trader is supposed to be certain on which conditions require to be met for trading to be executed. This entails the usage of charts such as the candlesticks that are efficient. The color green is used to signify buying, while red is a sign for a swing trader to sell his or her financial instruments. Some traders prefer other forms of technical analysis.

### *Deciding on How Many Shares to Be Purchased*

A trader who thinks of the size he or she is willing to trade before time is on a good business platform. He or she has the potential to avoid certain forms of risks that can be dangerous to the investment. One has to take note of the number of the amounts he or she is willing to trade. This will avoid overtrading, which dangerous.

### *The Setting of Specific Prices for Entry Points*

A swing trader can make several points that he or she will be certain while performing swing trading. These points include the price levels that will make the trader to either buy or sell the financial instrument that is being traded. One can minimize loss with this step.

### *Writing Down the Process to Monitor Each Trade*

Swing trading has charts that record trades after every fifteen to one hour. It is important to be certain to which time variance he or she is comfortable.

It is important for traders to set an alarm notification to remind them after every hour to check the market trends. This is in the event he or she is comfortable with a one-hour time variance.

***Deciding on The Trading Parameters***

There are several positions that swing traders can choose to enter, which are short positions and long positions. It is very crucial for a swing trader to have conditions that can make him or her to exit or enter either of these positions. A good trading plan is supposed to have a box that allows an individual to evaluate his or her trades.

CHAPTER 25:

# Psychology of a Successful Swing Trader

## Simplicity Always Beats Complexity

One thing you should note about the investment industry is the fact that it is filled with complex terminologies and very busy charts. Unfortunately, most beginner traders confuse complexity as a requirement for one to succeed in the market.

Well, the truth is, you don't need any complexity in trading. There is no need for complex charts, data, or even indicators for you to make a good trading decision of investment. It is often easy to get caught up in intellectual pursuits that we allow that to completely override our money-making efforts.

It is important that you stay simple when trading. Don't let being right or the desire to get great calls to override the real reason why you are in the market. Being successful in trading does not mean complex screens, methods, and tools, several technical indicators, or days staring at the screens.

What you need is the ability to adjust your opinion, have the fortitude to accept when you are wrong, get quality information, and have the ability to find confluences of support, resistance, and unique thoughts about them.

## How to Systematize Success

### *Plan–Do–Check–Act*

When you are trading, one of the most important things is to ensure that you have a trading plan.

**Plan:** What you need to do is plan a change and then test it. The main aim is to determine whether there is a need to modify the process for things to be more beneficial.

**Do:** The next thing is to implement that change and then try to test it on a small scale to ascertain the outcome.

**Check:** Once you test the change, the results you obtain are relevant in determining what the important lessons are. Here, it is critical to note what went right, wrong, and whether the change worked out well or not.

**Act:** Finally, it is important to note whether you would like to adopt the change, abandon it, or redo the whole PDCA cycle. When you do not get any significant value from the process as you had initially anticipated, then it is safe to terminate the decision. If the change is expected to create adherence issues or bring about minimal improvements, then it is safe to abort or repeat the cycle. In other words, you are repeating the process because the amount of improvement is not as much as you had anticipated. However, you might have already identified opportunities for change enhancement.

Once your main objective is met, then the final thing is for you to standardize the whole process. The power of this process lies in its simplicity and inductive use of logic. While it is also easy to understand, it can be challenging to attain on an ongoing basis, mainly because of difficulty associated with the analytical judgment of the hypothesis.

**Plan:** Setting your goals, targets, and strategies

When you start trading, there are so many questions you need to ask. The truth is, with all the information out there, it can be challenging to decide where to begin. However, you should set goals, targets, and strategize, but the chances are that most goals traders make are the wrong kind.

The goals that you set, in the beginning, will help determine whether you are going to make money or lose money. Therefore, it is important that you make your goals about the process and emulating all the traits professional traders portray.

The first one is by ensuring that you have a plan. In business school, we are taught to start any business with a business plan. If you didn't know, trading is a business! This means that each time you trade, you have to trade according to a well-thought-out and calculated plan.

Your trading plan should tell you how to enter trades and exit trades. It should include ways you intend to manage money. In other words, the whole plan should be well-detailed with risk parameters to look out for, markets to be traded, position size, whether you intend to use filters as trade signals, the market environments to trade, and how you intend to determine such things as trends and ranges among others.

In short, your goal should be to come up with a plan before you trade.

**Do:** Setting up your trading routine

When a certain dollar amount is your goal, you will ensure that you push to achieve that goal irrespective of opportunities being present or not. The truth is, the market does not present the statistical probability of trading opportunities always. In fact, you will be better off sitting on your hands in most instances.

However, this does not really work well for most people. Most people are looking to continually do something. The thing is, in the market, this can be slow and risks eroding your profits during good trading times.

Understand that trading when the times are slow or when you make impulsive trades that are out of scope requires your immediate attention. Therefore, one of your goals should be to be disciplined as much as possible so that you only trade as outlined on your plan.

### *Check and Act*

One thing that you need to note is that a complex strategy can be quite alluring. So many people think that just because something is complex, it is highly likely to work. You need to avoid being fancy with your analysis and trading strategies. Don't make your winning plan complex.

What you need to do is check the plan you have that it is realistic and simple, and then act on it. If you fail to check and act, the chances are that you will destroy the profitability of it. If you truly like the stock market, then ensure that you stick to trading stocks.

The bottom line here is for you to ensure that you are not constantly tinkering. This way, your performance will improve. Instead of always trying to switch the market, analysis method, or strategy, simply stick to your plan, check through it, and action. However, if you feel the need to rework it occasionally, ensure that you keep all revisions simple so that you don't end up making things overly complex.

## How to Set Up a Trade Journal

When trading, one of the most impactful and highly leveraged activities traders adopt is keeping track of their trades with the help of a trading journal. When you keep a trading journal, you ensure that you are keeping track of your experiences in the market so that you can come back to them later for lessons.

When you develop a trading journal/system, the most important thing is to save ideas in then and then test results. In other words, when you enter a certain position, you simply need to record everything about the trade. Ensure that you capture all your thoughts and contemplations when making a trade. This means that when you later have a "what was I thinking" moment in the future, all your answers will be found in the journal.

When setting up a trading journal, ensure that it has the following; trade date, number of shares and the reason you chose them, stock symbol, whether they are sold long/short, what triggered the entry signal and exit signal, where was your initial stop, did you move your stops and why, what were the reasons for your exit position?

Also, when you set up the trading journal, it is important that you keep track of not just your trades but beyond. For instance, the internet articles that influenced your thoughts, what the leading and lagging industries were, and the charts that helped you through the process.

Keeping a journal is key. Therefore, set aside some time each week or month to just go through your trades to identify key mistakes and missed opportunities. Ensure that you are brutally honest with yourself by simply stepping back, taking a cold and hard look at the decisions you made when trading.

In short, your trading journal should be the soil that nurtures your growth.

CHAPTER 26:

# Problems With Swing Trading Using Options

One of the most popular ways of trading the stock market is swing trading. In case you know it or not, you've likely been swinging all this time. Swing trading consists of occasionally buying a few days or weeks later when prices are higher or lower (in the case of shorts). Such an increase or decrease in prices is known as a "price fluctuation," hence the term "Swing Trading."

Most option trading beginners use options as a form of leverage for their swing trading. They want to buy call options when prices are low and then sell them quickly a few days or weeks later for advantage. Conversely, it applies to put options. Though, many of these newcomers soon discovered the hard way in which they could still make a significant loss in option trading, even if the stock eventually moved in the direction they predicted.

How did that happen? What are the problems associated with swing trading with options they have not taken note of?

While options can easily be used as a leveraged replacement for trading the underlying stock, most beginners do not consider specific options.

## Strike Price

It doesn't take long for somebody to know that there are many options available for many strike prices for all optional shares. The obvious choice that beginners generally make is to buy the "cheap" among the monetary options for higher leverage. Non-cash options are options that have no built-in value. These are call options whose hit price is higher than the current share price or put options whose strike price is lower than the current share price.

Problems with exchanging monetary options in swing trading are that even if the underlying stocks move towards your prediction (up for the purchase of call options and down for the call options). You can still lose all your capital if the shares did not exceed the hit price of the options you bought! That's right, and it's called "runs without money," which makes all the options you've bought useless. It is also how most beginners lose all their money in options trading.

In general, the more expensive the options, the higher the leverage, and the greater the risk that these options will expire worthless, causing you to lose all the money invested. The more options in cash, the less expensive they are because of the value integrated into them, the lower the leverage, the higher the risk of expiration. You need to consider the expected size of the move and the level of risk you can examine when deciding the strike price you want to buy for swing trading with options. If you expect a big step, the options out of the money will, of course, bring you huge rewards, but if the move does not exceed the hit price of these options after the expiration of the term, an unpleasant awakening awaits you.

## Expiry Date

Unlike swing trading with stocks that you can keep permanently when something goes wrong, options have a fixed expiration date. It means if you make a mistake, you will lose money very quickly at maturity without the benefit of being able to hold the spot and wait for a return or dividend.

Yes, swing trading with option battles against time. The faster the stock moves, the more confident you are in making a profit. The good news is that all optional stocks also have options to expire in several months. The closest monthly options are cheaper, and the extra monthly options are more expensive. So if you are confident that the underlying stock will move quickly, you can trade with shorter maturity options or what we call "month for options," which are cheaper, and therefore, have greater leverage. If you want to give more time to let the stock move, you can choose an extra expiry month, which will, of course, be more expensive and therefore has a much lower leverage.

As such, the expiration month choice for swing trading with options is mostly a choice between leverage and time. Note that you can sell profitable opportunities well before their expiration date. As such, most swing traders opt for options with a minimum duration of 2-3 months.

## Extrinsic Value

The extrinsic value, or commonly referred to as "premium," is the portion of the price of an option that disappears entirely upon expiration. It is why the monetary options we mentioned above expire worthless upon termination because their full price consists only of extrinsic value and not integrated value (intrinsic value).

The thing about extrinsic value is that it erodes under two circumstances; Through time and the volatility crunch.

Erosion or extrinsic value over time as it approaches expiration is known as "Temporal Decay." The longer you keep an option that is not profitable, the cheaper the option becomes and may become worthless. That's why swing trading with options is a race against time. The faster the stocks you choose to move, the more confident you are in making a profit. It's different from swing trading with the capital itself, where you make a profit as long as it eventually moves, no matter how long it takes.

The erosion of extrinsic value when "excitement" or "anticipation" of the stock falls is known as the "volatility crisis." When an action is expected to make an essential step at some point in the future, such as a profit publication or a judgment, implied volatility increases, and options for that action become increasingly expensive. The additional costs generated by anticipating such events will erode FULLY as soon as the game is announced and hit the wires.

It is what the tightening of volatility is for and why many new entrants to options trading are trying to trade stock through its profit publication to lose money. Yes, the erosion of extrinsic value due to the tightening of volatility can be so high that even if the stock moved strongly in the expected direction, you could not make a profit because the price movement was integrated into the value extrinsically itself.

As such, when trading options, you should consider a more complicated strategy when speculating on stocks or events with high volatility, and you should be able to choose stocks that move before the effects of time-lapse take away a large chunk of this profit.

## Bid-Ask Spread

The bid-ask spread for options can be significantly more significant than the bid-let range for their underlying stocks if the possibilities are not heavily traded. A large bid price spread introduces a substantial initial loss on the position, especially for cheap options outside monetary possibilities, leaving you with a significant loss from the start. As such, in options trading, it is authoritative to trade options with a tight bid-let spread to ensure liquidity and a small initial loss.

# CHAPTER 27:

# Preparing Your Mindset to Success

Even the most sensible swing trading strategies can fail without the right mindset. This is because the wrong attitude often leads to wrong decisions, which include not following the swing trading strategy chosen or worse, not choosing one at all, and just "winging" it.

## Flexibility

The bamboo is one of the strongest trees around, being able to withstand the strongest of storms despite its seeming frail structure. How's it able to do that?

By being the most flexible of all trees. When it is hit by the strongest winds one can imagine, it simply bends in the direction of such winds. Instead of resisting the inevitable, they adapt to it. Other bigger and stronger trees that aren't as flexible get uprooted while the bamboo remains where it is.

By flexibility, a swing trader must:

a. Not get attached to any of his or her trades.

b. Be able to change opinions and strategies when situations call for it because swing trading isn't about being "right" or firm but about making money.

c. Accept reality instead of always trying to "bend" it. No swing trader can control the market but can only surf its waves to profitability or get wiped out by trying to oppose it.

## Value the Importance of Proper Execution

Implementing swing trading strategies properly can substantially increase the chances of profitable swing trades. Improper or worse, the non-implementation of chosen strategies increases one's chances of losing trades. In fact, it can guarantee losing trades.

When it comes to the proper execution of swing trading strategies, the following are important things to prioritize:

a. Choosing the most appropriate tools and strategies for profitable swing trades.

b. Set demarcation lines and stick to them. Not all trades will be profitable, but losses can be minimized by setting stop-loss and profit-taking limits. Without such limits, swing trading losses can grow beyond reasonable limits, and profits that could've already been earned may be wiped out if held on for too long, waiting for prices to go up indefinitely.

c. Consistently executing strategies.

d. Taking reasonable and well-calculated risks.

## Use Numbers to Trade, Not Feelings

I remember over ten years ago when I let my emotions rule my swing trading. I bought shares of stock of a prominent real estate company, and within two months of holding it, I already had a paper gain of about 30%.

However, I felt really good about earning a 30% ROI in just two months and was very optimistic that I could double my money if I held on to my position for another couple of months. When its price dropped and reduced my ROI to only 15%, I justified it by saying, "It's just a correction." When the ROI became negative 10%, I still repeated the same mantra. Eventually, I cut my losses by 25%.

My optimism turned out to be nothing more than greed. Had I established a profit-taking point and stuck to it regardless, I would've locked in on my profits instead of losing money on that swing trade.

By setting limits both ways, i.e., profit-taking or stop-loss limits, you can minimize your swing trading risks because you rely on something objective and unchanging, unlike emotions.

Speaking of numbers, part of relying on numbers when swing trading focuses on overall swing trading results instead of individual trades. Why?

No trader is perfect, and there will always be losing trades. When you focus on individual trades, you can get discouraged. But when you look at it from a wider, general perspective, you can more accurately evaluate your swing trading results. For example, only three of your ten swing trades two years ago made money but overall, you accomplished an ROI of 50% for that year because those three winning trades made lots of profits while the losses of the seven other trades weren't big. The following year, six of your eight swing trades were profitable, and only two were losing trades. However, the losses on those two trades were so huge that you ended the year with an ROI of negative 10%.

Between the two years, which was better: the first year when only 30% of your trades were profitable, but you ended the year with an overall return of 50% (focus on overall trading results) or the second year when 75% of your trades were profitable (focus on individual trades), but you lost money overall? I bet you'll tell you that the first year was better – and you'd be right!

## Learn From Your Mistakes Instead of Being Discouraged by Them

If everybody makes mistakes, why should you think you're an exemption and beat yourself up over them? Consider Thomas Edison on successfully inventing the light bulb that forever changed human history for the better. He failed a thousand times before finally getting the working version of the light bulb right. When interviewed by a newspaper publication on how he handled those 1,000 failed experiments, he answered that those weren't failures but were simply 1,000 lessons on how not to make a working lightbulb. He didn't get discouraged by his mistakes because he knew that mistakes are valuable lessons on what not to do the next time.

When it comes to swing trading, nobody has a batting average of 100% - even computer programs. It's because price movements aren't governed by fixed laws of science but by finicky laws of human psychology. You only have to choices when you make mistakes: learn from them or quit because of them. It's up to you.

Successful swing traders remain unperturbed by losing trades but instead, they persist wisely by learning from their mistakes.

## Find and Stick to Trading Strategies That Work for You

While starting with the most popular trading strategies is a good place to start swing trading, you must come to evaluate the results you get from your chosen strategy to see if it's worth continuing, tweaking, or replacing.

What do you need to consider when evaluating whether a trading strategy is something that you should stick to, tweak, or ditch? One is risk appetite. If your risk appetite is on the low side, maybe you shouldn't even be trading at all. If it's moderate, your trading strategy must be one that carries a moderate amount of risk, too.

Your swing trading time frame is another consideration. If you want to earn big returns in a few days or weeks, then you must be ready to take on higher risks, as only highly volatile securities can give you opportunities to do so. If your risk tolerance is low to moderate, consider swing trading securities that aren't very volatile, albeit you'll need to extend your swing trading time frame to a few weeks or even a couple of months.

If you swing trade on a part-time basis only, it means you can't dedicate as much time for it as those who do it full time. That being said, it'd be better if you choose to swing trade securities that aren't very volatile. Very volatile, but potentially very profitable, securities require closer monitoring for optimal trading results.

Taking a swing trading position in a security that's very volatile and checking out its price once or twice a day only can put you at risk of either missing out on a potential bottom price for buying or a potentially high price for selling.

Worse, you may miss the security's profitable price level and end up with a losing swing trade when its price drops by the time you check it out again.

## Always Be Learning

Financial markets today are more complex and rapid today than ever before. If you're not always learning new things or if you're not keeping up to date with financial markets and the economy in general, you may run the risk of reading your chosen markets wrong and end up with more losing swing trades than profitable ones.

## Plan Your Swing Trades

As cliché as it may sound, failing to plan is indeed planning to fail. The worst swing trading strategy in the history of trader-kind is the wing-it strategy. Many traders make the mistake of just following the herd with nary a clue of why they're adopting the strategies of the trading herd and the risk-reward tradeoffs of such strategies.

The following are some of the most important things you must consider when planning your swing trades:

a. Your target profit or rate of return on the trade.

b. Your stop-loss price level at which you'll liquidate your swing trades to cut losses.

c. How much money you're comfortable losing on your swing trades, especially when you're just starting out.

d. Will you need the money you're trading at some point, and if so, when do you need it back.

e. Your swing trading time frame.

f. Can you afford to hold your position for a much longer period in case the price of the security you're holding is still underwater after several months?

Remember, the more detailed your plan, the lesser the tendency that you'll rely on your emotions and "gut" feel to execute your trades, which will greatly increase your chances of executing profitable swing trades.

## Practice a Lot Before Trading Actual Dollars

While practice doesn't make perfect, it does lead to excellence. When it comes to swing trading, excellence means a generally profitable collection of swing trades every year.

"But I don't have that much money to waste on practicing!" you might protest. Don't worry because practicing your swing trades, in the beginning, doesn't mean you'll have to stake real money.

You can practice what I refer to as "paper" swing trading. This means taking hypothetical positions using real-time market prices of financial securities. Let's consider paper trading shares of Apple, Inc.'s stocks.

Let's say that using technical analysis, you reckon now is a good time to take a swing trading position in Apple's stocks. On a spreadsheet like Excel or Numbers, input the number of shares you hypothetically bought (let's say 100 shares) at the actual closing price of Apple stocks today, which we'll assume to be $100 per share. Your hypothetical investment in that position would be $10,000.

For the next few days or weeks, monitor the daily closing price of Apple shares until it either reaches your designated profit-taking price or drops to or below your chosen stop-loss price. When that happens, "liquidate" or "sell" your hypothetical shares to close your position and complete your swing trade.

Through paper trading, you can get a very good feel of how to choose financial securities to swing trade and when to trade them without having to burn through your precious money. Only when you feel you've had enough paper swing trades and feel comfortable risking your own money already should you swing trade for real.

CHAPTER 28:

# Advanced Trading Strategies

Throughout this guidebook, we have spent some time looking at some of the different things that you can do when it comes to trading with swing trading. Now, it is time to take it a bit deeper and look at some of the more intermediate and advanced trading strategies you can use. As you progress with your swing trading, get a better idea of how it works, and get ready to take it a bit further to see what results you can get, these strategies will be the best options for you. Some of the different advanced trading strategies that you can use with swing trading include the following.

## Moving Average Trend Trading

The first strategy that we will take a look at here is the moving average trend strategy. This moving average is important because it is going to be the way that you can pick out when you want to enter and when you want to exit a trade for a specific stock.

There are many stocks that are going to start out the morning doing well in the morning trend, and they will have a strong upside or downside trend. You would then watch their charts and see where the moving averages go in the charts. This is beneficial to the traders because you will then be able to follow the moving average to figure out which trend is occurring, and you can ride out that kind of trend.

While this strategy does sound like it takes a bit of time to figure out, and it may seem complicated to work with, it is pretty easy to learn how to use it properly.

Some of the steps that are needed to make this one work for your needs include:

- When you take a look at the graphs that you want to use, and you are checking out the stock you want to use, make sure that you look to see whether or not a trend is forming near the spot that is the moving average. When you do see this, you will want to get into the market and use this strategy. You can then spend a bit of time looking at the trading data that shows up for that stock from the day before. This is important to see how the moving average changes and how the stock is going to respond to that average.

- After looking over the charts and getting a chance to see which moving average is the best one for the trade you are doing, it is time to purchase the stock. Some traders do choose to wait a little bit longer in order to confirm the moving average before they enter. But either way, try to purchase as close to the lines for the moving average as you can.

- Once you are ready, you need to pick out the stop points that you want to use. You may want to consider setting the stop just a bit below the moving average line to help protect your investment, but it still allows for a little bit of volatility of movement. If you are doing this strategy with a candlestick chart, then you need to make sure that you have a start that is close to the moving average and chooses to work with a long position.

- After you have these in place and have been able to enter the market, you can just ride on that trend until you see the moving average break and then take your profits.

For this kind of strategy, it is important to remember that you never want to work with a trailing stop on this strategy. This one is also a strategy where you need to pay full attention to the market or more than usual because there are times when the market can end up getting away from you.

While the scanner can be great for helping you get the right trades, you need to make sure that you use your own eyes rather than the scanner when you are ready to use this kind of strategy.

If you see that your chosen stock is moving really high from the moving average, this means that you are making a great profit. At this time, it may be best to take the half position rather than going all the way to your break. This will make sure that you make some profit, and sometimes, you will see the moving trend go down before the break. If you let this happen, it is possible to lose out on all of the profit. But, with the half position, you can at least make some profit.

## Resistance Trading

The next option that we will take a look at when it comes to trading is the resistance trading strategy. Support and resistance trading are also very popular when it comes to doing swing trading; you will probably find a lot of traders who choose to work with this method instead of one of the others. The support will be the price level when buying is really strong, so strong that it can interrupt or reverse the current downtrend that may show up in the charts.

When your current downtrend gets to a support level, it will bounce back at least a little. When you are looking at your graphs, this support line will be shown on a chart with a horizontal line that needs to connect together at least two bottoms together.

Then, we have to take a look at the resistance, which will be the opposite. This will end up being the price level where you see a strong selling position, one that is so strong that it can reverse the uptrend that is going on in the charts. When you see the uptrend hit this level, the trend will stop, and sometimes, it will go down. The resistance will be represented similarly to the support, but it will connect together two or more tops.

In some cases, it is possible to get a minor resistance or minor support. These are going to cause a little pause in the trend. But, when you work with the major support or resistance, it will be able to force the trend to reverse. Traders who are working with this kind of strategy will try to make a purchase as close to the support as possible, and then, they will sell as close to the resistance as possible. This helps them to get the most out of each trade.

In order to figure out these support and resistance levels, you need to take some time to look at the daily charts of your chosen stocks. Sometimes, this line is even hard to find, and you may have to wait a few days in order to find a clear line that you are comfortable using. This means that patience is needed with this kind of strategy, as you may have to wait a bit to get started with this strategy at all.

There are some steps that you can use the charts that you have available to help draw your own support and resistant lines. Some of the steps you can take to make this process easier and to really use this strategy include:

Remember those indecision candles? You are going to see these in areas of support and resistance. These candles often show that buyers and sellers are fighting each other to see who has the most control over the price.

Often, half dollars and whole dollars can be good support and resistance levels. This is especially true when you work on stocks under $10. If you can't find your support or your resistance lines, check here and see if your line would work there.

- When you make your own lines, you need to have the most recent data available. This ensures that you are getting the best information for that stock.

- The more that your line is able to touch the extreme price of the stock, the better option this line is for your support and resistance. If it is too far from this extreme point, then it is not going to have enough value to make it strong.

- Only look at any support or resistance lines that stay with the current price range. For example, if the stock's price is around $20 right now, you do not need to look at the region on the graph where the stock randomly jumped up to $40. This is not an area where the stock will probably go back to, so it doesn't make much sense to work from there.

- Many times, the support and resistance is not just one exact number. Often, it is more of an area. If you come up with a support or resistance that is about $19.69, then you know that the movement is somewhere near that number and not exactly that number. You can usually estimate that the area will be somewhere between five to ten cents above or under that line.

- The price you want to work from will need to have a clear bounce off that level. If you can't find that this price bounces at that level, then this is not a good support or resistance level for you to work with. Your levels need to be really easy to notice and need to make sense of the charts you look at. If you have any questions about whether you picked the right one or not, it's not the right one.

When you go onto the charts and create these lines, you may find that drawing the perfect line can be a challenge. You need to make sure that you are picking out the right lines for the support and for the resistance so that you know how to base the trades. But, the best way to ensure that you are doing this the proper way is to take the time to practice. Over time, you will get better, and this will be a great strategy to go with.

CHAPTER 29:

# Financial Instrument

Swing trading is a technique that has a general application. Therefore, it can be applied to the trading of any financial instrument that experiences price changes on the scale of days, weeks, or months. Once you understand the basic techniques used with swing trading, such as moving averages, then you can apply them to any financial asset you are interested in trading. Swing trading really isn't a strategy. In fact, it uses the same strategies used by day traders. Rather it's simply a time frame or style. So the same strategies are used, but they are applied to different time frames. This has significant implications, of course. Day traders are actually looking for the same types of price moves, just on different time scales. Since a swing trader is willing to hold their position overnight and out to weeks or even a few months, the risk is significantly lower. Some of the tools and strategies used by swing traders that are also used by day traders including:

- Looking for support and resistance
- Looking for chart patterns
- Moving averages
- Bollinger bands
- Trending and counter-trending
- Looking for signals in candlesticks

## Forex

Forex is short for foreign exchange and is a market where people trade one currency against another in pairs. Traders seek to profit from price swings of trading pairs and use a technique called long-term trend following. Swing trading also follows trends but does so over short periods, but periods that exceed those used by day traders.

On Forex markets, you can expect to hold positions for more than a day to a few weeks. Forex traders that use swing trading as a technique will study charts over the course of days to look for bring price swings they can take advantage of to earn profits.

Swing traders on Forex are looking for volatility. When there is more volatility, there is a greater chance that prices will have larger swings between high and low values, offering more chances for short term profits. Large price swings, as well as more frequent price moves, can aid the swing trader.

As a swing trader on Forex, you aren't going to be as concerned with specific currency pairs in terms of what currencies make up the pair, but whether or not the pair offers the types of price moves you are looking for, that is, big swings that offer a solid buy-low and sell-high possibility. Moving averages are frequently used when applying swing trading to Forex.

Swing trading is quite different than scalping, so you are not looking to profit from small price movements that occur over very short time periods. Scalping and day trading requires a lot of attention to the markets that will have to be focused whenever you hold a position. Because swing trading takes place over longer time frames, constant attention to the markets isn't necessary.

Of course, you still have to pay attention, but it is something that is far more amenable to part-time attention rather than having to go all in. When using swing trading on Forex, you will want to keep track of economic and political news that can roil the markets or cause rallies for one currency over another.

## Options

Options are a type of derivative that has an underlying financial asset, such as shares of stock. Most option traders are trading stock options. The option gives the buyer the right to buy or sell shares of stock at a fixed price, which is called the strike price. Options that give the buyer (of the option) the right to buy shares of stock are known as calls. If the option gives the buyer the right to sell shares of stock at the strike price, it's known as a put.

Options trading is amenable to swing trading because options are time-limited. Every options contract comes with an expiration date. The lifetime of an option can be quite varied, lasting from one week (so-called weekly) to a month, to several weeks, and even one year or more. Options that last one year or more are called LEAPs. However, no matter how long an option lasts, they all operate in basically the same fashion.

Unlike stocks, part of the pricing of an option is determined by "time value." The closer an option gets to the expiration date, the less time value the option has. That adds an extra wrinkle to trading options that other financial securities don't have – for example; you can hold stocks for however long as you like.

Since options (generally speaking) have a life that fits well within the periods that swing traders use, they naturally fit within a swing trading paradigm. A swing trader of options can use the same techniques of analysis that a swing trader of stocks or other financial assets will use to determine price swings. Puts offer an opportunity to short the market, so swing traders interested in shorting can use puts for that purpose rather than having to deal with the complexities and risks of using margin to borrow shares of stock.

Options have many strategies that specialists in options trading used to generate income, but those are not of interest to the swing trader. A swing trader will only be interested in using swings in stock price to profit from trading calls or puts at the right moment in time. This is a simpler approach rather than having to learn all the complicated schemes that have been put together to minimize risk with options. Instead, you will use the same tools to look for signals in the market that a swing trader of stocks is using, and then take advantage of buy and sell signals to buy or sell the appropriate options. The main difference will be focusing on the time value of the options and noting how that can impact pricing.

## Stocks

Swing trading obviously has an application to the stock market, and we will use it for many of our examples. You can use swing trading to profit from the moves of any stock, but high volatile stocks will work better because you are more likely to see large price swings in the stocks that you decide to take positions in. When using swing trading with stocks, there are different ways to approach it. At any given time, a stock may be fluctuating within specific ranges, and you can use this information to get a general idea of what the best share prices are to enter and exit trades. Big news can always cause a massive pricing move, and one thing you will look for is earnings reports. It's also important to study company fundamentals, but with an eye on profits during the current and next quarter rather than viewing them through the lens of a long-term investor. Earnings reports can offer opportunities to profit from swing trades, provided that you are correctly anticipating the way the reports are going to go. Something that you will be interested in doing is seeing what analysts are saying so that you know what the expectations are. Keep in mind that it's possible to make an incorrect judgment in this case, which can lead to significant losses.

Product news and even political and financial news can have a large influence on stock prices. If the FDA approves a new drug, then that could mean a significant rise in share prices. The introduction of a new smartphone might do the same, but if features were not as exciting as investors hoped, it could leave the stock moving sideways or even crashing low.

While paying attention to news is important, you don't want to give it the most weight. The fact is you are going to be the last person getting the news long after institutional investors or large hedge funds have gotten the information.

At best, you'll be getting the news at the same time, but they are going to be able to react to it instantly, long before you can.

So most of your focus should be directed at looking at the stock itself and how it behaved over recent time frames and out to a year. You don't necessarily want to look back too far since the behavior of the stock five years ago isn't nearly as relevant as the behavior of the stock in recent months.

Some of the tools used for analyzing the stock market are the same tools and techniques used on Forex. First and foremost, this will include using candlesticks and recognizing various chart patterns. You will also put a lot of emphasis on using support and resistance.

This can be used as an entry point for your trades.

Resistance is the upper price level. The stock may be unable to break like support; it's going to take a major change to get the stock to break above resistance. That major change could take many forms. It might be the introduction of a new product, an unexpectedly positive earnings report, or a change of CEO.

Therefore, you should spend time following the news related to companies you are trading, but don't let that be the final word or obsess over it too much. Just use it as one piece of information in your overall toolkit. To see why, go back to the spring and summer of 2008 and see what all the analysts were saying – most of them were dead wrong.

Of course, that doesn't mean they are always wrong, they are often right, but you have to take what they say with a grain of salt. So use your analysis and spot trends, know where the levels of support and resistance are, and then pay attention to special news items or events that could cause a major price change for the stock of the company.

CHAPTER 30:

# Finding a Broker

Some people reading this book may not have managed their own stock trading before. If it's your first foray into having an individually managed account, that can be intimidating, and you may not know where to begin. There are a few issues to consider and many choices available. Let's explore some of these briefly here.

## Commissions

These days, one of the biggest issues to consider when choosing a brokerage is whether they charge commissions, and if so, how big are they? Just a few years ago, this was not even a question that anyone would even bother asking, but today several brokerages don't charge any commissions at all. As a swing trader who frequently trades compared to your standard buy-and-hold investor, you might find that commissions can eat into your profits. Luckily, commissions are either dropping or even zero at many brokerages. The presence of zero-commission brokerages is also putting pressure on the old school brokers who have been used to charging high commissions and fees. Downward pressure on prices is a signal that market competition is good. One bit of advice is that you'll want to consider new brokerages. First, they tend to have zero commissions. Older stockbrokers like Charles Schwab are going to charge higher commissions as a rule. Do your research before making a decision.

## Resources

One thing you might consider is how much the broker devotes to providing resources that you can utilize to do your research without having to go somewhere else. Unfortunately, some of the no commission brokers fall short in this department. That may or may not be important since there are tons of free resources available on the internet. One of the best is Yahoo Finance, which has been around for more than two decades. It is very helpful with financial statements and nice interactive charts that let you use many of the tools we have been discussing in the book (and showing in many of the charts). It's all free, so there really isn't a need to have a broker provide that for you, but it's something to consider.

## Venue

Do you want an online broker? What about one with an app, or both? These days the old school way of doing things, going to an office where you actually meet a stockbroker, is something that has been replaced by electronic tools, and that makes perfect sense given the way the markets work. Recently many brokers have been expanding past the traditional internet to offer apps and an online presence, and some newer brokers have even moved completely into the app domain. That approach can have some drawbacks, especially for a swing trader. As a swing trader having a desktop computer will be an important part of your trading activities. At least right now, mobile apps don't seem to offer quite the same power.

## Educational Tools

Some brokers go above and beyond and offer educational tools as well as a trading platform. If you are a new trader, that can be a very useful thing for you to have access to. Educational tools often take the form of video courses, but some platforms even offer simulated trading, which means you can practice making trades – using the real stock market – without investing actual money. The simulator will let you see how your trade works out and learn from the experience without risking a dime of money. That might be overkill for some people who are anxious actually to get active with trading, but for others who have a lot more patience, that can be useful.

CHAPTER 31:

# Swing Trading Examples

Swing traders are not limited to stocks only. They can trade in numerous other instruments as well. These include bonds, currencies, options, futures, indices, and even ETFs or electronically traded funds. Swing trading is about holding either a short or long position in the markets for longer than one trading day but not longer than a couple of weeks or months.

Some trades are pretty brief and are executed in just over 24 hours. Others take longer and might last even two months or longer. Even then, they are both considered swing trades. Traders take profits via established risk versus reward ratios, which are based on profit targets as well as stop-loss points.

## An Example of Swing Trading

Here is a real-world example of a swing trading opportunity. This is a trading period where AAPL or Apple Inc. showcased an impressive period where the price moved upward strongly. This strong upward trend was then followed by another pattern, the cup and handle, indicating the strong upward trend is bound to continue. In our case, the price moves towards $192.70.

As a swing trader, with some technical analysis, we will place a stop-loss point right below the cup handle at $187. We also need to determine the entry point as well as the estimated risk. This is determined to be $192.50. To determine the estimated risk for this trade, we simply find the difference between the entry points and the stop-loss.

Estimated risk is $192.50 - $187 = $5.50

The possible or potential reward for this particular trade should be at least twice the estimated risk. As such, we expect to have the following potential reward.

Potential reward is $5.50 * 2 + higher price ($192.50) = $203.50

Apart from the risk versus reward ratio, other exit methods are available to traders. These include new lows by the price movement. Using this approach, the profit margins would alter slightly. However, the principle remains the same. Another way of looking at it is a profit margin of 12% compared to 3% risk or lower.

**Example 2**

Another important stock we observed is FAS, which is an ETF. Direxion Financial ETF is observed to form the cup with a handle figure. This is a sure sign that its upward trend is set to continue. The higher end of the handle is close to 74, which is a great place to watch out for a breakout. Any breakout beyond this point constitutes an excellent entry point.

In our case, the breakout was not seen until later the following day. There was a pullback on the ETF, so buying did not occur immediately. It was better to wait until the trend showcased more strength with sufficient confidence levels. It was observed that the ETF falling before eventually rising just above its original levels. The ETF was unable to build on its initial momentum and sustain growth as had been expected. As such, this particular trade was not pursued as it would not have been profitable.

**Example 3**

Let us take another example with company ABC whose stock is XYZ.

You decide to invest about $500 of your funds on this trade. This amount buys you 25 shares of ABC stock. If you did your assessment and analysis correctly, then you stand a chance of making money and with the capacity to limit losses. In this case, you can choose the value of $25 as the upper limit where you cease trading and first take profits. This is also known as the take profit point.

You can then choose the value of $17 as your stop-loss. This means that if the price drops to $17, then you will automatically exit the trade and count your losses. The maximum loss you can incur on this trade is $3 ($20-$17) * 20 shares = $60.

On the other hand, the maximum profitability in our case would be $5 ($25 - $20) * 20 = $100. So with this trade, you stand to gain $100 or lose $60. As such, the risk versus reward ratio is 100:60 or 1:0.6, which is close to 2:1. This ratio is considered acceptable even though it is the minimum acceptable risk versus reward ratio.

CHAPTER 32:

# Learning the Swing Trading Strategy

Online merchants are always vigilant for approaches to restrain speculator misfortunes. A standout amongst the most widely recognized drawback insurance components is a leave technique known as a stop-misfortune request. If an offer value plunges to a specific set level, the position will be consequently sold at the present market cost, to stem further misfortunes.

Be that as it may, merchants may improve the viability of a stop-misfortune by matching it with a trailing stop, which is an exchange request where the stop-misfortune cost isn't fixed at a solitary, total dollar sum, yet is somewhat set at a specific rate or dollar sum beneath the market cost. At the point when the cost builds, it hauls the trailing stop alongside it. At that point, when the value at long last quits was rising, the new stop-misfortune value stays at the level it was hauled to along these lines, naturally securing a financial specialist's drawback while securing benefits as the value achieves new highs.

Dealers may improve the adequacy of a stop-misfortune by matching it with a trailing stop, an exchange request where the stop-misfortune cost isn't fixed at a solitary, supreme dollar sum; however, is fairly set at a specific rate or a dollar sum beneath the market cost.

## Trailing-Stop/Stop-Loss Combo for Winning Trades

During transitory value plunges, it is pivotal to oppose the motivation to reset your trailing stop, or else, your successful stop-misfortune may finish up lower than anticipated. By a similar token, getting control over a trailing stop-misfortune is prudent when you see energy cresting in the graphs, particularly when the stock is hitting another high.

Trailing stops are only one approach to control the hazard compensation proportion when exchanging. Canny dealers keep up the choice of shutting a situation whenever presenting a sell request at the market.

## The Best of Both Worlds

When joining conventional stop-misfortunes with trailing stops, it's imperative to compute your most extreme hazard resilience. For instance, you could set a stop-misfortune at 5% underneath the present stock cost, and the trailing stop at 6% beneath the present stock cost. As the offer cost expands, the trailing stop will outperform the fixed stop-misfortune, rendering it excess or out of date. Any further cost increments will mean further limiting potential misfortunes with each upward value tick. The additional insurance is that the trailing stop will just go up, where during business sector hours, the trailing highlight will reliably recalculate the stop's trigger point.

## Utilizing the Trailing Stop/Stop-Loss Combo on Active Trades

Trailing stops are progressively hard to utilize with dynamic exchanges, because of value variances and the instability of specific stocks, particularly during the main hour of the exchanging day. Of course, such quick moving stocks ordinarily pull in brokers due to their capability to create generous measures of cash in a brief timeframe.

For this technique to deal with dynamic exchanges, you should set trailing stop esteem that will oblige ordinary value changes for the specific stock and catch just the genuine pullback in cost. This can be accomplished by altogether concentrating a stock for a few days before effectively exchanging it.

Next, you should probably time your exchange by taking a gander at a simple clock and taking note of the edge of the long arm when it is pointing between 12 p.m. also, 4 p.m., which you'll need to use as your guide. Presently, when your preferred moving normal is holding enduring at this point, remain with your underlying trailing stop misfortune. As the moving normal alters course, dipping under 4 p.m., it's an ideal opportunity to fix your trailing stop spread.

The trailing stop/stop-misfortune combo takes out the enthusiastic segment from exchanging, letting you soundly settle on estimated choices dependent on factual data.

## Broker Risk

Brokers face certain dangers in utilizing stop-misfortunes. First of all, advertising creators are definitely mindful of any stop-misfortunes you place with your intermediary. They can drive a whipsaw in the cost, accordingly knocking you out of your position, at that point running the value ideal back up once more. For this situation, the outcome will be where the stop will be activated by an impermanent value pullback, leaving dealers to fuss over the apparent loss. This can be an extreme mental pill to swallow.

Even though there are critical dangers required by utilizing trailing quits, joining them with customary stop-misfortunes can go far toward limiting misfortunes and securing benefits.

## Short Covering and Short Squeeze

Short covering and short squeeze are various terms to depict a circumstance, including short positions. A short squeeze is a circumstance where a security's cost increments fundamentally, making short venders close their short positions. On the other hand, short-covering includes repurchasing security to finish off an open short position.

A short squeeze includes a surge of purchasing action among short merchants because of an expansion in the cost of security. The expansion in the security value makes short venders repurchase it to finish off their short positions and book their misfortunes. This market movement causes a further increment in the security's value, which powers all the shorter venders to cover their short positions. By and large, protections with a high short intrigue experience a short crush.

For instance, the short interest for an organization is about a half. Assume numerous dealers and speculators are short from $30 because of awful profit, and the stock is as of now exchanging at $15. Be that as it may, throughout the following quarter, the organization reports excellent income and copies in an incentive of $60. Since numerous merchants are short, they would need to cover their short positions to constrain their misfortunes; this makes purchasing weight on the stock and makes the cost increment to $70.

In opposition to a short squeeze, short-covering includes acquiring security to cover an open short position. To finish off a short position, brokers and speculators buy a similar measure of offers in the security they undercut. For instance, a broker undercuts 200 portions of a company at $20 per offer, and after that, the company's value diminishes to $11 per share. The broker covers his short position by repurchasing 200 portions of the company's stock at $9. The merchant benefits significantly.

## The Trend Line

As a broker, you have presumably heard the familiar aphorism that it is ideal for exchanging with the pattern. The pattern, says every one of the intellectuals, is your companion. This is wise counsel as long as you most likely are aware and can acknowledge that the pattern can end. And after that, the pattern isn't your companion.

So how might we decide the bearing of the pattern? We have faith in the KISS rule, which says, "Keep it basic, inept." Here is a strategy for deciding the pattern and a straightforward technique for envisioning the finish of the pattern.

Before we begin, we need to make reference to the significance of time spans in deciding the pattern. As a rule, when we are examining long haul speculations, the long-haul period overwhelms the shorter periods. Be that as it may, for intraday purposes, the shorter time period could be of more noteworthy worth. Exchanges can be isolated into three classes of exchanging styles or portions: the intra-day, the swing, and the position exchange.

Huge business dealers, for example, those organizations setting up creation in an outside nation, may be keen on the destiny of the cash over an extensive stretch of, for example, months or years. Yet, for theorists, a week after week outline can be acknowledged as the long haul.

## Midpoints Moving in Pairs

With a week by week outline as the underlying reference, we would then be able to approach deciding the long-haul pattern for a theoretical merchant. To do this, we will turn to two valuable devices that will enable us to decide the pattern. These two apparatuses are the basic moving normal and the exponential moving normally.

## Catch a Wave

By setting up a momentary exponential moving normal and a more drawn out term straightforward moving normal, on week after week and a day by day graph, it is conceivable to check the bearing of the pattern. Realizing the pattern helps in taking positions; however, remember that the business sectors move in waves. These waves are called drive waves when toward the pattern and remedial waves when opposed to the pattern.

By including the waves or rotates in each wave, one can endeavor to foresee whether an exchanging opportunity will be against the pattern or with the pattern.

As indicated by the Elliot wave hypothesis, a motivation wave, for the most part, comprises five swings, and a remedial wave, for the most part, comprises three swings. A full-wave move would comprise of five swings with two of the swings being counter-pattern.

# Conclusion

Swing trading is a great strategy for any trader to enter, regardless of what their trading goals are. If you want to have the capacity to earn significant profits without having to wait so long to get them or endure the stress of day-to-day volatility quite so much, swing trading is the trading strategy for you.

This trading strategy is known for being one of the best strategies for beginners and experienced traders alike, as it has so many benefits to it. As well, there is so much that people can frequently learn from this strategy. It can take ages to master, yet you can still earn a huge profit from day one so long as you trade properly and follow the right strategies to keep yourself profitable.

After finishing this book, I strongly encourage you to engage in some practice trades before trying anything serious. Take out your trading book, take the knowledge you have learned here, and start going through your day as if you are truly trading. Create your watchlist, read the market and your indicators, time your entries, manage your practice trades, and time your exits. As you do, go through this book all over again, applying the knowledge to your practice trades along the way.

Once you begin to feel confident in practice trading, you can begin to engage in real trades. At this point, you will have a strong level of confidence behind you that will support you in staying out of a fear mindset when it comes to trading. Just make sure you do not switch into a greedy mindset as this would not be ideal and could cost you big time. Instead, stay humble and confident in what you are doing and maintain a healthy respect for the market.

After a few real trades, you will find that trading is not nearly as challenging or as intimidating as people make it out to be. While it certainly does have challenges and learning curves, it is something that anyone can do and that anyone can profit from. Plenty of people are earning consistent profits off of the market and creating high incomes for themselves using these strategies, which means you can absolutely do it, too.

Regardless of your level of experience, a swing trader gets to slow everything down, and that is an advantage, especially for new traders. You do not get caught up in a process where you need to make a decision in a matter of seconds. This type of pressure situation is where many day traders lose out and let their emotions get the better of them. Swing traders have the luxury of time to make their decisions and are less likely to make an impulsive trade move in the heat of the moment. Regardless, all of us have mental weaknesses that we must overcome as traders.

The final piece of advice I want to leave you with is to be serious about keeping your trading journals. Trading journals will help you track charts, patterns, prices, and positions in the market while also tracking your improvements. Every trader can benefit from keeping journals and keeping them organized, so do not overlook this trading tip. Also, make sure that you see your trade journals every so often so that you can recall all of the tips you have learned along the way, as writing them down only to forget them would not be helpful!

Lastly, if you have enjoyed reading “Swing Trading for Beginners.”

Thank you, and best of luck!

CPSIA information can be obtained
at www.ICGtesting.com
Printed in the USA
BVHW090202250621
610375BV00001B/319